Britannia's Glory

*A new series of books from Cassell's Sexual Politics list,
Women on Women provides a forum for lesbian, bisexual and
heterosexual women to explore and debate contemporary issues
and to develop strategies for the advancement of feminist
culture and politics into the next century.*

COMMISSIONING
Roz Hopkins
Liz Gibbs
Christina Ruse

Britannia's Glory

A History of Twentieth-Century Lesbians

Emily Hamer

CASSELL

Cassell
Wellington House
125 Strand
London
WC2R 0BB

215 Park Avenue South
New York
NY 10003

First published 1996

British Library Cataloguing-in-Publication Data
A catalogue record for this book is available from
the British Library.

ISBN 0–304–32964–9 (hardback)
      0–304–32967–3 (paperback)

Typeset by Chapter One (London)
Printed and bound in Great Britain by Biddles Ltd,
Guildford and King's Lynn

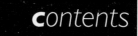

contents

acknowledgements

I would like to thank the following people for their help:

Diane Atkinson of the Museum of London, Michael Bott of Reading University Library, Sue Donnelly, curator of the Hall Carpenter Archives at the LSE, David Doughan and Rachel Emmett of the Fawcett Library, Jackie Forster, Liz Gibbs, Laura Gowing, Sarah Green, the Lesbian Archive, Mary Hamer, Tracy Hargreaves, Ruth Harman of Sheffield Archives, Roz Hopkins, Katrina Rolley, Emma Smith, Sarah Waters, Jeffrey Weeks, Elizabeth Wilson.

Any errors are entirely my own.

The quotations at the head of each chapter are taken from *Sappho: Poems and Fragments*, translated by Josephine Balmer (Newcastle upon Tyne: Bloodaxe Books, 1992) and are used with the permission of the publisher.

For Nic Williams,
Gudrun Limbrick and
Ann Burton

introduction

'No, not quite forgotten'
Sappho, Fragment 68

While I was looking for contemporary reviews of Radclyffe Hall's *The Well of Loneliness*, I came across a small but prominently featured item on the will of the Hon. Alice Coralie Glyn. This stated that the Hon. Miss Glyn had left a bequest of £25,000 (in 1928 a considerable sum of money) to establish homes for working-class women over the age of sixty, and it was this that the newspaper was reporting.[1] The concluding sentence, however, did mention that the remainder of the Hon. Miss Glyn's large estate had been left to her friend, Lois Tremlow. To the lesbian reader it is this postscript which grasps the imagination. Who was Alice Glyn? Where did her money come from? What prompted this large bequest to working-class women? Who was Lois Tremlow? Were they lovers? What did their families think? How long had they been together and what had they done with their lives? What was the relationship, and what were the politics, that Alice Glyn sought to mark in her will?

The history behind this private act of will-making is, potentially, lesbian history. Through the legal requirement that once it has gone through probate a will becomes a public document, the private life, loves and beliefs of Alice Glyn have been laid bare; we just have to put the flesh back onto the bones. Through public documents, like wills, through autobiographies, and through shared homes and shared graves, we can map lesbian history: a history of how lesbians thought of their lives, understood their experiences, and charted their commitments.

This book is concerned with the history of lesbians and lesbianism through the records that they have made. Lesbians have not been written out or missed out of history; it is rather that their lesbianism has not actually been written into their lives. My aim in this book is not to stamp 'lesbian' onto any woman who catches my eye. It is to use 'she was a lesbian' as an explanatory premise in trying to understand a woman's life, when that premise makes most sense of that life. If Alice Glyn was a lesbian and a suffragette and worked for better housing, her will makes perfect sense. Her will is so lesbian that if she were heterosexual it becomes almost incomprehensible.

Some of the women I discuss here are known to have been lesbians, because they identified themselves explicitly in public or in private as lesbians. Other women that I discuss never explicitly spoke of their sexuality. However, their lesbianism is tacitly known: 'She never had a lover; she lived with Margaret for forty years; they were so happy; she was devastated when she died.' In response to the question 'Why didn't they come out?' there can be many answers. One was given by Stella Browne in 1915, when talking of the relationship of women in general to their sexuality:

> The realities of women's sexual life have been greatly obscured by the lack of any sexual vocabulary. While her brother has often learned all the slang of the street before adolescence, the conventionally 'decently brought-up girl,' of the upper and middle classes, has no terms to define many of her sensations and experiences.[2]

To add to Stella Browne's point, they may have been literally unaware that the things they were doing at home with the woman they loved were the things that made one a 'lesbian'.

On the other hand these women may have been fully aware of their lesbianism. They may have been ashamed because they believed that to be a lesbian was bad (because the Church said it was) or it was a physical deformity or sickness (as the medical profession said it was) or mental illness or pathology (as the burgeoning profession of psychology said it was). They may have lied about what they did in bed with whom, but they may not have been ashamed at all of their lesbianism: many lesbians held their heads high. They may have been busy private women, who did not spend their time analysing what came naturally and happily to them. They may have been aware that to be a 'lesbian' was to take up a stigmatized identity, and may have balked at spending their lives draped on a cross of other people's design.

We cannot produce a history of lesbianism by simply writing down the names of women who wrote in their diaries 'I am a lesbian'. If this seems to beg a question, how do we know these women were lesbians? I would reiterate that we know that they were lesbians because this is the best explanation of their lives. Many critics of lesbian history have tried to argue that to know a woman was a lesbian requires an observer to witness that woman having sex with another woman. The standard of visibility is not a universal prerequisite for knowledge. We cannot see electricity but we know that electricity exists because electricity is the best explanation of why moving a light switch leads to the illumination of a light bulb. In the same way we do not require a witness to heterosexual intercourse in order to know that a woman is heterosexual.

I will lay my cards on the table: I have never seen any of the women whom I describe as lesbians in this book have sex. Generally it is accepted that we have the skills to deduce from the outward manifestations of a relationship its inner form. I see no reason why, when considering lesbians, this general presumption should fail to hold true. If a relationship looks like that of lovers, it usually is that of lovers. Lesbians are women who love women and this love of women is visible in how they have chosen to live their lives. Lesbians in history are recognizable through the lesbian lives that they have led.

I have tried to re-integrate the lesbianism of the women described in this book back into their lives. The women I discuss are women who have figured, sometimes albeit only in footnotes, in the feminist, political and cultural history of twentieth-century Britain. They are not necessarily role models; I do not condone their politics or how they spent their lives. They are linked to each other and to us because of their relationships with women. I have tried to show how they experienced their love and desire for other women emotionally and within a broad political framework. These women are interesting because they were lesbians who struggled to build and make sense of their lives, just as the rest of us are doing.

One of my aims has been to show that lesbian history already exists within published documents and public archives. I have not set out to record oral history or to trace and talk to older lesbians. Rather, I have used the records and documents already in the public domain. I have sought out the pre-existing accounts of lesbians, lesbian lives and lesbianism and tried to elucidate the history that these accounts represent. It seems that there is a lot of lesbian history waiting to be discovered. I hope that I have provided in this book a context which will help to illuminate subsequent oral history and first-hand accounts.

Certain sociological and historical facts have limited the scope of the lesbian history that I have been able to explore. 'History' has traditionally been about what people did in the public sphere. It has detailed and analysed what laws were enacted, what battles were fought, which industries were developed and who were the political leaders. The task of describing the private sphere has been relegated to 'social history'. Social history has documented social arrangements: marriage, divorce, childbirth, working conditions, housing, medical knowledge, and education. However, the major resource of social history is still *public* documentation: official registers, government reports, newspaper reports, medical case histories and so on.

Lesbian history largely lies outside this realm of quasi-official documentation. Lesbianism is not, as such, illegal so there is no legal case law specifically concerning lesbianism. Until 1956 it was not recognized in law that women could, let alone did, have any form of sexual interaction with each other.[3] Lesbianism remains outside a legal framework; lesbians can only be legally charged under generic indecency and public morality legislation and with indecent assault, even if their crime is specifically that of lesbian sex.[4] Lesbians cannot marry their female lovers, and while their births and deaths are registered their homosexuality goes unrecorded. Medical statistics have not been drawn up from medical notes on lesbians who have discussed their lesbianism with their doctors.

The records of lesbian history are the minor details of ordinary life: whom a woman lived with, who her friends were, what books she read, the clothes she wore, the work she did and her political and moral beliefs. This may seem to elide history with biography. However. as Liz Stanley has commented, 'it is *only* biography which can make available the detailed processes of historical change to us.'[5] The evidence of lesbianism is available in letters, diaries, photographs, magazine subscriptions, theatre programmes and so on. However, for most people it is just this kind of detritus which is thrown away when they die. The records of this day-to-day living are usually only preserved if the women involved were not ordinary. The value of someone's private life is measured against her public success.

Women who were important enough to have their lives preserved have not, in the past, been very common. Women have been debarred, both *de jure* and *de facto*, from education, the professions and power. Thus it is with the day-to-day minutiæ of men's lives that our libraries and archives have been overwhelmingly filled. In the last hundred years, however, the effect of feminist campaigning to allow women access to power in the public sphere has had a trickle-down effect. There is much more information on the lives of women since 1900 than there is on earlier generations.

However, it is still the private lives of *extraordinary* women that are documented. Women who were not deemed remarkable have dropped out of history. Becoming an extraordinary woman obviously depends on a combination of personal talent and supportive social structures.

Education is important. Education has a financial cost, not only in fees but in wages not earned. Women who were educated thus were almost inevitably from middle-class families. Education raises aspirations and offers increased access to positions of economic and professional power. On a practical level, illiterate women are less likely to be able to compose records of their lives which survive their own deaths.

Money is important. Educated women cannot leave records if they cannot afford paper and ink, let alone film and gravestones. These are luxury goods which require a certain degree of economic security to be seen as justifiable purchases. Having the time to record, for posterity's sake, your life or the life of your community requires a degree of economic privilege; time has a cash value. Lesbians need financial resources, either inherited or earned, if they are to set up homes with other women. Lesbians with neither family money nor a career have found it difficult to be self-supporting. Women earn less than men, so it is harder for a lesbian couple to set up a home together than for a gay male couple or a heterosexual couple.

Social attitudes to women living independently of their families or a husband have also affected the lives of lesbians. Many lesbians were simply unable to carve out another possible life for themselves, to live the life that they desired to live as lesbians. Social attitudes have also affected what happens to your belongings and papers when you die. A distaste for lesbianism by the person going through your papers when you are dead can result in the history of your lesbianism, an inalienable aspect of your life, being destroyed. Moreover social attitudes have influenced what counts as extraordinary achievement in women: being very good at a manual trade has not usually been enough to get one into history books.

It is within the limitations of these social and economic conditions that I have written this book. In practical terms this has meant that the majority of women I talk about are middle-class. This is the result of the material I could locate, not a personal or political bias. I am also aware that, as far as I know, all of the women in this book are white. In terms of my research it is white women, as it is middle-class women, that history has deemed extraordinary. My inability to find records of black lesbians is presumably due to a number of factors. The most obvious is that racism in British society has prevented black women achieving the success that white women have done.

Racism within homosexual organizations and informal groups may also have made them unappealing to black men and women. There may be specific ethnic beliefs about sexuality and gender which mean that black

touché

women have experienced their homosexual desire, and made it manifest, in different ways from white lesbians. Then it may also have been that black lesbians who were involved in predominantly white homosexual communities and organizations had their ethnic identity denied any significance, so that their identity as *black* lesbians is obscured. The absence of black women in this book is, again, due to empirical constraints, not personal or political prejudice.

This is a book about lesbians. I am only concerned with gay men, and homosexuality in general, in relation to lesbians. Terry Castle has written:

> As soon as the lesbian is lumped in – for better or for worse – with her male homosexual counterpart, the singularity of her experience (sexual or otherwise) tends to become obscured. We 'forget' about the lesbian by focusing instead on gay men...often the first question I would receive after delivering my talk was 'But what about gay men?' or some version thereof – as though I had implicitly committed an offence against good manners by daring to speak of lesbianism without mentioning male homosexuality.[6]

Gay men have always had easier access to the formation of social identity than lesbians have had, because they have always had the privileges that go with being a man. Sex between two men has much more commonly been admitted to the category 'sex' because it involves penises. This has had advantages and disadvantages: it has given men a basis for forming a gay identity and it has involved huge social and legal prohibition. Gay male sex has had a very long public history from the Bible through the ecclesiastical law and finally into criminal law. There are a number of books which focus mainly on the history of male homosexuality in Britain such as Jeffrey Weeks's seminal *Coming Out*. Lesbian experience has been different from that of gay men and deserves a history of its own.

Debates about what is a lesbian and the definition of lesbianism are extremely long-running. They occur both as an academic backdrop to the project of lesbian history and as recurring chapters within lesbian history itself. I will discuss how lesbians conceptualized lesbianism in different historical periods chronologically within the main body of the book. À *propos* the methodology I have used in deciding *who* are the subjects of this book, and *what* it was that they were doing which makes them subjects of this book, I have simply looked at the records of women's lives.

I have focused my attention on where women lived, whom they lived with, how they earned their living and what they did for pleasure. This examination has revealed the lesbians that I write about in this book. Once it is clear that a particular woman led a lesbian life, I have tried to assemble as much as possible about her in order to tease out the detail of lesbian life in Britain in earlier decades. This book examines lesbian history through the lives of individual lesbians. This collage of lesbianism shows how lesbian lives overlap, how lesbians have supported and loved one another, and how they have opposed and argued with each other.

In this book, then, I trace the lives of lesbians against the background of politics and history of their period, and I have tried to show the infinite variety of ways in which lesbians made their lives in Britain during this century. This history, made up of the lives of individual lesbians, is a constitutive element of contemporary lesbian life and has relevance to contemporary politics within the lesbian community.

A key area which has to be negotiated when doing historical research is where do you start and where do you stop. I focused my research on the following women: women who were involved in the suffrage campaigns; women who were involved in women's organizations; and women who were involved in homosexual organizations. From this large group of women I concentrated on those women who had close friendships with lesbians or gay men, women who had professional careers and did not marry, and women who lived with other women. Obviously this is only a partial history of British lesbians and lesbianism; there is a huge amount of British lesbian history which lies outside these parameters.

A major difficulty is identifying those lesbians who never had a long-term relationship. Without this, it is harder to distinguish the heterosexual or asexual spinster from the lesbian. I have no wish to co-opt heterosexual but celibate spinsters into lesbian history, and for this reason I have been wary of identifying women who did not have significant domestic relationships with other women as lesbians, unless there is other strong evidence. To those lesbians whom I have omitted because they were celibate, non-monogamous or inordinately promiscuous, I apologize.

There is much debate about whether we can know if lesbians existed in different historical periods. In *Surpassing the Love of Men*, Lillian Faderman appears to suggest that women probably did not have sex with each other before this century. Faderman states that

> women in centuries other than ours often internalized the view of females as having little sexual passion. Thus they might kiss, fondle each other, sleep together, utter expressions of overwhelming love and promises of eternal faithfulness, and yet see their passions as nothing more than effusions of the spirit.[7]

what about curiosity?

Few sexually explicit first-hand accounts of being lesbian have survived from before the middle of this century. The difficulty with Faderman's position is that she believes that the lack of such accounts means that women who loved women were not in fact having sex. The publication of Anne Lister's diaries in the late 1980s seems to show that Faderman is mistaken in this belief. Anne Lister was clearly having sex with women in the eighteenth century, and she felt and expressed her passion physically.

Faderman's position is that

> 'lesbian' describes a relationship in which two women's strongest emotions and affections are directed toward each other. Sexual contact may be a part of the relationship to a greater or lesser degree, or it may be entirely absent.[8]

This definition of lesbianism, which includes non-sexual relationships between women, is grounded in Lillian Faderman's own political beliefs about the nature of lesbian identity; her conception of lesbianism is evocative of lesbian-feminism. Sonja Ruehl has commented that

> to understand her account of this history the reader has to grasp Faderman's theoretical position, which is a lesbian-feminist one concerned to emphasise choice in relationship and also to demonstrate the continuity of friendship, emotional closeness and romance, and to de-emphasise the singling out of sexual expression as a particularly significant way of characterising women's relationships.[9]

Surpassing the Love of Men is an important resource for lesbian history. However, Faderman's belief that sex can be and may usually have been 'entirely absent' from lesbianism has had some unfortunate effects for lesbian history. One is that many studies of women's history do not bother to consider lesbianism as a specific mode of life, significantly different from that of having some good women friends. A paragraph is inserted into the introduction citing Faderman, which concludes along these lines: 'we cannot distinguish women's friendship from lesbianism, and there were not any lesbians as we know them today anyway, so we will just consider all female-female relationships as that of friends'. Lesbians and straight women, lesbianism and female friendship, are simply elided.

Lillian Faderman has also suggested that there were very few descriptions of lesbians in the culture at large so that women who loved other women simply would not know what to do with their passion. The first part of this argument has been undercut by Emma Donoghue's work.

Donoghue's *Passions Between Women* has highlighted the inaccuracy and elision in much of the history of British lesbians and lesbianism. Dictionaries are particularly inaccurate; according to the *Oxford English Dictionary* the words 'lesbian' and 'Sapphist' were not used in the homosexual sense until 1920 and 1908 respectively. Donoghue shows, however, that there are records of homosexual usage of lesbian and Sapphist for hundreds of years before this. There appears to have always been some space for, and acknowledgement of, lesbians in our culture.

The second point that Faderman makes, that we need to be taught how to relate desire to sex, that women who desired other women would be rendered impotent by lack of knowledge, is highly contestable. Babies masturbate; no one has to teach them how. Certainly, young lesbians without a physically explicit understanding of sex had to learn how to 'do' sex. However, this learning about the practicality of sex is not something which only lesbians go through. Young lesbians who had no access to books which instructed them in sexual techniques perhaps had less knowledge of how to do it at the beginning of their sexual careers but that does not mean that they never cracked it. Faderman's belief that women did not go 'down there', because they were socially conditioned not to, appears, in Terry Castle's words, to be a 'condescending belief in the intellectual and erotic naiveté of women of past epochs'.[10]

The fact that there are few autobiographical accounts which describe sex between women in graphic detail is explained more easily by the fact that women thought sex was private or that they knew that stories of sex between women would not add to their social respectability, rather than by the fact that women literally did not have sex with each other. To contend that women did not have sex with each other is to imply that sex and sexual desire are masculine, or only a female response to maleness. Historically in our culture a penis and penile penetration were generally required for something to count as 'sex': sex as a particular range of activities was constructed with the penis at the centre. This only means that nothing two (or more) women did together sexually was deemed to count as *real* sex. It does not mean that women did not have, and act on, burning sexual passions for each other, that women literally did not have sex.

These questions about sex and cultural beliefs about sex are central to a debate which has come out of Faderman's work, which is concerned with whether we can call women who lived in different historical periods from us 'lesbians'. The main issue here is that if lesbianism is a sexualized identity, can we then count as lesbians women who did not leave records of an explicitly sexual relationship? Can we in fact identify as lesbians women who did not explicitly identify themselves as lesbians?

As I have made clear, I believe that you can identify as lesbians women who have not left such explicit statements about their sexual identity. There is other information available to onlookers who are trying to see what a woman's life meant to her and how she thought of it which can show that she was a lesbian. It seems perverse for us to say that while a particular woman lived a lesbian life, that life is a conceptually separate question from that of whether she was a lesbian. Lesbianism is not, and has not been, a separate part of women's lives but an inalienable part of the fabric of their experiences and of their choices.

It is argued that only those women who thought of themselves as lesbians were lesbians. However, this does just seem wrong: being a lesbian is a theoretically observable aspect of a life. We may not have actually observed it in all cases but that does not mean that it is logically private. One is lesbian if the life that one lives is a lesbian life; what one thinks about that life is irrelevant to whether one is a lesbian. Of course, tracing the evolution of women being able to, or wanting to, describe themselves as lesbians is an interesting project. This evolution in publicly naming oneself as a lesbian is, however, separate from the history of lesbians and lesbianism *per se*.[11] In terms of this book I am fortunate; I do not actually have to engage in this debate. Nearly everyone is unanimous that women alive in this century would have been sexually aware and had sex.

There have been passionate debates about the cause of homosexuality since at least the middle of the last century. Lesbians, both now and in the past, have explained why they were lesbians in a number of different ways. These explanations have been the product not only of personal and autobiographical beliefs, but also of political expediency and broader scientific and political beliefs. I will discuss the differing explanations offered by lesbians for their lesbianism as they arise chronologically. It should be noted, however, that most lesbians whose lives I examine left no indication of their views on the genesis of their lesbianism.

Much of the history of lesbians, as written by lesbian historians, has accorded a key role to the development of the discipline of sexology in moulding lesbians' own perceptions of themselves. The sexologists who invented the new discipline of sexology in the mid-nineteenth century were mainly medics and scientists who took as their project the mapping of human sexuality. Work was done on homosexuality, and hence lesbianism, by the sexologists because homosexuality was seen as one of the anomalies and peculiarities that the discipline of sexology should be able to explain. Many of the key figures in the birth of sexology were German, such as Karl Ulrichs (1825–1895) and Richard von Krafft-Ebing (1840–1902).

I would argue, however, that the history of sexology has only an extremely tangential relevance to the lives and the history of British lesbians. The majority of sexological writing was not generally available to the British public or to British lesbians because it was not written in English, because it was published only in specialist journals, because such journals were very expensive, or because it was privately published, like J. A. Symonds's A *Problem in Greek Ethics* (1883), which had a print run of only ten copies. Thus care must be taken not to elide what the sexologists thought at any particular time about homosexuality with how lesbians thought about their sexuality, its meaning and their lives.

Moreover it should be remembered that the sexologists paid less attention to lesbians than they did to everyone else. Straight women, straight men and homosexual men were all seen as more exciting, perhaps even more sexy, than lesbians. Even Havelock Ellis's famous *Sexual Inversion* (1897) positioned lesbianism as a marginal subject. Sexologists believed that lesbians were very rare. As Jeffrey Weeks points out, in 1901 Krafft-Ebing believed that there were only fifty known cases of lesbianism.[12]

What is clear about the sexologists' accounts of lesbianism is that they had very little information to work from: there were no surveys of sexual behaviour and activity on which to base their work, and it was impossible to publicly advertise for lesbians to come forward to participate. The lesbians from whom sexologists drew their conclusions were known to the sexologists either because they moved in the same social circles or because the lesbian had presented herself to the sexologist. Lesbians who sought out sexologists were presumably troubled in some way by their lesbianism, and they cannot be taken as average representatives of lesbian experience.

It is important also to note that there were no sexologists, or none who figure in sexological history, who were lesbians. Sexologists did not know what it was like to be a lesbian, and had little vested interest in really finding out. In 1915 Stella Browne remarked that

> the psychology of homogenic women had been much less studied than that of inverted men. Probably there are many varieties and subtleties of emotional fibre among them.[13]

It was not until Charlotte Wolff's *Love Between Women* was published in 1971 that lesbianism got any significant psychological and sociological examination.

The sexologists do not, then, tell us what lesbian lives were like or what the vast majority of lesbians thought about their lesbianism. Radclyffe Hall was interested in the work of the sexologists (she read Havelock Ellis, Karl Ulrichs and Magnus Hirschfeld), but she seems to have been unusual. Lesbians with the interest in their lesbianism that Hall had in hers, and with the free time and the money to study sexological work, were rare. Very few of the lesbians I discuss appear to have read the sexologists.

In *The Spinster and Her Enemies*, Sheila Jeffreys's main thesis is that the sexologists created a lesbian stereotype which confounded lesbians and all women not engaged in heterosexuality. Sexology made the lives of women who were not actively heterosexual much harder. 'Spinster', she argues, became by the 1930s tarnished with connotations of lesbianism, perversity and repression. There does not seem to be overwhelming evidence in support of Sheila Jeffreys's view that the position of spinsters was made culturally untenable: in the mid-1930s a National Spinsters' Pension Association was established which published a magazine called *The Spinster*. By 1940 it had over 125,000 members and 97 branches. This does not indicate that 'spinster' was generally perceived to be a dirty word. Sexology is interesting in its own terms; but how some men conceptualized sexuality, gender and occasionally feminism does not make up lesbian history.

The most lasting benefit of sexology for lesbians and gay men was that it increased the vocabulary of homosexuality. While the words 'lesbian' and 'Sapphist' have been used for hundreds of years to describe women who love women, it was the sexologists who coined the term 'homosexual' in 1869, and the cluster of words from the root 'urania'. The language of urania filtered into radical and intellectual discourse via the work of Edward Carpenter. Ungoverned by long-established usage, there seem to have been hundreds of urania words that lesbians and gay men used: urning, uranian, uraniad, uraniand and so on.

I have tried as far as possible to use primary sources, that is the words of lesbians themselves, as the basis for this book. The descriptions of lesbians produced by investigating non-lesbians, including the sexologists, I have tended to use merely as light relief. While the description of 'social problems' by a well-meaning or salacious observer has a long history, it necessarily involves the experiences of the 'problem group' being re-interpreted. Even the most clinical observation and exposition tacitly introduces the views and beliefs of the analyst.

It became clear to me as I was writing this book that to follow the stylistic convention of consistently referring to an individual either by surname or by first name is actually not useful in the context of lesbian history. To refer to a woman by her first name implies a degree of intimacy and a lack of seriousness that does not feel appropriate. However, to refer to lesbians by their surnames actually elides their gender and their lesbianism. 'Smith and Jones go to bed' sounds like a gay male school story. I have resolved this difficulty by, inconsistently, using first name, surname and full name.

Finally, it is important to note the right of lesbians to privacy. There is an ethical dimension to naming women as lesbians to the general public without their express consent. I have followed the basic rule that if women who are still alive have not previously been publicly identified as lesbians, then I will not name them. I do not think that I have the right to out women regardless of their own preference for privacy, whatever I may think of the politics of that preference.

NOTES

1. *Sunday Times*, 5 August 1928. Glyn was the daughter of Vice-Admiral the Hon. Henry Carr Glyn.
2. Stella Browne, 'The sexual variety and variability among women', in Sheila Rowbotham, *A New World of Women: Stella Browne – Socialist Feminist* (London: Pluto Press, 1977), pp. 104–5.
3. See Susan Edwards, *Female Sexuality and the Law* (Oxford: Martin Robertson: 1981), p.45.
4. Cherry Smith, *Lesbians Talk Queer Notions* (London: Scarlet Press, 1992), p.23, re Jennifer Saunders.
5. Liz Stanley, 'Romantic friendship? Some issues in researching lesbian history and biography', *Women's History Review*, **1**(2), 1992, p.210.
6. Terry Castle, *The Apparitional Lesbian: Female Homosexuality and Modern Culture* (New York: Columbia University Press, 1993), p.12.
7. Lillian Faderman, *Surpassing the Love of Men* (London: The Women's Press, 1985), p.16.
8. *Ibid.*, pp.17–18.
9. Sonja Ruehl, 'Sexual theory and practice: another double standard', in Sue Cartledge and Jo Ryan (eds), *Sex and Love: New Thoughts on Old Contradictions* (London: The Women's Press, 1983), pp.216–17.

10. Castle, *The Apparitional Lesbian*, p.9.
11. See Leila J. Rupp quoted in Martin Duberman *et al.* (eds), *Hidden from History: Reclaiming the Lesbian and Gay Past* (New York: Meridan, 1990), for an interesting discussion of this issue.
12. Jeffrey Weeks, *Coming Out: Homosexual Politics in Britain from the Nineteenth Century to the Present* (London: Quartet, 1990, revised edition), p.88.
13. Browne, 'The sexual variety and variability among women', p.102.

2 lesbians and suffragists

'I don't know what to do — I'm torn in two'
Sappho, Fragment 48

In 1915 Kathlyn Oliver wrote to Edward Carpenter:

> I feel I must write to you, I have recently read with much interest your book entitled 'The Intermediate Sex' & it has lately dawned on me that I myself belong to that class and I write to ask if there is any way of getting in touch with others of the same temperament. I am a woman, 30 years of age & horribly lonely tho' I have a number of friends & acquaintances many of whom think quite a lot of me, but I unhappily feel quite out of touch with them. For about two years past I have longed intensely for a woman friend who would be to me more than anyone else in the world.[1]

There is little information available on Kathlyn Oliver. Her letters suggest that she was a middle-class woman who lived in London, that she was born about 1885 and was thirty when she wrote to Edward Carpenter.

After the death of her father when she was in her middle twenties she supported herself, unusually for a woman of her class, through domestic work. At this point although approximately 29 per cent of the officially recorded labour force were women, the majority of them were in domestic service – nearly 1,500,000 women in 1911. In the unindustrialized South employment opportunities for women other than in teaching and domestic service were rare. Domestic work, whether paid or unpaid, was not without real dangers: Lilian Barker nearly died in 1904 when some beeswax she was heating in the oven for polishing ignited; she suffered horrific burns and spent three months in hospital.

The life and beliefs of Edward Carpenter are well-documented. He was a utopian writer, a free-thinker, a socialist and a believer in rational dress. He was also homosexual and wrote widely on homosexuality and gender. In 1894 Carpenter published *Homogenic Love*; this was followed up by

The Intermediate Sex in 1908. He was the first President of the British Society for the Study of Sex Psychology (BSSSP), which was established in 1914. As Jeffrey Weeks notes:

> The discussion of homosexuality was inevitably at the heart of the society's work. Nor is this surprising . . . most of the leading lights who dominated the society from the 1920s, from Carpenter on his pedestal to Houseman and Ives, and later Norman Haire, were homosexual.[2]

The BSSSP served as a forum for both homosexual men and sexologists to meet and debate the nature of homosexuality. These two groups were not mutually exclusive; many sexologists were gay men.

Some women were involved with the BSSSP, such as Dora Russell, the leftist radical married to Bertrand Russell, and Stella Browne, the contraception pioneer. However, they were not lesbians; indeed they vigorously reiterated their heterosexuality. There seems to have been little lesbian involvement in the BSSSP. Discussions of lesbianism tended to occur as adjutants to the main issue, either male homosexuality or female heterosexuality. Lesbianism appears to have been perceived as either a mirror image of male homosexuality or as a route taken by women to avoid the more potent and potentially overwhelming nature of heterosexuality. The actual work of the BSSSP probably did not have much impact on lesbians; papers read at the BSSSP were not widely available, or even always published.

Carpenter had received correspondence from gay men for several years but following the publication of *The Intermediate Sex* he received a number of letters from lesbians. While many gay men, then as now, eulogized masculinity as the defining aspect of homosexuality, Carpenter wrote of the social constrictions of gender and dreamt of the perfect world where a median type with the best elements of man and woman would reign. Carpenter wrote positively of love between women and of the importance of women gaining the suffrage. Crucially, Carpenter was a visionary, not a doctor or scientist, and his books were written in a relatively popular sty!e. This, in conjunction with his widely known homosexuality and his involvement with BSSSP, made him a uniquely approachable figure for lesbians.

Many of Carpenter's homosexual contemporaries were not sympathetic to lesbianism. The American Edward Stephenson, who published *The Intersexes* in 1908 under the name Xavier Mayne, believed gay men were not only more spiritually and aesthetically pleasing than lesbians but, even more contentiously, that they lived longer. Particularly in light of the alternatives Edward Carpenter must have seemed profoundly lesbian-friendly. The letters Carpenter received from lesbians expressed gratitude: 'I should like to take this opportunity to say what I have always wanted to say to you, to try & express my gratitude for the splendid work you have done for Uranians.'[3] Kathlyn Oliver perceived him to be friendly and supportive to lesbians; she says, as she tells him the story of her life, that she hopes it 'doesn't bore you, but I believe you are sympathetic'.[4]

The letters Carpenter received were more than fan letters; lesbians saw him as a resource which they could use. What Kathlyn Oliver wanted was a lover:

> I have recently started a correspondence with a woman (about 30) in Scotland. She has been living for the last 4 years with a woman friend & they are very much in love & their relationship is physical as well as spiritual – they are intensely happy & I quite envy them – I long more than I can say to love a woman completely & absolutely & to have that love returned.[5]

She also hoped that Carpenter could help her to find one:

> It is possible that I shall have to leave my chances of meeting a kindred spirit to fate or luck but I am hoping you may know of some society or channel through which I may meet my other half.
> One of the correspondents in the appendix to your book speaks of having associated with Urnings *organised* & otherwise.[6]

Kathlyn Oliver was aware that wanting a lesbian relationship, and having one, would not be generally condoned: 'The world would say that a physical relationship between two of the same sex is an unspeakable crime,'[7] but Kathlyn was having none of this:

> But after a few weeks of consideration I have come to the conclusion that this relationship can *never* be as degrading as the *normal* sex relationship can be & *usually* is. I know it is a big thing to say that the normal sex relationship of men & women is *more* degrading than the other, but it will *be true wherever & so long as women are in economic slavery to men* – & I think you will agree.[8]

Clearly feminist thought had influenced how Kathlyn Oliver understood her lesbianism. As her correspondence to Carpenter and others makes clear, she identified as a feminist and a suffragist, a pacifist and a socialist.

In Britain at the turn of the century the most explicitly feminist focus of attention was the issue of women's suffrage. Organized suffrage activism had begun in Britain in the 1860s; in 1865 the Manchester National Society for Women's Suffrage had been established, and other groups quickly followed. From this date women, with some male support, had campaigned for female enfranchisement. Women, of course, were not the only group without the suffrage in Britain; enfranchisement was contingent upon a property qualification which effectively debarred both rural and urban working-class men from political participation. Universal suffrage was seen by many property owners as a dangerously radical fantasy which could destroy the nation.

The tactics of the women's suffrage groups, which were largely united in the National Union for Women's Suffrage Societies (NUWSS), were discreet and unaggressive. The NUWSS concentrated on Parliamentary lobbying and the regular presentation by sympathetic MPs of Bills in Parliament to enfranchise women. Historically, certain groups of women had been able to vote in Parliamentary elections, and this common law practice had only been finally eliminated by the Reform Act of 1832. It was this Act which 'by employing the term 'male person' for the first time in English history, expressly debarred women from claiming the franchise that it created'[9].

Women's Disabilities' Removal Bills were presented to Parliament through the 1870s and 1880s. The Bills were not successful and many suffrage activists shifted their efforts to campaign on other issues where women suffered from discrimination, such as the position of married women and divorce law. These efforts resulted in some advances, for instance in the amelioration of the position of married women, but by the beginning of this century the gaining of the vote for women seemed as far away as ever.

Suffrage activity, however, was reinvigorated with the establishment of the Women's Social and Political Union (WSPU) by the widowed Mrs Emmeline Pankhurst in Manchester in 1903. Her husband, Richard, had been a committed supporter of women's suffrage, drafting one of the early Bills presented to Parliament seeking to remove women's disabilities. Mrs Pankhurst's three daughters, Sylvia, Adela and Christabel, were raised in an atmosphere of political radicalism, and all did significant work for the cause of women's suffrage and female emancipation.

It was not by chance that so much political radicalism came out of Manchester. For both working-class men and women jobs in the Lancashire cotton industry were a spur to political activism. Wages were relatively high and, as Karl Marx and Friedrich Engels noted, the organization of industry provided a supportive structure for political organization. Manchester was the seed-bed of the trade union movement and the Independent Labour Party. Women received significantly higher wages in the cotton industry than they did in other non-professional jobs and they worked on relatively egalitarian terms with men. Many of the women suffrage activists came from Lancashire, where there was a tradition of political activism and female economic power.[10]

Mrs Pankhurst had been actively involved in the politics of the emerging Independent Labour Party and she was much piqued by their lack of commitment towards the enfranchisement of women. As Sylvia Pankhurst wryly commented, many socialists and Labour Party activists argued that

> it was not essential . . . that the whole people should be enfranchised. So long as the division were not upon class lines, their interests would be the same. There was no distinction of interest on sex, but only on class lines. It was not important that women should have the vote; for whilst some people would take an interest in politics, others would specialise in other directions.[11]

The Pankhurst women received these comments with bitter resentment.

Militant activism is dated from 13 October 1905 when Christabel Pankhurst and Annie Kenney tried to disrupt a Liberal Party election meeting in the Free Trade Hall in Manchester. After some difficulty they succeeded in being arrested – Christabel Pankhurst spat at a policeman in order to commit a technical assault. They were duly tried and sentenced to paying a fine or being imprisoned. They both refused to pay the fine: Annie Kenney was sentenced to three days in Strangeways, Christabel Pankhurst to five. Militancy, the aggressive disruption of order and the violation of civil and criminal law, gradually gathered steam. The militants, who described themselves as 'Suffragettes', a term not previously used, attempted to disrupt political meetings and government business, chained themselves to railings, refused to pay taxes, broke windows, set fire to pillar-boxes and also committed more serious crimes against property.

The development of militancy was not appreciated by the constitutionally organized suffragists, who felt that it did not help the cause but rather reinforced the preconception that women were immature and irrational. However, the militant suffragists gathered force in 1907 when the WSPU split, the majority accepting unconditionally Mrs Pankhurst's autocratic leadership and militant campaigning. The minority who wanted to maintain internal democracy established themselves as the democratic, and less militant, Women's Freedom League.[12]

From 1907 the WSPU belonged to Emmeline Pankhurst and Christabel, her best-loved daughter. Both women possessed great charisma and inspired great personal devotion. They saw themselves, and were seen by their female supporters, as the generals of an army fighting an almost holy war. They were not naïve; as one woman who had known them remarked, they were endowed 'with a fine sense of the dramatic and an appreciation of good stage management'.[13] By 1910 militant suffrage activism was perceived as a major nuisance by the newspapers and the government. Suffrage militancy in many ways provided the basis of modern direct action campaigns of groups such as ACT UP and OutRage!, but the suffragettes provoked greater government anger.

The suffragettes were usually arrested easily, for one of the aims of the campaign was to state the suffrage case in court. The authorities were unwilling to imprison women for these calculated attempts to infringe the law but as the suffragettes always refused to pay their fines they eventually had no choice but to incarcerate them, usually in Strangeways in Manchester and in Holloway in London, which were women's prisons.

The suffragettes further outraged the authorities by demanding that they be treated as political prisoners rather than common criminals for the duration of their sentences, a tactic shared by Irish Nationalists. It was as a protest against the government's refusal to treat them as political prisoners that the suffragettes undertook hunger strikes while in prison. No deaths directly resulted from their hunger strikes although a number of women, such as Lady Constance Lytton, had their health so undermined by the experience that their lives were shortened.

It was the WSPU, and to a lesser extent the Women's Freedom League (WFL), which was the home of the militant suffragettes; the long-established NUWSS continued to employ only constitutional tactics in its fight for the vote. Militant campaigning obviously served as a general tonic to the suffrage organizations by re-establishing women's suffrage as a topical and contested issue. This is shown by the growth in suffrage publications in the years between 1907 and the outbreak of World War I: there was The Suffragette published by the WSPU, Common Cause published by the NUWSS, The Vote published by the WFL, and the quasi-independent Votes for Women produced by Emmeline Pethick-Lawrence.

The relationship between the suffrage movement and lesbians is complex. The gaining of the vote would give women a symbolic equality with men, an equality which presumably was more important to lesbians than to women who were happy to be a man's wife. The acknowledgement of the worth and capability of women which the suffragists sought via the vote again may have attracted women who loved women, and who felt excluded and devalued in a society which saved its greatest approbation for women who had attracted a man.

The social change which the gaining of the suffrage would bring would allow lesbians more space in which to be independent of men; social pressures which forced women to marry might be eased if women were acknowledged to be competent and complete citizens. Micky Jacob, a lesbian and a suffragette, was to say:

> Looking back, I think that the Suffragettes helped me to – get free. I met women who worked, women who had ambitions, and some who had gratified those ambitions. I looked at my own position, and began to think and think hard.[14]

More prosaically, some of the concomitant aims of the suffrage movement, namely the opening of education and the professions to women, were clearly even more important to women who did not want to marry than to those who expected to marry and to be at least partially supported by a man's wage. Suffrage campaigning involved campaigning to improve women's economic and social position, which must have attracted many lesbians who could only gain in practical terms by such change. Many women were denied education and a career by social convention and external barriers: women were explicitly barred from many professions.

The situation of lesbians who were denied education and professional training, and hence the opportunity to be self-supporting, is vividly illustrated in the letters received by Edward Carpenter. Amy Tasker, who lived in Huntingdon, wrote to Carpenter in 1913. She described her experience of trying, and failing, to get an education:

> From the age of 16 to 30 I besieged my parents to let me make my own career, at first I begged for a higher education, then that I might specialise as a lecturer on history & literature or go the stage but it was useless, short of running away penniless there was no escape. Now my duty is fixed – to care for my mother & make the best her last years.[15]

As a result of her lack of education Amy Tasker was completely dependent on her family. This, as well as her acceptance of her social duty to care for her mother, had a catastrophic effect on her life:

[a further] Thirteen years passed before I met the woman of my dreams. For 6 years she has been all in all to me. [unreadable] I loved her as the mother of my children. When we were together the strength of my soul, mind & body was at its best.

She became engaged a month ago & I am widowed as no man was ever widowed. If I had had a house for my Love she would have been mine to her life's end, often she has said I filled her whole soul & being, that she desire no more of Life than my great Love [unreadable] to her. Her parents have lately lost almost all their income, I am bound hand & foot to [unreadable] (& have no money of my own) with no hope of freedom nor can I leave what little money I shall have out of the family. Terror of the future has taken her from me. The best in me thanks God for her happiness.

[unreadable] is an agony of suffering over which it is more decent to draw a veil & that is mine. – If it is possible to save others from this unspeakable pain in God's name let it be done. It is for this that I decided to reveal myself.[16]

Kathlyn Oliver had found herself in a similar position:

After that I lost my father, – who occupied a good position in the civil service, but though he was one of the best of men in a general way he did not think it necessary that his daughters sh[oul]d have more than a very secondary education & it happened that at the time of his death I was quite unfitted to earn my living which I had to do. I took up domestic work – the *conditions* & *spirit* of which I loathe. . . . But tho' I had other 'chances' to marry & tho' I was at times rather tempted to sell myself in marriage as a way out of work which I hated. I am indeed glad today that I did not yield to the temptation.[17]

The pressure upon lesbians to marry, in order not to literally starve or to be forced to work in grossly unsafe and poorly rewarded industries, was huge.

While there were strong ideological and economic motives for lesbians to support the campaign for the vote, there were also reasons of simple pleasure. The suffrage movement provided a forum where women could meet large numbers of other women. For women who were aware of their sexual desire for women, suffrage work provided a way of getting to know women and a conversational starting-point. Suffrage organizations contained women who had defied convention and who liked women: a positive lesbian environment. It seems likely as well that some women may have been awakened or converted to lesbianism through meeting lesbians in the suffrage movement.

Among the militant suffragists the camaraderie and emotional commitment was very strong: 'The spirit of the WSPU now became more and more that of a volunteer army at war.'[18] The historian Martha Vicinus stresses the junking of conventional femininity that took place in the ranks of the suffragettes:

> The leaders of the WSPU astutely tapped into the youthful desire for greater physical freedom and encouraged the exhilaration of battle among those who suffered from taunts, missiles, and unpleasant attacks wherever they attempted to speak in public. A 'hardened suffragette' knew, unlike many women, that she could 'take care of herself,' while the inexperienced learned to overcome traditional womanly inhibitions and fears.[19]

For a number of reasons, then, the militant suffrage movement attracted large numbers of lesbians: Mary Allen, Rachel Barrett, Eva Gore-Booth, Vera Holme, Evelina Haverfield, Esther Roper, Chris St John, Micky Jacob. They were not alone:

> Virtually all the full-time [WSPU] organizers were single women, and donations to the WSPU shifted from 45 per cent unmarried subscribers in the fiscal year 1906–7 to 63 per cent in the year 1913–14.[20]

The WSPU, as it gathered together women who wanted to cast off their shackles, became increasingly attractive to unmarried women. Not all unmarried women were lesbians, but lesbians appear to have made up a significant proportion of unmarried women who dedicated their energy to women's organizations and women's interests.

The most famous lesbian involved in the pre-war suffrage campaigns was the composer Ethel Smyth (1858–1944). It has been suggested that Ethel Smyth had an affair with Emmeline Pankhurst; they certainly had a very intimate relationship. If this is true it would put lesbianism at the heart of the suffrage movement. A longer-lasting gift was *The March of the Women*, Smyth's suffrage anthem, which she famously conducted with a toothbrush from the window of her cell in Holloway. Ethel Smyth was friendly with Radclyffe Hall and her lover Mabel Batten at this time and encouraged them to support the suffrage campaign.[21]

However, suffrage activism did not make a space which enabled Kathlyn Oliver, or indeed any other lesbian, to speak *as a lesbian*. This is illustrated by Oliver's correspondence with the feminist journal *The Freewoman* in 1912. Here Kathlyn Oliver engaged in a debate with Stella Browne on the subject of the importance of sexual desire and sexual activity in women's lives. In this very public debate Oliver makes it clear that she does not agree with Browne's view that women who live without (hetero)sexual contact are more prone to neurosis.[22] However, she certainly does not say that she is a member of the 'intermediate sex' or has uranian leanings. Rather, she sardonically emphasizes her potential heterosexuality:

> If I may give my own experience (which corresponds with that of most girls whom I have known), I had no serious desire to marry until I was 23, when I fell in love. Until this time, in sentimental moments I liked to dream about wifehood and motherhood, but I liked to contemplate them as I did heaven, as joys which awaited me in the *very far future*.[23]

In describing the same incident to Edward Carpenter she is more explicit about how she felt about marriage:

> I might mention that I have been engaged to marry on two occasions. The first affair was in my early 20s I liked the man a good deal & I suppose I thought I loved him but when the time came for him to talk of furniture & marriage I backed out. The thought of marriage & all that it meant repelled & disgusted me.[24]

Even though Oliver's life was economically precarious she just could not bring herself to marry; she could square it neither with her erotic desires nor with her feminist understanding of the nature of relationships between men and women in a patriarchal world. Kathlyn Oliver's disgust was not a neurotic fear of the mechanics of heterosexual intercourse. She believed that men and the world they had created, and hence their relationships with women, were extremely unpleasant.

Oliver made her views very clear in a letter she wrote to *The Freewoman*:

> From the 'natural' man, good Lord, deliver us. The very thought of him raises indeed a nightmare too horrible for words.
>
> Probably Mr d'Auvergre [an earlier correspondent] would like to revoke the law which makes rape and criminal assault on girls and women a punishable offence?
>
> But if the 'natural' man is to be encouraged, and if he is to roam at large in society with his natural instincts and desires ungoverned and uncontrolled, may I suggest as a woman that all girls and women be taught the use of firearms, which should be carried as regularly as a handkerchief?[25]

The Freewoman was a space where Oliver could articulate a robust and angry feminist political view. However, it was clearly not a space where she felt it was possible to come out as lesbian, for not only did she not come out, she 'heterosexualized' herself in her earlier letter. This is particularly interesting, given that *The Freewoman* was known to be sexually progressive, and had already run a series of sympathetic articles about homosexuality in the early months of 1912. Why was Oliver – and she was not alone in this – unable to identify publicly as a lesbian when she was supported by feminist politics and had access to a forum where discussion of homosexuality was accepted?

One strong restraining factor for lesbians such as Kathlyn Oliver who were committed suffragists and feminists must have been the public politics of much suffrage activism. A considerable force behind the suffrage movement was the belief that women should have the vote because of their special womanly qualities:

> Pioneers of the women's movement did not argue so much for the similarity of women to men as for the existence of women's special skills in regard to children, healthcare, education, and domestic morality.[26]

The public support that the suffrage campaign had was dependent upon the suffragists appearing just like normal wives, mothers, sisters and daughters. Whatever the reality of the sexualities of women within the Amazonian band of militant suffrage warriors, public support could not be alienated by a public discussion of lesbianism.

As far as the suffrage groups themselves were concerned, they seem to have seen lesbianism as a stick with which the cause could be attacked. Lesbianism was too potentially damaging to the cause to even be mentioned. The lack of lesbians coming out within the suffrage movement implies that they too, as Kathlyn Oliver clearly did, accepted the potential danger of suffragist lesbians becoming visible. Although some contemporary commentators did make vague imputations of lesbianism to suffrage activists, as George Dangerfield did in *The Strange Death of Liberal England* (1936), the suffragists' silence on lesbianism does seem to have indeed stopped accusations of lesbianism being flung at them.

The silence of the suffragists on the issue of lesbianism was not just due to political expediency and quite deplorable cowardliness. For feminists, then as now, lesbianism was problematic. Sheila Jeffreys notes, in *The Spinster and Her Enemies*, that much non-suffrage female activism in the public arena was orientated around the control of sex and sexuality.

> This period [1880–1930] witnessed a massive campaign by women to transform male sexual behaviour and protect women from the effects of the exercise of a form of male sexuality damaging to their interests.[27]

Issues like temperance, child abuse, and prostitution were all areas where women were key campaigners; not all these campaigns were feminist, but they were all gendered, with men cast as the sexual aggressors and women as their victims.

Attacks on male sexuality were also a feature of the suffrage campaigns. Christabel Pankhurst's *The Great Scourge* (1908) on venereal disease and Louisa Martindale's *Under the Surface* (1910) on prostitution were both exposés of how male sexuality was physically and psychologically damaging to women. Cicely Hamilton in *Marriage as a Trade* (1909) went further, by arguing that even within marriage women sold themselves sexually and economically. These pamphlets were revolutionary in their explanation of male sexual activity as a tool by which men dominated and exploited women.

As Jeffreys shows, feminists used the idea of men as sexed and women as sexless to justify their political and moral demands. One of their key political and rhetorical strategies was to stress the relationship between men, sex and danger. The extent to which feminists really believed in what was to a certain extent tactical propaganda remains unclear.

There can be danger for women in sex and in violent sexual desire; this does not mean that sex and sexual desire are necessarily dangerous to women and against women's interests. However, an implicit consequence of the suffragist tactics around sex, which Jeffreys fails to follow up, is that it made it extremely problematic for suffragists to then articulate their own sexual desire for women. Lesbian desire *as a sexual desire* 'preyed' upon women just as male heterosexual desire did. Against this background it would have been very hard to come out as a lesbian. Thus the feminist strategy of the period made publicly declaring one's lesbianism almost impossible for feminists.

Even the progressive *Freewoman* was affected by this feminist anxiety about lesbians. *The Freewoman* was established in 1911 under the editorship of Dora Marsden, herself formerly a militant suffragette. In the very first issue it was made clear, in the editorial, that *The Freewoman* was not going to toe the usual suffrage line. *The Freewoman* distinguished itself firmly from the politics of the suffragists, stating that its concern was with spiritual freedom for women, not the mere freedom to participate economically and politically in society. For *The Freewoman*, the vote was not a practical tool for helping woman to freedom but a symbolic sign of equality. The Freewoman was concerned with 'spiritual freedom', which was generally interpreted as the right to engage in sex and in attacks on chastity, the double standard and the marriage and divorce laws; among its contributors were the sexual radicals George Bernard Shaw and Rebecca West.

The Freewoman was outspoken in its defence of the validity and righteousness of women's heterosexual desire. It was much more circumspect about lesbianism. The debate which was run on homosexuality, under the title 'Uranians' in early 1912, largely ignored lesbians.[28] By discussing homosexuality relatively sympathetically and at length, The Freewoman was unique in feminist circles. The initial article by 'Harry J. Birnstringl' made the revolutionary public statement that 'women are forming romantic – nay, sometimes passionate attachments with each other'.[29] However, this sentence was practically the entire extent of The Freewoman's discussion of lesbianism.

It seems then that Kathlyn Oliver's life as a lesbian was deeply influenced by this contemporary feminist analysis of lesbianism as problematic. This feminist analysis both gave a theoretical and political justification for lesbianism, and simultaneously ensured that it remained the love that dare not speak its name. Whether Carpenter helped Oliver to find more lesbian friends or a lover is unknown and I have not been able to trace Kathlyn Oliver's subsequent history.

Many lesbians come to public attention, as Kathlyn Oliver did, for writing just a few letters that have been preserved; after these fifteen minutes of fame they disappear into the black hole of female invisibility. However, it is not necessarily easier to uncover the lives of lesbians whose lives are more consistently documented: many biographers have not been eager to disclose the lesbianism of their subject. In the last ten years this has begun to change – perhaps the most significant lesbian-friendly biography being Victoria Glendinning's biography of Vita Sackville-West, published in 1984. Glendinning, not a lesbian, took lesbianism pragmatically and explicitly into the mainstream of biography.

Some feminists have set out to write the biography of relatively undocumented feminist lives. Sometimes these biographies are explicitly open to the possibility that the woman in question might have been a lesbian. Ann Morley and Liz Stanley in their biography of Emily Wilding Davison, who was killed apparently during a suffragette protest, pose the possibility that Davison may have been a lesbian. Emily Wilding Davison (1872–1913) was educated at Royal Holloway College, Surrey, and at Oxford. She subsequently, between 1893 and 1906, worked as a teacher.

In 1906 she joined the WSPU and became extremely militant. She was arrested for window-breaking and setting fire to pillar-boxes; she was imprisoned and she suffered forced feeding. In 1913 she was killed at the Derby, by the King's horse, when she ran on to the racetrack. As a result of her death, reported as a vote-related suicide, Davies became the best-known contemporary symbol of the suffrage struggle.

Ann Morley and Liz Stanley show that various facts about Emily's life indicate that she may have been a lesbian: she was educated and had a career when these were not usual for women; she had very few male friends; she was a member of the significantly lesbian WSPU; and she was friendly with other lesbians. Morley and Stanley are painstaking in their efforts to shed light upon her life, and in particular to identify her women friends and possible woman lovers. However, they conclude, realistically, that there does not appear to be any evidence to suggest that she was a lesbian rather than a feminist with a lot of female friends.

Other biographers of women who shared the same interests as Emily Wilding Davison are absolutely determined that such 'circumstantial' evidence should not influence how they write up the lives of their subjects. Biographers of women who were active in feminist politics and active members of women-only groups, who lived with a woman partner and who had no obvious heterosexual interests, are suppressing the truth if they do not say that this suggests that such a woman may have been a lesbian. Certainly, in the past, biographers have actively suppressed material which explicitly showed their subjects to have been homosexual. This may be less common now but it has probably not disappeared entirely.

The markedly different reactions of biographers to the possibility of their subjects being lesbians is clearly illustrated in the work that has been done on the novelist(s) 'Somerville and Ross'. 'Somerville and Ross' was actually two Anglo-Irish gentlewomen, Edith Somerville (1858–1949) and Violet Martin (1862–1915), who were cousins. Somerville and Martin met for the first time in 1886, and their first volume of stories, *Some Experiences of an Irish RM*,* was published in 1899. They wrote collaboratively and produced a single authorial voice.

For the first twenty years of their partnership Edith and Martin, as Violet was known, lived in different parts of Ireland. They did, however, spend extended periods of time together. After Martin's mother's death in 1906, she moved into the Somerville home, Drishane. They lived here together for nine years until Martin's death. Somerville continued to write as

*Resident Magistrate

'Somerville and Ross', saying that Martin communicated her thoughts and creativity from beyond the grave.

The first biography of Edith Somerville and Violet Martin by Maurice Collis stresses the all-consuming love that these two unmarried cousins shared.[30] However, Gifford Lewis's 1985 biography appears to take as a *raison d'être* the scotching of these lesbian insinuations. Lewis spends considerable energy showing how both women had had unconsummated heterosexual 'romances' in their youths. The failure of these relationships purportedly explains why Somerville and Ross accepted the position of sexually and romantically inactive spinsters for the rest of their lives. According to Lewis it is against this backdrop of thwarted heterosexuality that Somerville and Ross's relationship must be considered.

Gifford Lewis is unshakeable in her belief that Somerville and Ross were not lovers. She writes:

> That Edith was a lesbian has gained general acceptance through an unlovely combination of affected liberalism, ignorant salaciousness and the sad assumption that huge vitality and strength in a woman implies masculinity.[31]

There is no affected liberalism here. One detail of the relationship which may have been particularly problematic to deal with, if Somerville and Ross were indeed lesbians, was its quasi-incestuous nature.

Lewis justifies her belief that Edith Somerville was heterosexual with statements like this: 'Edith had no desire to cut herself off from the society of men, as we can see from her speeches as President of the Munster Women's Suffrage League.'[32] While being president of the local women's suffrage organization may not mean that you are a lesbian, it surely cannot be used to show your simple and unproblematic love of men and heterosexuality. This is like citing one's Labour Party membership to show that one has a fondness for unadulterated capitalism.

Lewis also cites the correspondence between Somerville and Ross to show how they were not romantically or erotically committed to each other:

> The undemonstrative nature of their affection for each other is shown by a letter from Martin to Edith dated 23 January 1895. After nine years of knowing Edith, Martin is embarrassed to write of physical affection.[33]

The point here is moot. After a nine-year relationship, a brief absence from one's partner may well not drive one into rhapsodies of erotic poetry.

Moreover, Edith may well have destroyed any such letters that she had received from Martin, in the interest of maintaining the privacy of their relationship. Edith Somerville wrote, perhaps marking this fact, while Martin was dying, 'No one but she and I know what we were to each other.'[34]

Gifford Lewis's (heterosexual) version of Somerville and Ross is made more complicated by the relationship between Ethel Smyth and Edith Somerville. Somerville met Smyth after Martin's death when both women were in their fifties, about 1919. At the very least they shared a commitment to the women's suffrage movement. Smyth, who was notoriously blatant about her homosexuality, tried over a number of months to seduce Edith. According to Lewis, in this instance, Ethel Smyth's efforts were unsuccessful. However, other readers of the Somerville-Smyth correspondence strongly dispute Lewis's interpretation of the women's relationship, arguing that Smyth's letters suggest she had an affair with Emmeline Pankhurst and subsequently one with Edith Somerville.[35]

Another lesbian couple who have received some double-edged biographical attention are Christopher St John (1873–1960) and her lover Edy Craig (1869–1947). Edy was the daughter of the renowned actress Ellen Terry, and has thus received some attention in biographies of her mother. As well as this Edy and Chris appear as minor characters in a number of different autobiographies, reminiscences and biographies, including those of Sir John Gielgud: their range of friends was huge. Edy worked as a theatre and costume designer and Chris was a jobbing journalist and writer; their lives were quite ordinary, although avant-garde, and they were neither rich nor successful by the time they died.

Edy Craig and Chris St John were widely known to be lesbians and were physically recognizable as such; Vita Sackville-West remarked on first meeting Edy, the more feminine of the two, that she was the 'most tearing old lesbian'.[36] Vera Brittain, not a close friend, named them as lesbians as early as 1968. Presumably it was their public lesbianism which has led so many, superficially disinterested, commentators to attack them.

Michael Baker, a biographer of Radclyffe Hall, says of Edy: 'She had an undeniable streak of brilliance but she was too overbearing to reap the rewards her talent deserved.' If this appears to be a backhanded insult Chris comes off even worse: 'Chris was a heavy, ugly woman; clever, fastidious, stubborn, and cripplingly sensitive to her looks and cleft palate.'[37] This is remarkably perceptive as no photos of Chris in her prime appear to have survived, and in old age she looks neither 'heavy' nor 'ugly' but rather like a lesbian.

Chris St John is a particularly interesting woman. According to the *Somerville College Register* 1879–1971, she was educated at Clifton House School, Bristol, and abroad. She went to Somerville College, Oxford, in 1890 and she left in 1893, having gained a third in history.[38] She clearly came from a middle-class and progressive family, for she was one of the first women to go to Somerville, which was founded in 1879. By 1899 St John was apparently, according to the fallible *Times*, working as secretary to the Churchill family.

Chris appears to have replaced her given name, Christabel Marshall, with 'Christopher St John' before 1899; in the *Somerville College Register* she is listed as 'Christopher Marie St John (C.G. Marshall)'. As an adult she was always and in all spheres known as Christopher St John. This change of name is usually explained in terms of her Catholicism: 'She was a fervent Catholic convert; her 'St John' stood for St John the Baptist for whom she had a special devotion.'[39] This, however, cannot be the whole story. It is not standard Catholic practice to use one's saint's name in secular life, particularly if one has chosen a man's name.

When Radclyffe Hall converted to Catholicism in 1912 she took Antonia St Anthony as her baptismal name.[40] Thus, not even Radclyffe Hall took a man's name (and Christopher is indisputably a man's name) as her Catholic baptismal name. Neither did Hall take the male name she used in her secular life, John, as her baptismal name, or give 'John' as her name on her published work. The unexplained element of 'Christopher St John' is not the 'St John' but the 'Christopher'; what made Chris ditch Christabel for Christopher? One cannot gloss over the fact that Chris lived her whole adult life under a man's name by referring to her religious convictions.

Edy and Chris met as a result of Chris's crush on Ellen Terry. Although it was not love at first sight, their intimate relationship was quickly established. They lived together for forty-eight years, from 1899 until Edy's death. At the beginning of their life together they lived in Smith Square in Westminster; their friends referred to them subsequently as 'the squares'; even *The Times* in 1960 felt able to remark that Edy and Chris were anything but square.[41]

Both Chris and Edy were involved in the militant suffrage movement; one of them, probably Chris, was arrested for setting fire to a pillar-box in 1909.[42] Chris also wrote a number of extremely funny propaganda plays on women's suffrage with Cicely Hamilton. The most famous, *Votes for Women* (1909), concerns itself with what men would do if women really were totally dependent upon them as they were supposed to be. These plays were performed at suffragette events in London to a rapturous reception. Chris and Edy's public identification with, and commitment to, the enfranchisement of women was life-long. In 1937 Edy Craig was one of three invited speakers at the 'Annual Dinner for the Commemoration of the Passing of the Representation of the People Act 1918'.[43]

In 1911 Chris St John and Edy Craig also founded the Pioneer Players with Laurence Houseman (1865–1959), a gay man, who was the first chairman of the BSSSP. The Pioneer Players, even though they were run on a shoestring during their ten-year life, were an important theatre club. They specialized in new, foreign and feminist plays; the club was set up as private and this enabled it to put on plays which were otherwise unperformable. In 1912, for instance, the Pioneer Players staged Bernard Shaw's *Mrs Warren's Profession*, which was banned from public staging because it discussed prostitution; Radclyffe Hall appears to have attended this performance. For the Pioneer Players, Chris adapted and translated many now obscure plays, including St Georges de Bouhélhier's *Le Carnival des Enfants* and *Good Hope* by Herman Heijermans.

Chris earned her living through writing and she could turn her hand with considerable success to almost anything. Together with Edy, she wrote a biography of Ellen Terry and edited Terry's correspondence with George Bernard Shaw.[44] Chris wrote another two biographies; her biography of Ethel Smyth (1959) remains the best published account of Smyth's life and work. She was music critic at *The Lady* between 1897 and 1929 and wrote both drama and music criticism for *Time and Tide* between 1920 and 1931; Ethel Smyth had great respect for her music criticism.[45] Chris not only adapted works for the stage, she also wrote plays: *Erikkson's Wife* was performed with Ellen Terry in a starring role. Chris's least successful endeavour were her novels, most noticeably *Hungerheart*, published anonymously in 1915. *Hungerheart* has a number of good lines – 'No I never had a blind admiration for boys' and 'if a girl did not want to be married, there was only one explanation – sour grapes' – but it is generally rather pious.[46]

Victoria Glendinning appears happy to reduce all this activity to 'Chris supported herself inadequately by music criticism and by illuminated calligraphy'.[47] When I inquired about Chris St John, at what is now the Ellen Terry museum at Smallhythe, I was told by a curator, 'She was a very clever woman you know, and she has never been given her due.' Perhaps she had read Glendinning's summary of Chris's life. Of course many lesbians had lives in which they focused their energies far from suffrage activism or overtly feminist politics. Two fields where women could make a reasonable living and feel that they were contributing to society were nursing and teaching.

Agnes Hunt (1867–1948) dedicated her life to helping disabled children. Agnes was herself lame as the result of a blister on her leg which became septic when she was a child. She was never able to move or walk with ease again. Notwithstanding this, she overcame physical pain and social surprise and trained as a nurse. It may well have been the fact of her disability which has obscured her lesbianism from public view: the desexualization of people with disabilities is not an uncommon phenomenon. Not even her Eton crop has raised much posthumous comment.

Agnes was born and brought up in Australia. However, after the death of her father, her mother travelled the world with her children for four years. Mrs Hunt and several of her children finally settled in England in the late 1880s. Agnes Hunt was unusual in that she came from a comfortably off middle-class family where her mother actively encouraged her, a woman with a significant physical disability, to have a career. Although it was fear of her mother's anger which had led to Agnes concealing the fateful septic blister and thus becoming crippled, she always stressed her gratitude to her mother for insisting that she could do anything that her brothers and sisters could do.

Agnes Hunt started her training as a nurse in 1887, at the age of twenty, and over a period of some four years she qualified as both a nurse and a midwife. Her training took longer than that of most of her contemporaries because the effect of a strenuous nurse's training in conjunction with her disability led to several prolonged and debilitating bouts of illness. In 1891 Agnes Hunt met Emily Selina Goodford, whose father had been the Provost of Eton. Emily was some ten years older than Agnes (she was born about 1856) and she too was training as a nurse.

Meeting Emily, or Goody as Agnes called her, was the turning point in Agnes Hunt's life. The slightly disjunctive sentences in this passage, written after Emily's death, show rather clearly her place in Agnes's heart:

Had she been well-dressed and her hair done in a later fashion, she would have been an exceedingly handsome woman. As it was she was unique, and a most arresting personality. Gradually I won her friendship, and we worked and quarrelled and loved each other for thirty glorious years.[48]

Their relationship, and its seriousness, was quickly established and in 1882 Emily and Agnes went together to the Midlands to undertake their first job; within weeks of their arrival a typhoid epidemic broke out, a harsh induction into the realities of nursing. After eight years' nursing, Agnes

Hunt and Emily Goodford had an opportunity to fulfil their shared dream; to live permanently together and to concentrate their energies on the care and rehabilitation of children who had been crippled by accident and disease.

It was in 1900 that Agnes and Goody established the Baschurch Home for Cripples at Florence House in Baschurch. They settled here with their family of an orphaned Goodford niece and an orphaned Hunt nephew, and the elderly Mrs Hunt, who had given the Baschurch Home financial backing. The relationship between Emily Goodford and the formidable Mrs Hunt appears to have had moments of tension (Emily had not wanted Mrs Hunt to live with them), but they managed to rub along.

The Baschurch Home for Cripples was quickly established as a revolutionary orthopædic hospital. It was important for several reasons. Firstly because Agnes Hunt recognized that the material circumstances of the children's families were profoundly influential in the quality of medical treatment that children received, and in the subsequent education and training that they had. Children from working-class families who did not receive special education or training were pauperized by their disabilities. Unable to do manual work, they were unable to earn a living. Agnes Hunt tried to offer free medical attention to children from poor families and to provide them with after-care which would equip them with skills that would enable them to be self-supporting.

The cause of physically disabled children became, as she said, her obsession:

> I have seen children with tuberculosis, with poliomyelitis, with osteomyelitis, and many other crippling diseases, go into hospital, and return to their wretched homes no better, or, perhaps with an arm or leg amputated. No proper treatment, or after-care, no hope for the future, except the gloomy portals of the workhouse – a burden to their loved ones, wretched and utterly helpless, alternatively spoilt and smacked by their people, and systematically cold-shouldered by a world which had no room, and little sympathy for the physically disabled.[49]

Treatment for children who had survived crippling diseases was just beginning to be effective, and Agnes herself benefited from the doctors she came into contact with in her search for cures for her patients. In 1901 she was confined on her back for three months in a 'Jones abduction frame'; after this she was able to ride again, which cheered her greatly. It continued to shock Hunt that many children were crippled from poor health caused by poverty; tuberculous joints were a common cause of disability among poor children. For twenty years Emily Goodford and Agnes Hunt worked to alleviate both the physical pain and social ostracism suffered by disabled children.

Emily Goodford died in 1920, two years after the death of Mrs Hunt. While Agnes was saddened by her mother's death it was nothing in comparison with that of Emily:

> Even now, after eighteen years, it is difficult to write of her [Emily] and what she was to me. It is given to few to live and work, to laugh and play with one beloved friend for thirty years in perfect love and unity. Mother once said that I was very lucky in having such a friend, because every virtue I lacked (and there were many!) Miss Goodford provided, and so we made one fairly satisfactory whole.[50]

In the late 1920s, Agnes was involved with the Derwent Cripples' Training College, which dedicated itself to providing physically disabled people with skills by which they could earn their own living. In 1924 Agnes Hunt developed the extremely painful condition lupus and had to retire from active work. She received a damehood in 1926, and was celebrated in a number of books discussing remarkable women, such as *Heroines of Our Time* (1939). Hunt died in 1948 at the age of eighty-two.

Lilian Barker (1874–1955), while not apparently a suffrage activist, was motivated by a profound commitment to women. She was one of seven children and was born and brought up in Kentish Town where her father had a tobacconist's shop. Her father, James, was a good-looking, charming man and an alcoholic. The family, during Lily's childhood, was balanced on a knife-edge of lower-middle-class respectability, always in danger of being disgraced by James Barker's behaviour. James was deeply conservative with a strong dislike of Impressionist art and a distaste for the campaign for women's suffrage.

Lilian, or Lily, as she was known by her family, was always considered the brightest of the children but she was also the most wilful and difficult. She left school at fourteen and started training as a florist. However, she decided that she wanted to teach and by the time she was sixteen she was working as a pupil-teacher. In 1894 when she was twenty she was accepted for two years' residential training at Whitelands Teachers' Training College in Chelsea on a scholarship. She was voted 'the most popular girl of the year' in both of those years.[51] A photograph of her around this period shows her with cropped hair, some twenty years before it became a daring fashion.

After her training Lilian returned to teaching in the deprived areas of London, where she taught classes of sixty children and specialized in teaching those who were considered retarded or delinquent. She was a successful teacher and appears to have been loved for her innovative methods by her pupils, taking them on walks, to museums and galleries, and providing clothes and shoes to those without them, and plentiful supplies of pear-drops to all. However, in 1899 her widowed mother became confined to a wheelchair as a result of a progressive paralysing illness. Lilian, as the daughter whose career was perceived by the family to be most dispensable, gave up work to look after her. Mrs Barker lingered on for seven years, while Lilian cared for her mother and those of her siblings still living at home. The strain of sacrifice seems to have been bravely borne but not inconsiderable: this period of her life is referred to as 'the lost years' by her niece.

One important consolation emerged and that was Lily's meeting with Florence Francis at the Sunday School where they both taught, Lilian's one opportunity to exercise her teaching skills. Florence was 'exceedingly good-looking, with sculptured features, blue eyes and long golden blonde hair. She was tall and slim, and carried herself proudly erect'.[52] Florence was in social terms completely out of Lilian's class but although this seems to have caused problems for Florence's family it was never a problem for Florence or Lilian. When they met, both women were in their early thirties. Their relationship was to be lifelong.

In 1913, following her mother's death, Lilian Barker became the Principal of a new evening school for working girls and women. Her management of the Bell Street Evening Institute was highly praised. She offered working-class women classes in art, literature, music, history and politics as well as beauty, dress-making, and cookery. The Institute started most evenings with dancing led by Miss Barker, and always provided tea and penny buns for the women who came straight from work. Lilian Barker also organized classes for the women patients at the Lock Hospital for Venereal Disease. She had a strong sympathy for 'fallen women', unmarried mothers and women with venereal disease, and was outraged by the contempt with which they were treated by the medical profession.

Many of these lesbian lives were affected by the outbreak of World War I in 1914, which shattered the established political, social and economic status quo. Perhaps most crucially it broke the suffrage campaign. However, the war gave many women, and lesbians, new and undreamed-of opportunities.

They had the chance to show their mettle, by taking up the space left by the men who went to fight. In prosaic terms this was a physical space in industries where the work force had gone to war – in factories, the civil service, and the education system. However, these new possibilities that were opened to women as a result of the massive military mobilization brought with them more profound freedoms. Change and confusion were in the air and many women grasped the opportunity that the disturbance of war had provided.

Women's reaction to war was not a simple matter; they did not unthinkingly 'rally to help their country'. As Christopher St John noted:

> [Women] needed an outlet for their feminist energy when a truce was called in the fight for the vote. Moreover, as old antagonists of the Government, it came naturally for them to defy the Government to keep women in their place.[53]

As St John makes clear, there was a subversive pleasure in women doing 'men's jobs'. It allowed women the chance to work and organize in ways which had been ideologically and practically closed to them.

The 'truce which was called in the fight for the vote' was widespread. The WSPU, still under the autocratic leadership of Mrs Pankhurst and Christabel Pankhurst, swiftly moved from being an organization fighting the state to being a bulwark of the Establishment. Sylvia Pankhurst, a pacifist and not a great fan of Christabel or her mother by this point, remarked that 'Giving its energies wholly to the prosecution of the War, it [the WSPU] rushed to a furious extreme, its Chauvinism unexampled amongst all the other women's societies'.[54] The WSPU paper *The Suffragette* was patriotically renamed *Britannia* in the summer of 1915. Jacqueline de Vries has argued, however, that the patriotic jingoism of the Pankhursts during World War I drew strongly upon their feminism. Christabel's speeches, declaring that the war was the result of German valorization of masculinity and denigration of womanhood, simply recast the suffrage campaign on a larger stage.[55]

NOTES

1. Oliver letter, 25 October 1915, Carpenter Collection (Sheffield City archives).
2. Jeffrey Weeks, *Coming Out: Homosexual Politics in Britain from the Nineteenth Century to the Present* (London: Quartet, 1990, revised edition), p.134.
3. Chambers letter, 19 August 1921, Carpenter Collection (Sheffield City Archives).

4. Oliver letter, 25 October 1915, Carpenter Collection (Sheffield City Archives).
5. Ibid.
6. Ibid.
7. Ibid.
8. Ibid.
9. See Sylvia Pankhurst, *The Suffragette Movement*, 1931 (London: Virago, 1977, reprinted 1988), p.30.
10. See J. Liddington and J. Norris, *One Hand Tied behind Us: The Rise of the Women's Suffrage Movement* (London: Virago, 1978), for a full discussion of this.
11. Pankhurst, *The Suffragette Movement*, p.167.
12. The most prominent members of the Women's Freedom League were Mrs Charlotte Despart, Nina Boyle and Theresa Billington Grieg.
13. Naomi Jacob, *Me: A Chronicle about Other People* (London: Hutchinson, 1933), p.59.
14. Ibid., p.60.
15. Tasker letter, 2 July 1913, Carpenter collection (Sheffield City Archives).
16. Ibid.
17. Oliver letter, 25 October 1915, Carpenter collection (Sheffield City Archives).
18. Pankhurst, *The Suffragette Movement*, p.265.
19. Martha Vicinus, *Independent Women: Work and Community for Single Women 1850–1920* (London: Virago, 1985), p.261.
20. Ibid., p.261.
21. Michael Baker, *Our Three Selves: A Life of Radclyffe Hall* (London: Hamish Hamilton, 1985), p.48.
22. Stella Browne initially wrote under the pseudonym 'New Subscriber'.
23. Oliver letter, *The Freewoman*, 11 July 1912.
24. Oliver letter, 25 October 1915, Carpenter collection (Sheffield City Archives).
25. Oliver letter, *The Freewoman*, 19 September 1912.
26. Vicinus, *Independent Women*, p.x.
27. Sheila Jeffreys, *The Spinster and Her Enemies: Feminism and Sexuality 1880–1930* (London: Pandora, 1985), p.1.
28. *The Freewoman*, 4 January, 18 January, 25 January, 8 February and 22 February 1912.
29. Harry J. Birnstringl, *The Freewoman*, 4 January 1912.
30. Maurice Collis, *Somerville and Ross* (London: Faber & Faber, 1968).
31. Gifford Lewis, *Somerville and Ross: The World of the Irish R.M.* (London: Viking, 1985), p.203.
32. Ibid., p.208.
33. Ibid., p.205.
34. Collis, *Somerville and Ross*, p.172.
35. I would like to thank Dr Tracy Hargreaves for this information.
36. Quoted in Victoria Glendinning, *Vita: The Life of V. Sackville-West* (London: Penguin, 1984) p.251.

37. Baker, *Our Three Selves*, p.264.
38. *The Times* in its obituary is four years out on the years when St John was at Somerville.
39. Glendinning, *Vita: The Life of V. Sackville-West*, p.250.
40. Baker, *Our Three Selves*, p.44.
41. *The Times*, 25 October 1960.
42. Vera 'Jack' Holme collection, Fawcett Library Archives, newspaper clipping: there is contradictory evidence about whether it was Edy or Chris.
43. Vera 'Jack' Holme collection, Fawcett Library Archives, invitation to the 'Annual Dinner for the Commemoration of the Passing of the Representation of the People Act 1918' on 6 February 1937.
44. *Ellen Terry and Bernard Shaw: A Correspondence* (London: Constable & Co., 1931).
45. *The Times*, 20 October 1960, and the *Somerville College Register*.
46. Anon. (Chris St John), *Hungerheart* (London: Methuen, 1915), p.33 and p.36.
47. Glendinning, *Vita: The Life of V. Sackville-West*, p.250.
48. Agnes Hunt, *Reminiscences* (Shrewsbury: Wilding & Son, 1935), p.77.
49. Agnes Hunt, *This Is My Life* (London and Glasgow: Blackie, 1938), pp.145–6.
50. *Ibid.*, p.178.
51. Elizabeth Gore, *The Better Fight: The Story of Dame Lilian Barker* (London: G. Bles, 1965), p.23.
52. *Ibid.*, p.33.
53. Christopher St John, *Christine Murrell*, M.D. (London: Williams & Norgate, 1935), p.69.
54. Pankhurst, *The Suffragette Movement*, p.593.
55. Jacqueline de Vries, 'Gendering patriotism: Emmeline and Christabel Pankhurst and World War One', in Sybil Oldfield (ed.), *This Working-Day World: Women's Lives and Culture(s) in Britain 1914–45* (London: Taylor & Francis, 1994).

lesbians and the outbreak of war

'You, yes you, will be my ally'
Sappho, Fragment 78

Among those women who rushed eagerly into the breach created by the war were lesbians. The opportunities and salvation that the hiatus of the war offered to lesbians were recorded, with a certain wry humour, by Radclyffe Hall:

> Side by side with more fortunate women, worked Miss Smith who had been breeding dogs in the country; or Miss Oliphant who had been breeding nothing since birth but a litter of hefty complexes; or Miss Tring who had lived with a very dear friend in the humbler purlieus of Chelsea....Yet now even really nice women with hairpins often found their less orthodox sisters quite useful. It would be: 'Miss Smith, do just start up my motor – the engine's so cold I can't get the thing going'; or: 'Miss Oliphant, do glance through these accounts, I've got such a rotten bad head for figures'; or 'Miss Tring, may I borrow your British Warm? The office is simply arctic this morning!'[1]

Some of these lesbians were drawn from the ranks of the WSPU, where they had already been inculcated in the mental and physical disposition of combatants. The role of waiting, loving and supporting women was not particularly attractive to them. Mary Allen probably spoke for many when she said:

> To those of us who had been leaders and organisers in the tumultuous tide of the suffrage campaign, the ordinary channels of usefulness for the weaker sex in war-time – nursing, canteen work, sewing societies etc. – made preciously little appeal.[2]

However, if the militant army of suffragettes was generally committed to carrying on as an active fighting machine, there were significant differences in where these soldiers thought the battle lay. The 'suffragette army' was to be as fractured by the experience of World War I as any pre-war group. The lesbians within this army did not react uniformly to the arrival of war; a shared feminism did not hold these women together under the shattering force of war.

Mary Allen (1878–1964) and Margaret Damer Dawson (1874–1920) were two lesbians liberated by the war. Together they established one of the earliest groups of women police in Britain. There has been heated debate about who were the very first women police, and as there is only a couple of months in it, I do not think it is worth making the grand and contestable claim that women police were established by lesbians, although they probably were. Margaret Damer Dawson's early death appears to have precluded her leaving a record of her experiences. However, Mary Allen produced three volumes of autobiographical writing which describe her experiences as a woman police officer and her political views.

While we do not now conceive of policewomen as an emblem of political radicalness, for Mary Allen, setting up a police force of women was an explicitly feminist goal. She was not alone in this: Sylvia Pankhurst, whose politics were far to the left of those of Allen, also saw the establishment of women police as an important feminist achievement.[3] The opening up of police work to women was an important expansion of women's opportunities. As Allen pointed out:

> Many of the women attracted by the idea of women police had been prominent workers for women's suffrage in the militant days before the war. Their efforts – whether rightly or wrongly exercised, is fortunately no longer in question – had not only shaken vast numbers of women out of their normal indifference to political question, but had brought some into close, sometimes, painful touch with the police, teaching them how very unpleasant it is for an alleged woman culprit to be handled by men.[4]

Sexual assaults, as well as more general beatings, had been a common feature of police intervention and arrest during the pre-war suffrage campaigns.

> The police snatched the flags, tore them to shreds, and smashed the sticks, struck the women with fists and knees, knocked them down, some even kicked them, then dragging them up, carried them a few paces, and flung them into the crowd of sightseers .... For six hours this continued .... We saw women go out and return exhausted, with black eyes, bleeding noses,

bruises, sprains and dislocations. The cry went around: 'Be careful; they are dragging women down the side streets!' We knew this always meant greater ill-usage [i.e. 'violence and indecency'].

Infamously, on 'Black Friday' in 1910, three suffragettes received such vicious handling from the police, who were supposedly keeping the peace, that they died shortly afterwards.[5] If women were going to be free to be arrested they needed a police force that would not assault them while doing so.

The establishment of women police was also designed to show that women were responsible citizens, and hence worthy of the suffrage. With hindsight, Mary Allen said:

> It was, perhaps, both logical and inevitable that the desire to undertake civic duties should develop simultaneously with the movement for the political enfranchisement of women.[6]

The implication here was one that to contemporaries might seem outrageous: that the terroristic militant suffragette movement was an appropriate training ground for those who worked to enforce law and order. Mary Allen's experience was not in lobbying and diplomatically arguing the case for women's suffrage as the tone of her words might suggest but in fire-bombing, resisting arrest and going on hunger strike.

Mary Allen came from a comfortable middle-class family – her father was the Manager of the Great Western Railway.[7] She received a relatively good education for a woman of her time, at Princess Helena College in Hertfordshire. What she did between leaving school, in about 1894, and 1909 is unclear. However, by 1909, at the age of thirty-one she was

> in the heat of the woman suffrage movement . . . I could not resist throwing in my lot with the belligerent element, who were prepared to risk everything, even life and limb, in order to secure parliamentary representation.[8]

Allen was imprisoned twice between 1909 and 1912 for suffrage activism.

Mary Allen went on hunger strike on both occasions, and suffered force-feeding as a result. Going on hunger strike left women at the very least dangerously run down and at the worst close to death from starvation. Forced feeding not only required the brutal restraint of the struggling victim but often resulted in food being misdirected into the lungs, where, unsurprisingly, it caused significant damage. The combined effects of going on hunger strike and then being force-fed were enough to undermine the long-term health of even a robust woman. Allen had been a delicate child, and after the brutality of her force-feeding she was forbidden by Mrs Pankhurst to risk imprisonment again. She was sent by the WSPU to Edinburgh, a safe zone, to recruit for the cause there.

When war broke out, May Allen was still in Edinburgh:

> She was invited to join a needlework guild, a prospect which filled her with horror: she wanted action. While in this state of limbo, she overheard two people on a bus discussing the risible idea of women police. Mary was enchanted by the notion and immediately investigated and volunteered.[9]

The women police which were being discussed were those just established by Margaret Damer Dawson. Not only was the idea of a women's police force appealing to Allen, but so was Margaret Damer Dawson, 'blonde, blue-eyed, of a delicate complexion', herself.[10]

Margaret Damer Dawson was a woman of independent means. In 1914 she had both a house in Chelsea, London, and a country residence, 'Danehill' at Lympne in Kent. She had studied music at the Royal Academy of Music, gaining a diploma and a Gold Medal, but she was no effete artist. She enjoyed riding, mountain climbing and motoring, a more challenging pastime then than now. Insulated by her private income from the world of paid employment and its demands, she had dedicated much time and effort to working for animal protection. In 1906 she had organized an international congress for the protection of animals, and later received decorations for this work from Finland and Denmark; her home doubled as an animal sanctuary.[11]

By 1914 Damer Dawson had extended her interests from animal protection to include the protection of women. She was involved with the Criminal Law Amendment Committee and the National Vigilance Association. Both of these organizations worked to keep women out of organized prostitution or, as it was more luridly called, the white-slave trade.[12] Damer Dawson was frustrated by the inability of the police to respond effectively to the threat that this traffic in women posed to women's safety, health and welfare. She therefore decided to devote her considerable personal wealth to the training and development of a women's police force which would be able to deal with this problem, among others.

Damer Dawson and Mary Allen came from different political and social positions but they shared a common aim, to establish women police.

An effective working and intimate personal relationship between them was quick to form. Margaret Damer Dawson was not the only woman keen to set up a women police force in 1914. Nina Boyle of the Women's Freedom League had also begun to advertise for women police; as Sylvia Pankhurst said,

> The Freedom League never approached the WSPU in membership, means or influence, but occasionally it intervened with a bright, effective strategy.[13]

Women police was one of these strategies and Boyle and Damer Dawson met, discussed their plans, and together formed the Women Police Volunteers (WPV).

Initially, the Women Police Volunteers was headed by Margaret Damer Dawson, as Commandant, with Nina Boyle as her Deputy; Mary Allen had the number three position. However, the WPV suffered an early internal split. In November 1914, its first two officers, one of whom was Mary Allen, were seconded to Grantham in Lincolnshire. Grantham was the home of the Army's newly established Belton Park Camp which had added 20,000 to the town's population. Almost as soon as the police women had arrived at Grantham, a curfew on civilian women in the town was implemented under the Defence of the Realm Act. The curfew was instituted in order to stop 'vice', i.e., prostitution and female drunkenness, around the camp.

The NUWSS and the WFL attacked the curfew, which they rightly saw as an example of the sexual double standard in action and an untenable restriction on women's freedom. Moreover, they were fiercely critical of the WPV for enforcing it. As Nina Boyle was one of the critics of the actions of the WPV, an internal vote of confidence was called on the matter. The vote overwhelmingly supported the implementation of the curfew. At this point, Nina Boyle, popularly defeated, quit the WPV, and Damer Dawson renamed the force the Women Police Service (WPS).

Damer Dawson and Allen were aware of the sexist implications of the Grantham curfew.[14] However, they felt it would severely undermine the credibility of the WPV in particular, and women police in general, if they refused to enforce a government decision during wartime. Furthermore, they felt that the administration of the curfew was better carried out by women if women were its objects. For as Mary Allen said, 'The protection of women by women was the root principle [of the WPV]'.[15] Other women felt that the WPV had been duped, and there were feminist demonstrations against the WPV in Grantham.

As a result of the WPS's decision to police Grantham in these circumstances, feminist historians of the women police have tended to ignore or deride the WPS. Margaret Damer Dawson, Mary Allen and their women police are seen as politically suspect. Much feminist time is spent on Nina Boyle, who is perceived as a 'proper' feminist in contradistinction to Allen and Damer Dawson. Nina Boyle, however, never had more than a marginal role in the establishment of women police. She certainly had no role at all in the long-term administration, financial support, training, and development of a force of women police.

Distaste for Margaret Damer Dawson and Mary Allen is shared by feminist historians and by police historians. Joan Lock, author of *The British Policewoman*, says of Margaret Damer Dawson: 'Her character seems to have been an amalgam of upper class silliness and tactlessness, shyness and gentleness, high intelligence and toughness, over-confidence and, above all, utter determination.'[16] That somebody could actually exist with this surreal amalgam of characteristics seems unlikely. Lock also describes Mary Allen as 'a little given to dramatization' and, repeatedly, as 'silly'.[17] No other British policewomen seem to displease Lock to the same extent. It seems plausible that this distaste for Allen and Damer Dawson is caused not only by their putatively dubious politics but also by their lesbianism. The 'council of three' who ran the WPS from the point of Nina Boyle's departure, Damer Dawson, Allen and Isobel 'Toto' Goldingham, another ex-suffragette, were all lesbians, as were a number of women in the lower ranks.

Mary Allen is the main focus of this antipathy as she was, following Damer Dawson's early death, the most well-known policewoman in Britain until World War II. Mary Allen made her lesbianism flamboyantly visible through the public presentation of her body. Her hair was Eton-cropped, she wore a monocle and she wore her police uniform at all public appearances. The subject of Mary Allen's clothes rouses Joan Lock almost to fever pitch:

... the aggressively uniformed Mary Allen

[Allen] seems never to have taken her uniform off, even wearing it for travelling and attending banquets in her honour.

She had the utmost aversion from dresses...

Mary's uniform, complete with peaked hat, navy-blue breeches ('I haven't worn a skirt for six years,' she told avid newsmen), knee-high shiny black boots and monocle, caused a sensation.[18]

Contemporary lesbian opinion, however, was that Allen was 'exceedingly attractive' and that her uniform merely added to the allure:

> Her uniform, a severe military 'frock coat' in dark blue which fell just below her knees, breeches and riding boots, with a field service hat with a gold band round the peak, was both dignified and arresting.[19]

While we may now have reached the stage where out lesbians no longer wear recognizably 'lesbian' clothes, this is a recent development. Certainly, earlier generations of lesbians seem to have often chosen to mark their lesbianism through their clothes, their shoes, their hair-cuts and their jewellery. They made themselves visible to their contemporaries, and to us, by how they publicly presented themselves, through how they placed their bodies within the fields of sex, gender and sexual desire. As Katrina Rolley has said:

> Clothes can, in fact, take on a heightened significance for lesbians. Self-presentation allows the expression and communication of an otherwise invisible identity. Through dress, lesbians can reconstruct their bodies and transform themselves from 'heterosexual women' into 'lesbians'.[20]

The most obvious way of dressing like a lesbian was dressing mannishly. This is not to say that lesbians felt like men, but rather that to be identifiable as a lesbian, as a woman who was not heterosexual, a woman had to distance herself from heterosexual femininity. In a world of two genders you can only distance yourself from conventional conceptions of femininity by gesturing towards masculinity.

Before the mid-1920s the only way a middle-class woman stood any chance of wearing clothes which were not feminine, let alone trousers, was by wearing a uniform. Belonging to an organization such as the WPS which required members to wear a military-style uniform gave to the watching heterosexual world a justification of why a woman was wearing men's clothes. A cap or a helmet also provided a spurious justification for short hair. As one of the hierarchy of the WPS, Mary Allen had the luxury of being able to design a uniform of her own choosing, a uniform which required her to wear knee-high boots, breeches and a peaked cap.

Uniforms gave lesbians visibility without putting them in positions of danger, for they also explicitly provided a reason for wearing men's clothes – membership of a particular group – which was not simply lesbianism. Given this, it is not surprising that lesbians had more than sartorial reasons for preferring to help the war effort via uniformed work rather than by knitting. Radclyffe Hall was aware of how the opportunities provided by uniforms were attractive to lesbians:

> One great weakness they [lesbians undertaking war work] all had, it must be admitted, and this was for uniforms – yet why not? The good workman is worthy of his Sam Browne belt.[21]

There is a certain ambiguity in this passage. By 'The good workman is worthy of his Sam Browne belt' Hall seems to be saying that uniforms went some way to alleviating lesbian exclusion from the world of action, courage and heroism, the male preserve of the battlefield in wartime. However, this language of belts and the good workman is evocative of sex: belts with notches in, and the good workman who makes his lover come. Perhaps Hall is suggesting that uniforms, particularly men's uniforms, were the least that women who took the place of men in sex with women deserved. For the uniform is a sexual tool to the lesbian, by making her visible, as the Sam Browne belt is a tool to the workman. As a reward for her life-enhancing sexual work the lesbian deserves the uniform which advertises her sexual desire.

Leaving aside such close textual reading, it is clear that wearing a uniform only partially excused the rejection of femininity which went with it. Micky Jacob remarked that:

> I remember the last war, when women who wore uniform – unless they were nurses – were regarded as something strange, eccentric, and a fine target for jokes.[22]

As Jacob was a friend of Mary Allen's, it is likely that her comment was informed by the experience of Allen and the women police. Damer Dawson and Allen's fondness for their uniforms does seem to have been understood contemporaneously as sexually perverse. It was undoubtedly a factor in their lack of success with the police establishment. General Sir Nevil Macready, Commissioner of the Metropolitan Police in 1918, did not think that Margaret Damer Dawson, Mary Allen or the WPS were a suitable basis for an official female police force.

One of Macready's main objections to the WPS was that it was full of militant suffragettes, and obviously this would never do for a police force. However, Macready also seems to have had explicit anxieties about sexual debauchery in the ranks. Joan Lock describes a bizarre episode where

Macready obtained a photograph of members of the WPS. This photograph appeared to show a man among their number. However, given that the WPS consisted only of women, Macready was forced to conclude that the 'man' was a woman parading in a sexually perverse manner in men's clothes and with masculine accoutrements.

Macready used this photograph as evidence, at two official committees, against the WPS. He argued against the formal incorporation of the WPS into the official police force, saying that it was obviously important 'to eliminate any women of extreme views – the vinegary spinster or blighted middle-age fanatic' from the ranks of potential women police. Vinegary spinsters and blighted middle-age fanatics were clearly equated by Macready with lesbians.[23] Even though the WPS were highly thought of by many Chief Constables and had enjoyed considerable success, from this point they were gradually eased out of the employment they had found, working under contract for police forces. Mary Allen resisted the strong pressure brought to bear by the official police to give up her public role as the face of police women in Britain until the 1930s. Eventually, however, she was, against her will, forced to retire from her police work.

In 1920 Margaret Damer Dawson died at the age of forty-five from a heart attack. Mary Allen believed that the stress and attack under which she had been placed by the police establishment was a significant factor in her death and spoke very positively of her in obituaries. Joan Lock dismisses both Margaret Damer Dawson's death and Mary Allen's life by saying that 'such fulsomeness might suggest a homosexual affection, particularly since the writer [Allen] was, by now, grotesquely masculine in appearance'.[24] From existing photographs both Margaret and Mary appear equally butch, and not noticeably grotesque. It does seem that Damer Dawson and Allen were lovers, and between 1914 and 1920, they appear to have lived together in London.[25]

Mary Allen did not have to face the impotent misery of her exclusion from the official world of the police, and Damer Dawson's untimely death, alone. By the early 1930s Mary Allen was living with another woman, a Miss Tagart, at 'Danehill' in Lympne with two St Bernards. By this point Mary Allen was known to her lesbian friends as Robert. Miss Tagart had been a Sub-Inspector in the WPS; she had accompanied Mary Allen on an official trip to Germany in 1928. As 'Danehill' was originally owned by Damer Dawson, the fact that Mary Allen lived there in the 1930s indicates that she was a major beneficiary in Damer Dawson's will.[26]

Allen had not just lovers but also lesbian friends, such as Radclyffe Hall and Una Troubridge. Hall and Troubridge offered lesbian solidarity and a community in which she could share her anger and disappointment at her treatment by the authorities:

> John [Hall] and Una sympathized, agreeing that the authorities were against her because she was an invert (all they wanted, Una declared contemptuously, were 'fluffy policewomen'). The two couples were heartened to find that they shared common beliefs on the subject of homosexuality. 'To feel that they are in sympathy with John's aims & mine is good indeed for they are fine citizens,' Una confided to her diary.[27]

The very fact that there was to be no formal women's police force until World War II meant that the police could only interfere with Mary Allen's activities and those of the WPS to a limited degree. Throughout the 1920s and 1930s, Mary Allen continued to lecture on women police all over the world and the WPS remained active for some time. A force from the WPS served in Ireland in 1920, invited at official request to help to maintain the peace during Sinn Fein agitation. A force from the WPS was also invited to go to Germany in the 1920s to help to maintain order in the depression-torn cities. In 1927 Mary Allen launched *The Policewoman's Review*.

Joan Lock, while trying to play down both Allen's dynamism and success, has to concede, albeit in a throwaway paragraph, that:

> In the mid-twenties she stood for Parliament as a Liberal candidate but was defeated, wrote her first book, learned to fly, set up a Women's Emergency Corps during the General Strike...and continued with her speaking tours abroad, visiting Holland, Poland, Hungary, Czechoslovakia, Egypt, Finland, France, Germany, Greece and Brazil.[28]

Mary Allen received an OBE, and her friend, colleague, and fellow lesbian, Isobel 'Toto' Goldingham, received an MBE. Mary Allen was not solely interested in the police and law and order. She and her colleagues set up a home for the babies of unmarried mothers in Aldington in Kent in the early 1920s. Here women could leave their babies until they had established themselves in a home in which they could take care of their children. Allen insisted that the home was designed to keep mother and child in contact rather than break this bond. Mary Allen maintained a number of suffragette anxieties about the dangers of male sexuality; she was very worried about children's minds being warped by popular films shown at cinemas.

While the war allowed women to establish such innovations as women police, at the end of the war many such new organizations were disbanded under pressure from the authorities; the WPS was unusual in that it continued to operate for a good ten years after the coming of peace in 1918. While war provided opportunities for women, it was not accepted that these new opportunities would persist after the war had ended. While working women were praised for their response to the war, there was a negative effect on women that Christopher St John astutely realized:

> While the War gave women the chance of manifesting potentialities with which they had not hitherto been credited, it did not raise their status. Rather it lowered it, by emphasizing a disability. Women could not be soldiers.[29]

In no circumstances were the War Office prepared to employ women as soldiers. The only way women could attach themselves to the British Army was via the Women's Army Auxiliary Corps which was established in 1917. The WAAC performed domestic duties within the Army such as cooking and cleaning, and some administrative tasks. However, they were legally ranked merely as 'camp followers', like prostitutes, not as members of the British Army itself. The War Office employed the members of the WAAC at a lower rate of pay than that received by soldiers in the Army, and co-ordinated their movements. While members of the WAAC were sent to France, they were kept safely away from any actual fighting. No women from the WAAC were officially permitted to go to the Front.[30]

Many women were keen to go to the Western and Eastern Fronts because it was here that the war was being fought. While most women accepted that they could not fight, they knew that there was a need for doctors, nurses and ambulance drivers at the battlefields. A number of women's organizations organized medical teams and left Britain, heading for the battlefields of Europe. In 1917 Barbara 'Toupie' Lowther began to set up an all-women ambulance unit, with the intention of taking the unit to the Front in France. This ambulance unit would ferry the wounded from the battlefields to hospitals. Toupie was the eldest daughter of the sixth Earl of Lonsdale and a close relative of Claude Lowther, the MP. These aristocratic and wealthy connections enabled Lowther to get her ambulance unit up and running. Working with her on the project was Norah Desmond Hackett, who came from Liverpool.

Lowther appears to have had a good education; she was a Bachelor of Science from the Sorbonne.[31] Michael Baker says of her:

> A bulky, tall woman of extremely masculine appearance, she had a considerable reputation as a fencer and tennis player. A story about her, probably apocryphal, told how she was once arrested at the Franco-Italian frontier for masquerading as a man. On the return journey she wore skirts but was again arrested – for masquerading as a woman.[32]

This apocryphal story emphasizes again the vexed relationship between lesbians and dress. A woman with an Eton crop, no jewellery and a severe style looked unlike a (heterosexual) woman in women's clothes, but did not pass as a man in men's clothes. Lesbian style marked out a visible difference from both men and heterosexual women.

Toupie Lowther had married Lieutenant-Colonel James Innes in 1914, and at the time of the foundation of the Hackett-Lowther unit was the mother of two small babies.[33] Lowther and Innes were to divorce in 1921. Neither marriage nor motherhood appears to have restricted Toupie's activities, or her nicknames: she was also known to her lesbian friends as 'Brother'. No account of her mentions her children, and few mention her marriage. She used only her maiden name when she was recruiting staff for the ambulance unit, while in France and when interviewed by *The Times* on her return home.

In London, Toupie Lowther and Norah Desmond Hackett assembled a number of cars to serve as ambulances. These were donated by a Miss Mary Dexter, the Misses Hancock, and a Miss Rachel Ripton, among others. They then collected a multinational team of women drivers via newspaper advertisements. From Britain there was Miss Francis Demisthorpe, Miss K. Hodges, Miss Enid Elliot, Miss B. Sterling, Miss Murphy, Miss G. Stuart Richardson, Miss Gartland, Miss Plimsoll, Miss Chappel Hodge, Miss C. Meade, Mrs A. Cox, Mrs Hanna, Miss G. Bailey, Miss Salvage, Case de Bellenoche, Miss Rachel Ripton and Miss Harvey. From Ireland there was the Hon. Eileen Plunket, from France there was Mlle de Montgeen, and from America there was Miss M. Dexter, Miss Moore, Miss Fitch, Miss Clarfts, Miss Smith, Miss Reid, and Miss Hawthorne.[34]

The lives of these women appear to be largely untraceable. However, certain things about them as a group are clear. They must have been free of domestic ties to have volunteered to go to France and place themselves in great danger by working on the Front. Certainly some of the women appear to have taken their domestic and erotic ties with them. The Hon. Eileen Plunket and Enid Elliot were lovers in the 1930s. It is unclear whether they met in the Hackett-Lowther unit or if they were already lovers when they joined. Only two members of the Hackett-Lowther unit used the title Mrs, and it seems likely that a significant number of the women in the unit were lesbians. Given Toupie's arresting 'masculine appearance' it seems unlikely that women who had conventional views about the duties of motherhood, sexual morality or the role of women in society would have wanted to join the unit. Toupie Lowther advertised for women who could drive and repair cars. In 1917 this was an unusual and unladylike female skill. There were few cars in Britain, and women who could drive were either wealthy or working-class, determined chauffeurs and mechanics. Rachel Ripton and Mary Dexter both donated cars to the unit and then served in it. The fact that they had cars to donate suggests that these women were relatively wealthy.

Once equipped with women and cars the Hackett-Lowther unit proceeded to France. The fact that the Hackett-Lowther unit got to France without any official authorization illustrates how accessible to the general public World War I was. Once in France, however, Toupie found, to her incredulous anger, that the British Army refused point blank to have anything to do with them: the British Army did not employ women. However, the arrival of the Hackett-Lowther unit in France was not in vain. The French agreed that the unit could serve at the front under the French flag. Moreover, the French employed the women as soldiers and paid them the wage of regular French soldiers.

Toupie Lowther was employed as a lieutenant and all the women received the 'indemnité de combat', an allowance French troops received while they were serving at the front. Thus the French Army gained from the dedication and bravery of the Hackett-Lowther unit rather than the British. While the Hackett-Lowther unit was not the only all-female ambulance unit working in France in World War I, it was the only unit of women which was employed by an army as soldiers and which worked on the battlefield, not safely behind the lines. Toupie Lowther said of her work in France, 'It was a wonderful time. We were often 350 yards from the German lines awaiting the wounded, under camouflage.'[35] Lowther was mentioned in dispatches and decorated, as were fifteen other women in the unit, and she received the Croix de Guerre.

In an Author's Note in The Well of Loneliness Radclyffe Hall acknowledges that: 'A motor ambulance unit of British women drivers did very fine service upon the Allied Front in France during the later months of the war.' Hall then provides the usual disclaimer, saying that the ambulance unit described in The Well of Loneliness is not supposed to be a portrait of this particular unit. However, Radclyffe Hall was a close friend of Toupie

Lowther right through the 1920s and it is likely that Hall drew upon Toupie's descriptions of her time in France in both *The Well of Loneliness* and *Miss Ogilvy Finds Herself*. Lowther, in later life, apparently came to believe herself to be the model for Stephen Gordon, although this was to be hotly refuted by Una Troubridge.

The Hackett-Lowther unit did not arrive back in England until the summer of 1919. On her return from France, Lowther was quickly re-integrated into London lesbian life, and by 1920 she was having an affair with a woman called Nellie Rowe. Toupie Lowther, wealthy and apparently carefree, was involved in an extravagant and pleasurable lesbian subculture. In 1923, for instance, she gave a lesbian fancy dress ball. In the early 1920s Toupie Lowther was at the cutting edge of lesbian chic – she wore trousers of black satin. This so shocked Una Troubridge that she noted it in her diary.[36] Toupie also acquired a motorcycle, one of the first in Britain to be owned and ridden by a woman.[37] It was not the first, however: that distinction may lie with Mary Allen. In a pre-1920 publicity shot for the women police, Mary Allen is shown astride a motorcycle, with Margaret Damer Dawson and a young child in a side-car, driving through the streets of London. A shockingly lesbian image, outrageously incorporating a child, this must have re-enforced Nevil Macready's anxieties about Allen and Damer Dawson, and their relationship.

Another lesbian who undertook war work was Vera 'Jack' Holme (1882–1969).[38] Vera Holme had also trained with

> the WSPU guerrilla army, [which] toughened from years of discipline and sacrifice, transformed itself with remarkable ease into a fighting force for England.[39]

She was the WSPU chauffeur from 1909, driving Emmeline and Christabel Pankhurst and other organizers around the country. One of the WSPU publicity postcards sold to raise funds for the vote was of Vera in her chauffeur's uniform.

Vera Holme came from Birkdale near Liverpool. She had moved to London as an actress at some point prior to 1909. Sylvia Pankhurst describes Vera as:

> an orphan educated in a French convent, and now singing in the chorus of the Gilbert and Sullivan operas, who presently became chauffeur to the W.S.P.U., a noisy, explosive young person, frequently rebuked for her elders for lack of dignity.[40]

This romantic past may have been an invention. As well as the WSPU, Vera was involved in the Actress' [sic] Franchise League. Vera Holme was involved in a number of militant suffragette actions. She was arrested and charged with obstruction three times during 1910 and 1911, and she was imprisoned in Holloway gaol. Among her papers she kept her three charge sheets from Cannon Row and Bow Street police stations, and sketches of her cell in Holloway.[41]

Vera Holme was physically at the centre of WSPU activities and part of the London feminist theatrical circles. Through these networks she knew not just the Pankhursts and Annie and Jessie Kenney, but also women like Chris St John and Edy Craig. Holme left a collection of newspaper clippings on Ethel Smyth. She had presumably known Smyth at the time of her passionate liaison with Emmeline Pankhurst. Whether the clippings mark an admiration for Smyth as a composer or are a record of the life of a fellow and famous lesbian is now unclear. Vera Holme played the role of Georgina, the feminist, in Chris St John and Cicely Hamilton's play How the Vote Was Won. Her friendship with Edy Craig and Chris St John was long-lasting, and she regularly stage-managed plays for Edy in the 1930s. Through Edy and Chris, she was to meet Radclyffe Hall and Una Troubridge.[42]

It was also presumably through the WSPU that Vera Holme first met the Hon. Evelina Haverfield (18??–1920). Haverfield is described by David Mitchell as 'one of the first and most vigorous of the upper-echelon suffragettes, stepping into the breach and the breeches, with a will'. Evelina Haverfield was married with several children but motherhood did not curtail any of her activities. She was, for instance, 'one of the most brilliant and daring horsewomen of her day'.[43] She was also a militant suffragette, and had been imprisoned for her part in a suffragette assault on Parliament.

In 1914 Evelina Haverfield was a founder member of the Women's Emergency Corps. She was also Commandant in Chief of the Women's Reserve Ambulance Corps and had founded the Women's Volunteer Reserves.[44] All these organizations sought to train and to organize women so that they could support the war effort and step in to fill the gaps left by men gone to war. These organizations also empowered women by giving them new skills and experience. The Women's Legion, for instance, founded in 1916 by Lilian Barker, trained women as cooks, and thus gave them an *entrée* into the male world of professional chefs. These organizations were all entirely independent of the government, and were financed through public and private donations.

The WVR specifically advertised for women motorists and aviators to come forward to undertake civilian jobs in Britain. By October 1914, Vera Holme, with her experience as a professional motorist, had achieved the rank of major. Although Evelina Haverfield and Vera Holme came from very different backgrounds, they were united by their feminism, their wish to make an active contribution to the war effort and by their lesbianism. According to Naomi Jacob, the Women's Volunteer Reserves 'were referred to by wits as Kitchiner's Lizzies'; by a Freudian slip of the eye I misread this.[45] However, Haverfield and Holme obviously felt that their skills were not being fully utilized on the home front, and in 1915 they went together to Serbia with the Scottish Women's Hospital.

The history of the Scottish Women's Hospital shows again the resistance of the War Office to women working, under dangerous conditions and abroad, for the war effort.

> The Scottish Women's Hospitals owed their existence to Dr Elsie Inglis. Women's suffrage work was for the moment at a standstill [due to the war]: why not, she thought, use the whole force of the well organised National Union of Women's Suffrage Societies to inaugurate a unit of women surgeons and physicians and offer it to the War Office?

The offer was made but was immediately declined.[46] The Allies, however, accepted and units were established in Calais, Royaumont, Serbia, Troyes, Salonika, Corsica, Ostrovo, Vranja, Russia and Sallanches. Public support for the Scottish Women's Hospital was strong. On one occasion alone, at a fund-raising meeting in Calcutta, over £13,000 was raised. Elsie Inglis was Scottish and had been involved with the non-militant NUWSS; in 1914, she was the secretary of the Federation of Scottish Suffrage Societies. She had lived with Dr Flora Murray for a number of years in Edinburgh. Not surprisingly Dr Elsie Inglis's Scottish Women's Hospital attracted many former suffragists and lesbians.

One unit of the Scottish Women's Hospital was stationed in Royaumont Abbey in France. Here the former suffragettes Cicely Hamilton, Dr Louisa Aldrich-Blake (Dean of the London School of Medicine for Women) and Dr Louisa Martindale spent much of World War I. While Martindale and Aldrich-Blake lived with women (Ismay Fitzgerald and Rosamond Wigram respectively), Cicely Hamilton's sexuality is less clear, although she certainly knew a great many lesbians.[47] Between 1914 and 1919, the small SWH unit at Royaumont cared for 10,681 patients and performed 7,024 operations. There were only 184 deaths, a remarkably low death rate. The

British authorities were so impressed by the performance of the female medical team at Royaumont that they invited a number of them to establish the Endell Street Military Hospital in London.

Elsie Inglis herself, however, travelled to Serbia with a unit of the SWH. In Serbia the fighting was terroristic, the weather appalling, civilian deaths numerous and disease rampant. Communications were very poor, medical supplies were limited and there was little indigenous healthcare. In Serbia Vera Holme and Evelina Haverfield worked closely with Inglis; in the 1940s, Vera Holme would give talks for the BBC on her memories of Elsie Inglis.[48] Both Elsie Inglis and Evelina Haverfield were to receive Serbia's highest decoration, the Order of the White Eagle, as a mark of public gratitude for their work there.[49]

In 1917 Dr Inglis died in Britain after a physically gruelling journey across Siberia to the Russian port of Archangel pursued by the invading Central Powers. Vera Holme stayed on with Evelina in Serbia. At the end of the war Evelina Haverfield opened a hospital for tubercular and orphaned children at Bajuna Bostc on the Bosnian border.[50] In 1920 she died and was buried in Serbia. On her headstone is inscribed 'She worked for the Serbian people, with untiring zeal. A straight fighter, a straight rider, and a most loyal friend. RIP.'

After Evelina's death Vera Holme had to remove her belongings from the home in Britain which they had shared; the house had been owned by Evelina. Vera sent a list of her belongings, which were to be returned to her, to the executors of Haverfield's estate. A copy of this list survives among Vera Holme's papers. Among the things that Vera Holme wanted back were presents that she had given to Evelina and things with particular sentimental value. Chief amongst these was '1 bed with carved sides [inscribed with] E.H. and V.H.'. A bed with the initials of you and your dead lover carved into it would indisputably have sentimental value. How public Vera Holme and Evelina Haverfield were about their relationship is hard to know; Vera was certainly on friendly terms with Evelina's surviving son, remaining in contact with him and his family for many years.

Also among Vera Holme's papers is an illustrated scroll which sets out the membership rules for a group called the 'Foosack League'. The mock-heraldic jokey language used suggests that the women involved were very intimate. The scroll states that only women, and only women who are suffragists, could be members of the Foosack League. The exact nature of the tie that binds these women remains unspecified, but it does look as though the Foosack League was a lesbian secret society. The scroll is signed by Vera Holme, Evelina Haverfield, Alice Embleton and Celia Wray.

I have been unable to trace Alice Embleton or Celia Wray.[51] The scroll is undated but it must have been drawn up before Evelina's death in 1920.

Evelina's death, as a result of illness exacerbated by the deprivations of war, did not persuade Vera Holme to return to Britain, and she remained in Serbia until the mid-1920s working as an ambulance and relief lorry driver. It was in Serbia that Vera Holme met the women who were to replace Evelina Haverfield in her affections, Margaret Greenless and Margaret Kerr. On their return from Serbia in the late 1920s, Vera Holme and the two Margarets set up home together in Lochearnhead, Scotland. They quickly established themselves as local figures, as Holme's collection of newspaper clippings demonstrates, performing in local amateur dramatics and fishing prolifically. During the 1930s the *ménage à trois* must have become untenable for some reason; by 1939 Margaret Kerr had moved out. In 1964 Vera made a second broadcast for the BBC on her experiences in Serbia. By this point, she was eighty-two and living in a nursing home in Glasgow.

Naomi 'Micky' Jacob (1889–1964), the actress and writer, was another lesbian who took her war work seriously. Micky ran a munitions factory during World War 1 in Willesden in London, where she supervised 500 men and women making, among other things, lamps and aeroplane engines. She said that this was the 'most enjoyable' job that she had ever had.[52] Jacob was the child of a middle-class and rather bohemian Yorkshire family. Around 1905 Jacob's mother, the writer and journalist Nana Collinson, who wrote as 'Nina Abbott', went to work in America. Micky refused to go with her and instead, at the age of sixteen, launched into a career as a pupil-teacher.

However, by the time she was twenty, Micky Jacob had left teaching to become 'secretary, companion, manager, courier' to Marguerite Broadfoot, a touring comedienne and Scottish gentlewoman. It seems likely that Marguerite Broadfoot was Jacob's first serious love affair; Broadfoot died in 1915. Micky Jacob had joined the WSPU around 1912 and quickly asked if she could be involved in illegal suffragette activities. She was invited to an interview with Sylvia Pankhurst who said to her, 'You might be quite a useful person if you would overcome your idiotic love of popularity, Jacob.'[53] Presumably it was via the suffragettes or through London lesbians generally that Micky came to know Vera Holme, whom she invited to provide one of the Friday lunch-time 'entertainments', a talk on the Serbian retreat, at the munitions factory in 1919.[54]

Micky Jacob was not the only lesbian running a munitions factory. In 1916, Lilian Barker was appointed Lady Superintendent of Woolwich

Arsenal with the brief of supervising the work and welfare of the women who took up the jobs vacated by men in this key munitions site. Woolwich Arsenal had not employed women since they were squeezed out by government legislation in 1892. However, within a year of Lilian's appointment, 30,000 women were working at Woolwich Arsenal. The Arsenal was vast, covering nine square miles. The accumulated effect of women undertaking war work was that by 1918 the number of women in work had gone up by over a million, an increase of more than a quarter.

By the start of the war Lilian Barker was living with her lover, Florence Francis, and Francis's mother, in Hampstead. Barker's biographer Elizabeth Gore says, in one of the very few passages in which she directly refers to a love affair which lasted forty years:

> Her [Barker's] relationship with the Francis brothers and sisters although it became cordial was never close for there were certain things about Lily that they could never accept; but Lily and Florence were completely at ease together, each a perfect foil for the other: Lily talked, Florrie listened, Lily remonstrated, Florrie gave way, Lily laughed, Florrie smiled. Yet the domination which this suggests never really existed, for each provided exactly what the other required.[55]

It seems plausible that it was Lilian Barker's 'gay masculine figure' which the Francis siblings found hard to swallow as much as her working-class background.[56]

Just as there were lesbians actively engaged in the war effort, there were a number of lesbians who fiercely fought for pacifism and internationalism during World War I. In terms of feminist politics there seems to be some evidence that it was the militant suffragettes of the WSPU who took up war work, and the less militant suffragists of the WFL and the NUWSS who took up pacifism, but records are too few to make any certain generalizations. Certainly personal friendships and old suffrage links were not completely shattered by the politics of war. It was, for instance, Mrs Margaret Corbett Ashley, a committed pacifist and internationalist, who suggested to her old friend Mary Allen that a team of her women police should go to help in Germany in the 1920s.

Two of the most active women campaigners for peace in World War I were Eva Gore-Booth (1870–1926) and Esther Roper (1868–1938). Gore-Booth and Roper met while on holiday in Italy in 1896 and lived together until Gore-Booth's death thirty years later. For the major part of their life together they lived in Manchester, and they moved to Hampstead in London, just before the war started, believing that the Lancashire climate was exacerbating Eva's poor health. Eva and Esther spent their life together working for the political, economic and cultural empowerment of women.

Esther Roper was the daughter of a working-class missionary and she spent her childhood boarded out at a church school in London and staying with her grandparents in Manchester, while her parents fought for heathen souls in Africa. When Edward Roper died his young family were left entirely dependent upon the charity of his employers, the Church Missionary Society. From the age of eleven, Esther would have known that she would have to earn her own living to survive. Esther Roper was one of the first women to be awarded a degree, from Owen's College in Manchester, one of the first colleges to admit women on equal terms with men. It is unclear when Esther became interested in the questions of feminism and female suffrage. However, her very first job was as a paid organizing secretary for the National Society for Women's Suffrage.

Eva Gore-Booth was a daughter of the Anglo-Irish gentry; the Gore-Booth home was Lissadell in County Sligo. Her sister was Constance Markievicz, the Sinn Fein revolutionary. The sisters were immortalized by Yeats in his not particularly flattering poem 'In Memory of Eva Gore-Booth and Constance Markievicz'. Both Constance and Eva were brought up within the conventional dictates of their class: they were presented at Court and did the 'season' in London. Before meeting Esther Roper, Eva appears to have spent her time reading the classics, writing poetry and travelling with her parents.

Gore-Booth, when in her thirties, was described by her contemporary Sylvia Pankhurst as

> tall and excessively slender, intensely short-sighted, with a mass of golden hair, worn like a great ball at the nape of her long neck, bespectacled, bending forward, short of breath with high-pitched voice and gasping speech, she was nevertheless a personality of great charm.[57]

When Eva Gore-Booth met Esther Roper she was twenty-six and Esther was twenty-eight. Within two years Eva had left Lissadell and joined Esther in Manchester.

Eva Gore-Booth and Esther Roper worked, both paid and unpaid, for a wide variety of organizations which were working to politicize, educate, enfranchise and unionize working-class women. As they held many positions simultaneously and sources of information conflict on when they were working for whom, an exact breakdown of their careers is not easy. Esther Roper certainly worked for a number of different suffrage organizations and Eva worked both as a teacher at a women's night school and for the Women's Trade Union Council. However, both women were equally committed to the suffrage and trade union movements.

Much of their work centred upon women workers, where the questions of unionization and women's suffrage intersected. Roper and Gore-Booth were both involved in the establishment of the Manchester and Salford Women's Trade Councils about 1900, 'the foremost purpose of which was to do battle for the representation of women's labour'.[58] Also involved with this project were their close friends Sarah Reddish and Sarah Dickenson, who had started their lives working in the Lancashire cotton mills. Reddish (1850–1925) and Dickenson (1868–1954) always appear as a couple in contemporary records, and although Dickenson had married in 1896, her husband appears to have played little part in her life. It seems likely that these women too were lesbians.

Eva was a particularly close friend of Christabel Pankhurst in the first years of the century; it was Eva Gore-Booth who encouraged Christabel to train as a lawyer. On the important public occasion of the release from prison of Christabel Pankhurst and Annie Kenney, after the first militant outrage in 1905, it was Esther Roper and Eva Gore-Booth who led the suffragettes and presented them with flowers. During World War I both Eva and Esther became involved in pacifist campaigning; in Esther's words, they were 'extreme pacifists'.[59]

Their approach to pacifist politics was built on the belief that national identity was unimportant and meaningless in the face of an international common humanity. Their pacifism was applied in a very practical way; in the autumn of 1914 they spent their time visiting, with food and money, the families of Germans who had been interned as enemy aliens. Esther described the distress among German women and children, and the few older men who had not been interned, as ' heartbreaking'.[60]

Eva and Esther also worked for the No-Conscription Fellowship during the war, an organization which aided and abetted men avoiding conscription. Ironically the fight against war was closed to women just as the war itself was closed; by virtue of their sex, women could not be conscientious objectors for no-one was seeking to conscript them. In joining the No-Conscription Fellowship, unsurprisingly a largely male organization, Eva and Esther carried on the fight for women's equality. They did not want to fight but they wanted the right to be seen as equal participants in the movement against war.

Eva and Esther were concerned as well on behalf of their male friends and colleagues who were resisting conscription:

> Many of our friends were imprisoned for refusing Military Service. Many were court-martialled, constantly tried by tribunals or deprived of posts.[61]

Conscientious objectors were in real physical danger during the war. They risked not only attack in the streets but also illicit press-ganging; once in the forces they could be shot for desertion if they refused to fight. The NCF was one of the most radical of the pacifist organizations as it rejected not only military service but also non-combatant alternatives to military service. Within the NCF all forms of conscripted war work were viewed as part of the war machinery; non-combatant work forces were no better or cleaner than regular military service.

The NCF not only gave advice and support to conscientious objectors in preparation for tribunal hearings, they also lobbied for fair tribunals, for instance those which accepted that there were valid reasons for refusing to participate in the war effort. Although there were more than a hundred pacifist groups in Britain during World War I, the NCF was one of the most subversive. It published inflammatory articles and pamphlets attacking the Allied powers, arguing, for instance, that the war was being fought for no more moral reason than a false economic boom and the expansion of capitalism.

The NCF also accused the Allied powers of inhumane and illegal treatment of conscientious objectors. NCF leaders and even some of the common membership were kept under government surveillance between 1914 and 1918.

> With relatively little money and almost no popular support the fellowship attracted a remarkably able band of social activists and political organizers. Together these men and women shaped an organization that caused the government more grief than any other body of dissenters against the war.[62]

Both Eva and Esther were also involved in specifically feminist pacifist organizations. During 1915 and 1916 they travelled through Britain speaking as members of the Women's Peace Crusade: 'supporting the efforts of those who sought to end the war by negotiations, not by further slaughter'.[63] Esther Roper was among the women who demonstrated at Grantham against the presence of women police.[64] Presumably Esther was motivated here not simply by her feminist politics but also by her pacifism;

women police, although non-combatant, were an active part of the machinery of war.

Eva Gore-Booth and Esther Roper were among the British women involved in the Women's International Congress at the Hague which took place in the spring of 1915. The Congress had two aims:

1. To demand that international disputes shall in future be settled by some other means than war.
2. To claim that women should have a voice in the affairs of nations.

Eva and Esther's old friends and allies Sarah Reddish and Sarah Dickenson was also members of the British Organising Committee for the Women's International Congress.

The writer 'Vernon Lee' was another of the signatories to the Women's International Congress. Vernon Lee was the pseudonym of Violet Paget (1856–1935). Paget was a lesbian, and she lived with her lover, Kit Anstruther-Thomson. She was loosely tied into London lesbian circles through her friendship with Ethel Smyth. Violet Paget had been born in France, which might have induced her to be more internationalist in outlook than the mass of British womanhood. In 1915, Paget published a pamphlet *Peace with Honour – Controversial Notes on the Settlement*. This pamphlet correctly foresaw that implementing a punitive peace settlement, as the 1919 Treaty of Versailles was to be, would only serve to hasten further war.[65]

The end of the war was a mixed blessing for women, particularly for lesbians, whose lovers had not been at risk. The opportunities to earn good wages, learn new skills and take fresh responsibilities were over. Hilda Martindale, Louisa Martindale's sister, was a peripatetic Inspector of Factories during the war and saw at first hand the positive experience that the war offered to women:

> During the war women's powers and capacities were called into full play, and no one denied that there was a response beyond all expectation. Soon, however, interesting work was taken out of their hands, and they were forced back into the routines of their hitherto normal occupations, and the splendid work they did in industry was forgotten.[66]

Women were forced back into the poorer-paid, less-skilled, and less-responsible positions they had occupied before the war.

Much women's employment disappeared altogether. All the 30,000 women who had worked at the Woolwich Arsenal were dismissed at the end of the war. Women attached to the armed forces, the WAAC and the WRNS, were also compulsorily demobilized in 1919. The demobilization of women was not received without anger. For many women, and particularly for lesbians, the war had offered them work and pay which enabled them to lead independent lives, no longer hemmed in by old social codes. However, not everything which had been gained was lost, to turn again to Radclyffe Hall:

> A battalion was formed in those terrible years that would never again be completely disbanded. War and death had given them a right to life, and life tasted sweet, very sweet to their palates. Later on would come bitterness, disillusion but never again would such women submit to being driven back to their holes and corners. They had found themselves – thus the whirligig of war brings in its abrupt revenges.[67]

NOTES

1. Radclyffe Hall, *The Well of Loneliness*, 1928 (London: Virago, 1982, reprinted 1985), p.275.
2. Sophia Mary Allen, *The Pioneer Policewoman* (London: Chatto & Windus, 1925), p.17.
3. Sylvia Pankhurst, *The Suffragette Movement*, 1931 (London: Virago, 1977, reprinted 1988), p.593.
4. Allen, *The Pioneer Policewoman*, p.13.
5. Pankhurst, *The Suffragette Movement*, pp.342–4: 'Black Friday' was 18 November 1910 and the demonstration which was its putative cause consisted of 300 women attempting to deliver a petition to Asquith at the House of Commons.
6. Allen, *The Pioneer Policewoman*, p.6.
7. Joan Lock, *The British Policewoman: Her Story* (London: Robert Hale, 1979), p.15, and Sophia Mary Allen, *Lady in Blue* (London: Stanley Paul & Co., 1936), pp.15–25.
8. Allen, *The Pioneer Policewoman*, p.17.
9. Lock, *The British Policewoman*, p.20, and Allen, *The Pioneer Policewoman*, p.17.
10. Allen, *The Pioneer Policewoman*, p.10.
11. Lock, *The British Policewoman*, p.19.
12. *Ibid.*
13. Pankhurst, *The Suffragette Movement*, p.265.
14. See Allen, *The Pioneer Policewoman*.
15. *Ibid.*, p.19.

16. Lock, *The British Policewoman*, p.19.
17. *Ibid.*, pp.61 and 149.
18. *Ibid.*, p.150.
19. Naomi Jacob, *Me – and the Swans* (London: William Kimber, 1963), pp.153 and 158.
20. Katrina Rolley, 'The lesbian sixth sense', *Feminist Art News*, **3**(5), p.11.
21. Hall, *The Well of Loneliness*, p.272.
22. Naomi Jacob, *Me in War-Time* (London: Hutchinson, 1940), p.208.
23. Lock, *The British Policewoman*, p.110.
24. *Ibid.*, p.128.
25. Allen, *The Pioneer Policewoman*, p.267, 'both of No.3, Little George St West'.
26. Michael Baker, *Our Three Selves: A Life of Radclyffe Hall* (London: Hamish Hamilton, 1985), p.267; Allen, *The Pioneer Policewoman*.
27. Quote from diary of Una Troubridge, 9 January 1931, in Baker, *Our Three Selves*, p.267.
28. Lock, *The British Policewoman*, p.156.
29. Christopher St John, *Christine Murrell*, M.D. (London: Williams & Norgate, 1935), p.58.
30. The WRNS, the women's branch of the Navy, was also established in 1917. It had a similarly circumscribed remit.
31. *The Times*, 5 August 1919.
32. Baker, *Our Three Selves*, pp.125–6. His precise source of this description remains unclear.
33. *Debrett's Peerage*, 1920.
34. See the Hackett-Lowther papers, Women at War Collection, Imperial War Museum, London.
35. *The Times*, 5 August 1919.
36. Baker, *Our Three Selves*, p.126.
37. *Ibid.*
38. All material on Holme not otherwise given a source comes from the Vera 'Jack' Holme collection held at the Fawcett Library.
39. Martha Vicinus, *Independent Women: Work and Community for Single Women 1850–1920* (London: Virago, 1985), p.279.
40. Pankhurst, *The Suffragette Movement*, p.225.
41. Dated 22 November 1910, and at Bow Street 22 and 24 November 1911.
42. Baker, *Our Three Selves*, p.264.
43. David Mitchell, *Women on the War Path* (London: Cape, 1966), p.88.
44. *Ibid.*
45. Jacob, *Me in War-Time*, p.175.
46. Louisa Martindale, *A Woman Surgeon* (London: Gollancz, 1951), p.163.
47. See Rosemary Auchmurty, 'By their friends we shall know them: the lives and networks of some women in North Lambeth, 1880–1940', in Lesbian History Group (ed.), *Not a Passing Phase: Reclaiming Lesbians in History* (London: The Women's Press, 1989), p.96.

48. 'I knew Elsie Inglis', 25 May 1941, recorded in Glasgow.
49. Roy Terry, *Women in Khaki: The Story of the British Woman Soldier* (London: Columbus, 1988), p.33.
50. Monica Krippner, *Quality of Mercy* (Newton Abbot: David & Charles, 1980), p.210.
51. This name is particularly indecipherable: it could be Alice Guildon. However, Embleton is a more common surname.
52. Naomi Jacob, *Me: A Chronicle about Other People* (London: Hutchinson, 1933), p.127.
53. *Ibid.*, p.193.
54. Jacob, *Me in War-Time*, p.131.
55. Elizabeth Gore, *The Better Fight: The Story of Dame Lilian Barker* (London: G. Bles, 1965), pp.61–2.
56. *Ibid.*, p.258.
57. Pankhurst, *The Suffragette Movement*, p.164.
58. *Ibid.*, p.167.
59. Esther Roper (ed.), *The Prison Letters of Countess Markievicz* (London: Longman, 1934), p.103.
60. *Ibid.*
61. *Ibid.*
62. Thomas C. Kennedy, *The Hound of Conscience: A History of the No-Conscription Fellowship, 1914-1919* (Fayetteville: University of Arkansas, 1981), p.56.
63. Roper, *The Prison Letters of Countess Markievicz*, p.103.
64. See Anne Wiltsher, *Most Dangerous Women: Feminist Peace Campaigners of the Great War* (London: Pandora, 1985).
65. Sybil Oldfield (ed.), *This Working-Day World: Women's Lives and Culture(s) in Britain 1914–45* (London: Taylor & Francis, 1994), pp.90–3.
66. Hilda Martindale, *From One Generation to Another* (London: Allen & Unwin, 1944), p.158.
67. Hall, *The Well of Loneliness*, p.275.

4 lesbians after the great war

'There is no place for grief'
Sappho, Fragment 76

Bob Rodgers was a young woman living in Derby and she wrote to Edward Carpenter in 1925:

> I feel I am acting as the spokesman of thousands who think and feel as I do, in writing to express my deep gratitude for your 'Intermediate Sex' and 'Towards Democracy'.
>
> Although I am known as Bob, physically I am a girl, still in my twenty-first year. I have been teaching slum boys since I left college nearly two years ago.
>
> It was at college that I met and learned to love a girl, who, in almost every respect, is quite different from me. Small, dainty, and essentially feminine, she is a great contrast to me. Until I met her, I had no idea that love between two of the same sex could possibly exist.

Although Rodgers makes clear that lesbianism was not a subject commonly discussed in front of girls and young women, she also indicates that lesbianism was not something that women needed to be instructed in. Significantly too, Rodgers saw herself as a butch dyke in isolation from public butch lesbian stereotypes; in 1925 *The Well of Loneliness* was not available as a manual for lesbian living. Derby is not known to have had a large lesbian scene in the 1920s and Rodgers was too young to have been involved in the lesbian networking of suffrage activism or war work. Yet Bob Rodgers was a lesbian: those who spoke publicly about homosexuality did not create homosexuals, they rather reinforced the pride and identity of lesbians and gay men who had previously felt isolated through public silence.

Bob Rodgers was friendly with a number of gay men and believed that lesbians and gay men shared a common condition.

> During the summer holidays my friend came to spend a month in Derby with me, and during that time, we made the acquaintance of six boys who are lovers in the same way. They introduced us to your books, and thereby earned my undying gratitude.

This is very different from the feminist-informed lesbianism of Kathlyn Oliver. Oliver makes no reference to gay men at all in any of her correspondence. Carpenter seems to have preferred Bob Rodgers's understanding of her lesbianism to Kathlyn Oliver's: he made very enthusiastic notes in the margins of letters that Bob Rodgers sent him. While friendships between lesbians and gay men have not been uncommon, it is unclear if they were predicated upon the belief that gay men and lesbians were simply two sides of the same coin. Lesbians and gay men may have felt united by social disapproval rather than united by an ungendered homosexuality.

One of the clearest cases of lesbian and gay unity in the early part of this century was the magazine Urania which was founded in 1915. The principal movers behind Urania were Esther Roper, Eva Gore-Booth and Thomas Baty, although a J. Wade and a D.H. Cornish were also listed as contacts in the magazine.[1] Urania was initially published six times a year, dropping to three times after 1920, and it ran until 1940.[2] The magazine was privately circulated, and neither a complete run nor the mailing list appears to have survived. Eva Gore-Booth and Esther Roper were, as I have discussed, important figures in the trade union, suffrage and internationalist pacifist movements. They appear to have met Baty through the suffrage movement at some point between 1908 and 1912.[3]

Thomas Baty (1869–1954) was a successful London lawyer. He practised at the Bar and was the author of a number of legal texts. In Who's Who he listed his recreations as 'music, heraldry, the sea; extreme feminist, would abolish all sex distinctions; conservative; vegetarianism'.[4] The first public indication of the nature of Baty's feminism and views on sex and gender was the publication of the novel Beatrice the Sixteenth in 1909. This novel was published under the name 'Irene Clyde'. Correspondence between Thomas Baty and George Bell, the publishers, indicates that Baty was Irene Clyde.[5] It is possible, although I have found no supporting evidence, that Baty merely represented 'Irene Clyde' to George Bell: 'Irene Clyde' was certainly not the name of a real woman.

Beatrice the Sixteenth is the story of a Mary Hatherley, M.B., explorer and geographer, who finds herself in an undiscovered land where gender does not exist. The novel is firmly positioned within the genre of science-fiction/exploration fantasy which had been established by writers such as Rider Haggard and H. G. Wells. By virtue of its position within this fantastic genre *Beatrice the Sixteenth* was protected from the kind of attack that realist novels, such as *The Well of Loneliness*, which dealt positively with what was perceived as perverse, received. *Beatrice the Sixteenth* made a scathing attack on a number of aspects of contemporary British society such as meat-eating, the disenfranchisement of women, the treatment of the poor and the British legal system. However, the major focus of the book is the iniquity of gender distinctions between men and women, and the cultural dominance of heterosexuality.

Beatrice the Sixteenth is a lesbian love story:

> I [Mary] looked at Ilex, and she was smiling. I moved backwards, and laid my head on her shoulder. She clasped me close in her arms. My thoughts flew back to the first time when I had quivered at her touch.
>
> 'Oh, my sweet!' she said, speaking with tense utterance as her heart beat near mine. 'In the whole gamut of human emotion, is there any such a thrill as that of knowing that one has someone one loves close − close − to one? Wilder, there may be, but anything so satisfying and perfect − no!'
>
> I trembled with delight in her arms.[6]

It is the surrealness of a man, even a gay man, choosing to write a lesbian love story under a female pseudonym which makes me wonder if Baty, a lawyer, was acting as the intermediary for a lesbian, perhaps Esther Roper. For a man, certainly in this period, to choose to write under a female pseudonym was unusual; it would be likely to decrease a novel's sales, review coverage and claims on serious critical analysis. Whether Baty actually was the author of all 'Irene Clyde's' writing or not, he certainly had an intimate relationship with 'Miss Clyde' and her work, and agreed with her views on gender, feminism, sexuality and vegetarianism.

For whatever reasons, its female author or its lesbian and feminist subject matter, *Beatrice the Sixteenth* sold extremely badly: copies were still held by the publisher in the 1950s.[7] Baty was, however, undeterred by this apparent failure and remained committed to getting gender and sexuality raised as issues of debate in feminist circles and the public arena. In 1911 he was in correspondence with Mrs Millicent Garrett Fawcett, the doyenne of suffrage campaigning, about a new group called the 'Aëthenic Union' which was working for the elimination of gender distinctions. Baty asked Mrs Fawcett if the NUWSS would adopt the elimination of gender distinctions as one of its aims. By the NUWSS's standards of radicalism

Baty must have seemed a bomb-carrying revolutionary; Mrs Fawcett refused his request.

Baty also wrote a letter to *The Freewoman* in 1912 publicizing the existence of the Aëthenic Union.[8] The most explicit statement Baty makes about the Aëthenic Union is that it will have as its ideal 'Penthesilea, Sappho and Pallas Athëne'.[9] Penthesilea was a warrior queen, Sappho the lesbian teacher, and the goddess Pallas Athëne was born from her father's forehead, without the bloody marks of woman's struggle: a combination of mythic women which is evocative but not easily decipherable. There is a flier for the first meeting of the Aëthenic Union, entitled *The Phoenix*. It lists among the group's supporters Eva Gore-Booth and Esther Roper. No further records of the Aëthenic Union exist and it appears it existed only for a few months. Undaunted by the rejection of his views by mainstream suffragists and of the apparent collapse of the Aëthenic Union after its first meeting, Baty re-emerges with the launch of *Urania* in 1915.

Each issue of *Urania* was headed with the statement:

> Urania denotes the company of those who are firmly determined to ignore the dual organisation of humanity in all its manifestations.
>
> They are convinced that this duality has resulted in the formation of two warped and imperfect types. They are further convinced that in order to get rid of this state of things no measures of 'emancipation' or 'equality' will suffice, which do not begin by a complete refusal to recognise or tolerate the duality itself.
>
> If the world is to see sweetness and independence combined in the same individual, *all* recognition of that duality must be given up. For it inevitably brings in its train the suggestion of the conventional distortions of character which are based on it.
>
> There are no 'men' or 'women' in Urania.

The politics of *Urania* were, then, to work against the belief that men and women were innately different. *Urania* argued that gender was a cultural construction which worked against the true realization of an individual's potential. By inculcating femininity in women and masculinity in men, society served to limit their true development as people with aspects and attributes of both the conventionally male and conventionally female. A corollary to this argument was that when women and men became people and escaped the limits of gender, heterosexual relationships would no longer be prioritized over same-sex relationships. It was this attack on heterosexuality, as well as the constructed and artificial nature of gender, that made Roper, Gore-Booth and Baty appear so dangerously radical to many suffragists.

One of Eva Gore-Booth's favourite sayings was 'sex is an accident'. By this she did not mean that we fall into bed but that biology is arbitrarily and non-causally related to cultural ideas of maleness and femaleness. It was the truth of this belief that *Urania* was designed to illustrate. Each issue was between ten and twenty pages long and consisted almost entirely of clippings of articles, from newspapers from all over the world, on cross-dressing, life-long transvestism, passing women, hermaphrodites, transsexualism, and same-sex 'marriages'. Attention was also paid to women who achieved success in male fields such as those who won open scholarships, built ships or beat off attackers, and to men who knitted exquisitely and so on. Baty had close links with Japan, links which were exploited to full advantage in *Urania*, which included numerous Asian press clippings.[10]

With the exception of the opening statement reproduced in each issue, which I have already quoted, *Urania* contained very little editorial or analytical commentary; all the press clippings were reproduced without comment. Original articles were published infrequently and were usually unsigned; the notable exception were articles with Irene Clyde's by-line. It is possible that the name 'Irene Clyde' was used by more than one of the contributors; a shared alias indicating shared sympathies. Irene Clyde continued in *Urania* to celebrate love between women, for instance, in the article A *Railway Idyll*, which appeared in 1922. It is unclear whether A *Railway Idyll* was fiction or reportage; it describes a genderless narrator travelling on a train. The climax of the journey is the sighting of 'two ordinary girls' who 'behaved like an engaged couple':

> Their evident absorption in each other – the indulgent protective face of the elder – the anxiety of the younger to be entertaining and attractive and pleasing would have been amusing if they had not been transcendentally beautiful.

Clyde asks 'Why do not poets celebrate this beautiful thing? Why do not artists praise it?' and she concludes:

> Does the world not know it, this love? Or are men too jealous to notice it? Ovid could not be content without metamorphosing Iphis into a conventional shape; Wilkie Collins' heroine entreats her friend not to marry, 'unless you meet somebody you like better than me'; plaintively recognising the

possibility. Henry James' Olive loses her lover to Basil Ransome. Lady Eleanor
Butler and Miss Ponsonby are treated as eccentrics . . .

For all that it is a real thing: love of like by like . . . [11]

It is interesting to see that Clyde invokes women who continue to be called
upon as legendary lesbians. This indicates that it was a specifically lesbian
legacy, not a history of female friendship, with which Clyde is identifying.
Clyde's argument also reiterates the imagery of 'the love that dare not
speak its name' to make the point that the existence of lesbianism is
denied; it is the love that will not be heard.

However, the relationship between *Urania* and lesbianism was complex,
as is shown by the anonymous review of *The Well of Loneliness* which was
published in *Urania* in the summer of 1929. Giving a reaction to *The Well of
Loneliness* was obviously perceived to be very important; the review takes up
the entire front page of the issue. It begins appreciatively:

This absurd world in which two perversely imperfect types must exist, in
order that by their mutual craze for each other, the perverse imperfection
may be renewed, is beginning to be found out for the sham that it is. [12]

However, it criticizes Hall for making Stephen Gordon masculine and Mary
Llewellyn feminine. Given that *Urania's raison d'être* was the elimination of
masculinity and femininity this criticism is not unexpected.

There is no attraction for anybody in mannishness or effeminacy. It was a
gratuitous concession to popular foolishness on Radclyffe Hall's part, to make
her heroine a little mannish.

The belief here appears to be that Hall has made her lesbians too
heterosexual, political criticism which was to be shared by later lesbian-
feminists.

Overall, it is a positive review:

We venture the hope that Radclyffe Hall will give us another book in which
no imitation men need figure. For she has a wonderful pen. The descriptions
of Nature are delightful: the insight into character is penetrating: her style is
sympathetic and her language beautiful.

However, the review does include some passages which are hard to make sense of, for instance after stating that 'There will inevitably be spirits in each garb who prefer their own type to the other', it continues:

> That they do not find expression in the violent and brutally limited physical form styled by the world 'perversion', is equally natural.
> In Radclyffe Hall's novel they do. The fact is not insisted on in any detail by her. Seven words – 'and that night they were not divided' – sums up the whole offending.

This appears to distance those spirits who find happiness in same-sex relationships from those perverts who have homosexual sex. It is not clear whether the review does not want lesbianism to be simply reduced to a sexual activity or whether it seeks to exclude sex from same-sex happiness entirely. When the review talks of 'violent and brutally limited physical form' does it mean that lesbian sex is violent and brutally limited or is it satirizing the public conception of sex as violent and brutally limited? Similar confusion is engendered by the concluding sentence of this two-page review: 'We think Sapphism contemptible: but we find "The Well of Loneliness" a triumph of art and delicacy.' From the perspective of the 1990s this sentence appears to be nonsensical, unless 'Sapphism' is being used ironically to mark a particular conception of lesbianism.

It is impossible to try to infer the politics of a magazine which ran for twenty-five years from one book review, particularly given the potential danger of unequivocally supporting a book which had been successfully prosecuted for obscenity, and of seeming to endorse sexual activities some of which were illegal. It is unclear too whether the review of *The Well of Loneliness* was the work of a committee stating the *Urania* line or of an individual. *Urania* cannot simply be thought of as an early version of *Gay Times*. It was powered by a political and philosophical agenda, the intricacies of which have been made obscure by the passage of time.

That said, in general *Urania* had a lot in common with *Gay Times*, the very name of the magazine being most important. The vocabulary of 'urania' was, I have already said, used widely by both professional sexologists like Havelock Ellis and homosexuals themselves, as Edward Carpenter's writings and correspondence show. 'Uranian' was widely known to be a synonym for homosexuality by the early years of the twentieth century. In 1908, Stephenson explicated the 'problem of homosexuality' as 'the problem of homosexualism, simisexualism, urningism, inverted sexuality, [and] uranianism as it is variously termed'.[13]

Stephenson explains the 'urania-' root of this vocabulary as being

> derived from the classic fable of the 'Venus Urania', and from the Platonic discussions concerning a mystic 'nobler Venus' the divine patroness of simisexualism, passional loves, especially between males' re-affirming the theory of there having been created only one single human sex of old, that only later came to subsist two types with their separate sexual instincts in mankind each by divine insinuation.[14]

The links between *Urania* and this mythical heritage are clear; *Urania* was dedicated to overthrowing the hegemony of sexual duality and (re)turning to the single sex which unites all that is best in humanity. The classical root of urania that Stephenson claims fits into the characterization of homosexuality as 'Greek love' that draws upon the descriptions of same-sex love in Greek classical texts. Eva Gore-Booth and Thomas Baty were both well-versed in the classics; Eva Gore-Booth had read Sappho in the original Greek.

Thomas Baty, Eva Gore-Booth and Esther Roper cannot have been ignorant of the contemporary understanding of the meaning of urania, uranian and uranianism: the 1912 discussion of homosexuality in *The Freewoman* took place under the title 'Uranianism' and Thomas Baty corresponded with *The Freewoman* on the subject of the Aëthenic Union during this very debate.[15] Eva Gore-Booth and Esther Roper, given their membership of the Aëthenic Union, must surely have read those issues of *The Freewoman*, although they undoubtedly read *The Freewoman* on a regular basis anyway. *Urania* was quite simply the magazine for uranians.

Gifford Lewis, the biographer of Roper and Gore-Booth, suggests that it was because of Eva and Esther's interest in astrology that they called their magazine *Urania*, since Urania was a muse of astrology. This theory appears unlikely as astrology does not feature in *Urania*. Gifford Lewis is vehemently opposed to the suggestion that Esther Roper and Eva Gore-Booth were lovers, contending, for instance, that 'they put aside sexuality from their lives as an irrelevance'. Rather surprisingly, Lewis's justification for this is 'Eva calmly noting in a manuscript book of dream images that she had not bothered to record any that were "obviously sexual"'.[16] Having obviously sexual dreams does not in a straightforward way imply that one has cast aside sex and sexuality as an irrelevance. Given the relative rarity of women who are well-known for their female partnerships, Lewis's choice of subjects seems unfortunate. However with Gore-Booth and Roper, Gifford Lewis faces an impossible task: their sexuality could not be clearer.

In 1900, Eva had altered her will, making Esther the sole beneficiary; this will was unchanged at her death twenty-seven years later. Esther Roper and Eva Gore-Booth are buried together in a single grave in Hampstead churchyard. The headstone gives merely their names, dates and a quotation 'Life that is Love is God'. This quotation Esther Roper believed, probably mistakenly, to be from Sappho.[17] The fact that Esther Roper chose for herself and Eva to be commemorated together by a line from Sappho cannot, in the context of their lives, simply be attributed to chance. Eva knew the works of Sappho well and not just through bowdlerized translations: in 1926 no confusion existed at all about what Sappho stood for, and what Sapphism meant.

While Eva and Esther were unfortunate in their biographer they were luckier with their own relatives. Esther's brother Edward was very close to them as was Eva's sister, Constance Markievicz; Constance seems to have been very accepting of her sister's choices about sex and love. Constance said of Esther:

> She is wonderful, and the moment one knows her, the moment one loves her, and I feel so glad that Eva and she were together and so thankful that her love was with Eva to the end.[18]

After Eva's death in 1926 Constance wrote to Esther:

> It is only because you were so much in touch with her human form that you miss it so, and your mind can't rest: but it will find rest, and her, only it will take time.[19]

She reiterates this theme in other letters at this time, accepting that Esther's grief for Eva is of a different order than her own because Esther 'was so much nearer her body than I was'.[20]

As feminists, Esther Roper and Eva Gore-Booth were unusual in that the partial winning of the suffrage in 1918 seems to have made little difference to their political activities. For many women who had campaigned actively for the vote, the triumph of 1918, the vote for women over thirty, caused new problems. Whether the gaining of the suffrage was the result of women's vital contribution to the war effort, or to the fear that militancy would re-emerge, or due to broader political changes which accepted the need for a more universal suffrage remains hotly debated. However, the gaining of the vote undisputedly shattered many suffrage and feminist groups and alliances which had existed before the war. Once the vote was won the uniting common cause was gone.

Many women, who believed that further political and social changes were necessary, turned their energies towards the mainstream political system which was now open to them. The first women MPs were elected in the 1920s with Labour women predominant. Constance Markievicz was the first woman MP, though as a Sinn Fein member she did not take her seat. Micky Jacob became involved in Labour party politics, and was selected as the prospective candidate for Sevenoaks, although she had to withdraw as a candidate because of a recurrence of her TB. This is sad for lesbian history, for the election of Micky Jacob would undoubtedly have brought Vita Sackville-West, conservative, anti-Semitic and snobbish, and whose heart lay in Sevenoaks, to a state of apoplexy.

Between 1918 and 1928, when all women over the age of twenty-one received the vote, professional and educational opportunities, most importantly law and accountancy, were gradually opened up to women. More universities began to admit women as undergraduates on the same terms as men, although Cambridge was to resist absolute equality until 1948. This expansion of possibilities for women led to many women diverting their energies from politics to building successful professional lives. For working-class women the employment position did not change dramatically, although moves were made by the government to institute some training schemes for women. Lilian Barker was among those who pressed for this kind of initiative from her position within the Home Office; she felt that the government had a duty to those women it had picked up during the war and flung aside at its end. Not all these initiatives were appealing; one was designed to train women to be better domestic servants.

Lilian Barker built an impressive career after the war on the basis of her experience as a teacher and at Woolwich Arsenal. In 1923 she was appointed Governor of Aylesbury Girls' Borstal, and in 1935 she was the first woman to be appointed Assistant Commissioner of Prisons. When it was decided in the 1920s that women should be able to receive an honour on a par with a knighthood, it was Lilian Barker, again from her position within the Home Office, who suggested that the title should be that of Dame. With the vote and the acceptance of women into the body politic came new duties as well as new rights, such as jury service. Lilian Barker was, in 1921, one of the first women to serve on a jury.

Many women had discovered, through the war itself, causes which they believed were now more urgent and pressing than feminism. Vera Holme, for instance, concerned herself with the politics of Yugoslavia and the Serbs as a result of her experiences there during and after the war. Her interest in Serbia was to be life-long; in the 1940s, she was on the West of Scotland committee of the Yugoslav Relief Society.[21] Vera Holme maintained her connections with feminist activism, she was still a member of the Women's Freedom League in 1942, but not on the level of her suffragette days.

Feminism did not disappear in the 1920s and 1930s but feminist activity was only a shadow of its engrossing pre-war self. Some pre-war suffrage groups such as the Women's Freedom League persisted, and new feminist groups such as the Six Point Group and the Open Door Council were established. These groups were concerned with ensuring that the principle of women's equality, now enshrined by law, was respected and re-enforced through all other pertinent legislation. Thus exciting and involved direct action politics was replaced by parliamentary lobbying and what must have seemed like tedious minutiæ.

Feminist politics in the 1920s split into two camps. On the one hand there were 'equality' feminists who wanted women to have exactly the same rights and privileges as men, no more and no less. Chief concerns in this area were equal access to education and the professions, and equal pay. One of the most pressing changes in economic and social conditions still waiting to be implemented in 1918 was the principle of equal pay for equal work regardless of sex. While feminists from all political groups supported this principle, it was bitterly opposed by the trade unions; they believed that men should be paid a family wage, enough to support a wife and children, while women should be paid a lesser rate as they had no dependants to support. It was of course not until the Equal Pay Act of 1970 that women were to win the legal right to equal pay.

The Open Door Council worked towards equal rights for women in employment; Esther Roper was one of its officers.[22] The Six Point Group concerned itself more generally with equal rights for women; it campaigned on six points of female equality at a time: as an issue was won, it was replaced by a new feminist goal. One of the best-known 'equal rights' feminists was Lady Rhondda, the long-time companion of Theodora Bosanquet, who founded the feminist magazine *Time and Tide* in 1920. *Time and Tide* was known as 'the Sapphic Graphic', presumably because there were so many lesbians involved with it.[23] Winifred Holtby and Vera Brittain were another influential feminist couple who were involved in a wide variety of campaigns for equal rights in the 1920s and 1930s, and who were also closely involved with *Time and Tide*.

The alternative to the equal rights feminists were the 'new' feminists, who were, in fact, in many ways not new at all. Eleanor Rathbone (1872–1946) was the most famous 'new' feminist and she had perhaps the greatest practical effect on women's lives of any of the feminists of the inter-war period. She had been a committed suffragist, and although she was never militant, she was on the NUWSS executive committee in 1912. Born and brought up in Liverpool, she returned there after three years of studying at Somerville College, Oxford. Although she did not need to work for a living, Rathbone was active in both social work and politics; she was the first woman to sit on Liverpool City Council in 1909.

After World War I Eleanor Rathbone moved to London with her 'best-loved friend' Elizabeth Macadam, a Scottish social worker.[24] Elizabeth and Eleanor had met in Liverpool in 1902; Mary Stocks, Rathbone's biographer, does not equivocate about their relationship: 'Elizabeth Macadam became in due course the friend and companion of Eleanor's existence until death did them part, and at no subsequent period was Eleanor lonely.' Stocks, who had known the couple intimately, quotes a poem to show what their meeting meant:

And none will know the gleam there used to be
About the feast days freshly kept by me
But men will call the hour of golden bliss
'About this time' or 'Shortly after this'[25]

After the war the NUWSS was reborn as the National Union for Societies for Equal Citizenship (NUSEC), which saw its mission as equipping women with the skills and knowledge to put their political enfranchisement to maximum use. In 1919 Eleanor Rathbone was elected as the president of the NUSEC, following the resignation of Millicent Garrett Fawcett. The feminism with which Rathbone and the NUSEC were identified argued that women's aims were not simply equality, but the appreciation of women's difference from men. Equal opportunities, the new feminists argued, were not always the right answer; women by virtue of their biology, and perhaps their desires, had different social needs from men, and they had a right to have those needs met by the state.

One of Rathbone's main political objectives was to raise the status and improve the lives of mothers and children. Throughout her political career she campaigned for a family allowance to be paid by the state to the mother. Rathbone's scheme was eventually incorporated, with much of its guts missing, into the Beveridge legislation, introduced after World War II.

Rathbone's political influence was strong, for not only did she head the NUSEC, which had a membership of tens of thousands of women, but also in 1929 she was elected as an Independent MP for the Combined Universities. The Combined Universities seat was an anomaly, a parliamentary seat which represented not a geographical area but the graduates of the older universities, supposedly the intellectual opinion of Britain; Eleanor Rathbone held it until her death.

Rathbone's feminist politics were pragmatic not idealistic; changing the world would take time and in the interim mothers needed more practical help in order to have a better quality of life for themselves and their children. Sheila Jeffreys, and others, have accused Eleanor Rathbone of betraying true feminism:

> Rather than struggle for equal pay, she suggested that women should campaign for the endowment of motherhood, envisioned by Rathbone as a wage, rather than a small allowance. Thus she betrayed the cause of spinsterhood and the independent woman. She deserted a feminist option because it was too difficult and embraced the simpler alternative of emphasising woman's mission of motherhood.[26]

However, this is to misrepresent Eleanor Rathbone, who was with the equal rights feminists on the issue of equal pay; in her major economic polemic *The Disinherited Family* she produced 'a powerful and comprehensive dismissal of the family wage as an economic ideal'.[27] Carol Dyhouse points out that Eleanor Rathbone 'was vehemently opposed to any idea that the payment of family allowances should depend upon a mother staying at home'; her aim was not to provide an incentive for women to leave the work force but to give them some economic security if they became mothers, not always a decision over which they had great control.[28]

Another of Eleanor Rathbone's objectives, and one shared by many feminists in the 1920s, was to educate women politically so that they could exploit their new rights as citizens. It was with this in mind that she anonymously donated £100 to establish the National Union of Townswomen's Guilds (NUTG) in 1928. The aims of the Townswomen's Guilds, which were initially backed by the NUSEC, were:

> To encourage the education of women to enable them as citizens to make their best contribution towards the common good.

> To serve as a common meeting ground for women irrespective of creed
> and party for their wider education including social intercourse.

Obviously women who had been in the suffrage campaigns, the anti-slavery campaigns, the campaigns against the contagious diseases legislation, or who had been involved in trade union organization and the formation of the Labour Party, knew and cared about public policy, as did the hundreds of thousands of women who were teachers, civil servants and social workers, and those women who served as local councillors or on school and hospital boards. However, a significant number of women were alienated from the world of public debate and politics and much feminist work in the 1920s and 1930s centred upon bringing women into full political participation. The granting of the vote in 1918 was seen by many feminists as the winning of a battle, not the war.

The NUTG, the Women's Institutes, established in 1915, and other women-only organizations were enormously important in a country with few mass membership organizations where women had any power or authority. Together they formed a network of empowering women-only spaces which allowed women to organize and to debate and to gain skills which they could take into the outside world. They also kept alive the memory of the early feminists, publishing pamphlets with titles such as *Women Who Defied Prejudice*. Today the NUTG is a pale shadow of its former self and is thought of, with the Mothers' Union and the Women's Institute, as one of the family-centred, Christian, and right-wing institutions of middle England. However, in their early days these groups were much more overtly feminist and provided considerable lesbian space.

A woman remembering her life in this period emphasizes the important role these apparently staid institutions played in women's lives:

> I knew I was a lesbian when I was fourteen [about 1930]. I accepted it as natural. It was natural to me that I loved women – I was never interested in boys, men, it was always women. When I was fourteen, I left elementary school, and went to a Women's Evening Institute. It was a club, we were all women together, did everything together – holidays, swimming, netball. I was in a netball team and went all over London playing. We spent holidays together – we were in the atmosphere of caring for women – in gym classes, etc. A lot of us had crushes on other women and a lot of us have never married. Four of us quickly formed an exclusive group. We were all lesbians and there were many more we were aware of among the wider group of

students. We four did everything together and even broke the ice at the Women's Pond at Highgate one New Year's Day.[29]

The NUTG is interesting not only because of Eleanor Rathbone's involvement with it. The honorary secretary and treasurer of the NUTG for many years was Alice Franklin, a woman with a resolutely feminist background. Under her leadership, the NUTG had a distinctive flavour all of its own. Alice C. Franklin (1885–1964) was the daughter of an upper-middle-class intellectual Jewish family. With her sister Helen Bentwich and brother Hugh Franklin, she became involved in suffrage activity while a young woman; she is listed in the 1913 *Who's Who of Women's Suffrage* as a secretary of a Jewish women's suffrage group. According to Mary Stott, Franklin was also 'a Socialist and honorary secretary of a group of young intellectuals who called themselves "The Utopians"'. She later worked as the secretary of the Society for the Overseas Settlement of British Women, an organization which helped women who wanted to emigrate.[30]

Alice Franklin worked for the NUTG in a full-time but unpaid capacity for twenty years. In *Organisation Woman* Mary Stott describes how the other women there remembered her:

> When I first met Miss Franklin I had to look twice – she looked so like a man with her short-cropped hair. She was rather abrupt and short in her manner – a real character. She and Mrs Horton used surnames without prefixes and would call upstairs for 'Elias' or whoever.[31]

As Stott makes clear, while Alice Franklin was admired by her colleagues for her dedication to the Townswomen's Guilds, she also made them uneasy:

> Alice Franklin's sense of fun did not always go down very well with her committees. Some members were antagonistic to her, and objected when she teased them by saying 'What a nuisance your husbands are'.[32]

Franklin fell out with the executive committee in 1948 and left the NUTG on a note of considerable bitterness. Although she lived for another sixteen years, dying when she was seventy-nine, her name never again appeared in NUTG annual reports, or in any accounts of events in *The Townswoman*.[33] She was awarded the OBE in the 1930s.

Lesbians, however, were not content merely to establish themselves in (heterosexual) women's organizations; they were keen to create new spaces just for themselves. There were some lesbian haunts by the middle of the 1920s in London. As early as 1908 Stephenson mentions the London 'vapour bath' on Ladies' Day as a frequent place for lesbians to meet, and in the 1920s well-off lesbians could meet in straight but bohemian night clubs, such as the Cave of Harmony, the Orange Tree and the Hambone.[34] However, none of these was a dedicated lesbian space and some women wanted more than they offered. In 1921 Enid Chambers wrote to Edward Carpenter 'about the idea I have had in my mind for some time of getting together a group of Uranian women to form the nucleus of a club'.[35]

Chambers wondered if Carpenter could help her by giving her 'the names & addresses of any Uranian women you know whom you think would be glad of companionship & the chance of meeting others like themselves'. For as she said:

> I know only too well the loneliness that most Uranians have to go through, & the utter impossibility of speaking of their problems to those who do not understand.
>
> I know one or two & have been able to help one or two, but I want to meet & know more. There must be very many others round me here in London: some who think themselves alone; others who do not even understand their own natures & still others who have been taught to think of themselves as freaks or criminals. Only a Uranian can really understand a Uranian, & I do understand so well from my own experiences the complex nature of a Uranian woman.

Chambers was not motivated solely by the wish to help depressed and isolated lesbians, or to find more friends or lovers. She was also eager to start a political group which would defend the interests of lesbians and gay men:

> Another reason why I think it would be good to get a collection of Uranian women together is that there will be more Uranians during the next ten years than ever, & as the question comes more before the public there will be greater opposition, & there may be attempts made for the law to interfere considerably with our freedom. In which case there is all the more need of comradeship. I believe there's a club for men in London but I don't think anything has yet been done in that way for women.[36]

It is unclear why Chambers thought that there would be more Uranians in the next ten years; perhaps she believed that there would be a cultural move towards a unity of masculinity and femininity which would lead inevitably to more homosexuality.

Although I have not been able to identify precisely which Uranian 'club for men' Enid Chambers was referring to, it is indisputable that there was a greater number of gay male spaces than lesbian spaces in London in this period. Some of these spaces were private clubs, but there were also strong gay male social networks, such as those centred around the BSSSP and the Order of Chaeronea, a kind of gay male Freemasons. While the BSSSP and the Order of Chaeronea largely linked gay men, some lesbians were peripherally involved with them. Jeffrey Weeks suggests that Una Troubridge and Radclyffe Hall may have been members of the Order of Chaeronea as well as the BSSSP.[37] It was members of these two groups who published *The Quorum: A Magazine of Friendship* in 1920. *The Quorum* contained homoerotic, although not explicitly sexual, pieces eulogizing same-sex love. All the male contributors, E.E. Bradford, Arthur Gardner, Leonard Green, Kenneth Ingram, and J.G. Nicolson, are known to have been homosexual or paedophile in their sexual desires.[38] There was one woman contributor, Dorothy L. Sayers (1893–1957), then an almost unknown young poet.

Sayers's contribution to *The Quorum* was 'Veronica':

> You have not hurt me. If I dared to say
> That I approached nightly for your sake,
> My vigils would reproach you in that day
> When all we sleepers wake.
>
> Let not your shamed and seeking fingers cease
> My heavy hands, my listless hands to lift –
> They are but listless with exceeding peace
> And heavy with a gift.
>
> Be not afraid, most dear and weariest,
> To take what comfort you can have of me;
> Have I not told you that my quiet breast
> Is cooler than the sea?

I swear that never till the end of ends
Shall you have drawn one veil across the blue,
I am not sadder that we have been friends,
Nor lonelier, loving you.

Never believe that I could betray you so,
Could add one smallest burden to the heap,
Not God Himself, Who knows all things, shall know
That you have made me weep.[39]

While 'Veronica' is not explicitly lesbian it is homoerotic and obviously was seen as a positive and relevant addition to The Quorum by its editor, C. Kairns Jackson. It is hard to see why Sayers would have known of the existence of The Quorum if she had not been friendly with the gay men who established it. Only one edition of The Quorum was produced and it was privately circulated largely to the membership of the BSSSP. There appears to have been no interest in circulating the magazine to a larger or more general audience; publication in The Quorum was not then an obvious way for Sayers to pursue her literary career. It is inconceivable, given the well-justified fear that gay men had of the police and the law, that the poem was published without Sayers's express permission.

None of the biographers of Dorothy L. Sayers betrays any knowledge of Sayers's involvement with The Quorum or mentions any of the men involved with it, but it is possible that Dorothy knew these men from Oxford. Leonard Green (1885–1966), for instance, may have been there at the same time. In 1920 Dorothy L. Sayers had just moved from Oxford to London, and her biographers seem to have little information on the friends of Dorothy in this period. Sayers was certainly aware of lesbianism and lesbians: one of her friends in this period was Evelyn Irons, a lesbian who was relatively open about her sexuality.[40] Evelyn Irons's friendship with Sayers is also not mentioned by Sayers's biographers.

Janet Hitchman, one of her biographers, is prepared to admit that by 1927, when Unnatural Death was published, Dorothy 'knew all about lesbianism. Mary Whittaker is quite the nastiest of her villains and is obviously a lesbian.'[41] However, Hitchman maintains that

in spite of her masculine style of dress, which became more pronounced as she grew older, there is no evidence that she [Sayers] was ever in love with a woman. Indeed, had she noticed such tendencies in herself she would have fought against them, for any kind of homosexuality was the 'unmentionable' sin in the circle in which she had been raised. However broadminded she was to become later in life, as a young girl the only permissible love was that between the members of opposite sexes.[42]

This is internally rather incoherent, implying that Sayers was not a lesbian and could never be one because of her upbringing, and that she became less constrained by her upbringing and more broad-minded about homosexuality as she became older. The most obvious reason for Dorothy L. Sayers's knowledge of lesbians, her friendships with lesbians and gay men and her identification with homoeroticism is that she had been involved in a lesbian relationship. The fact that Dorothy L. Sayers had written a poem which was clearly addressed to a woman and which was published in a highbrow homoerotic magazine cannot easily be heterosexualized.

Although *The Well of Loneliness* is so notoriously the great British public's introduction to lesbianism, it was of course not the first book by a woman writer about lesbianism. It was rather the first book by an author who was publicly prepared to say that she herself was a lesbian. Not only did *Unnatural Death* have lesbianism as its plot but so did other novels published between the war and 1928. In 1917 Clemence Dane's first novel, *Regiment of Women*, was published to much popular acclaim. Clemence Dane was the pen-name of Winifred Ashton (1887–1965). Dane had been educated privately, and had then spent some time at the Slade studying art and was briefly an actress. In the period before writing the *Regiment of Women* she had taught at a girls' school in Ireland.

Regiment of Women concerns the experiences of two women teachers and a young female pupil at a girls' school. The (anti-)heroine is Claire Hartill, who is a proud, sensitive and intelligent woman. The novel describes how Claire charms the new teacher Alwynne Durand and her young pupil Louise Denny. The climax is reached when Louise, thinking that Claire no longer loves her, commits suicide and Alwynne succumbs to the marriage proposal of the insensitive and rather stupid Roger Lumsden.

Regiment of Women is not a cheerful lesbian love story, indeed it is often cited as being a profoundly anti-lesbian book.[43] However, this quick reaction is, I think, an over-simple response. The first 264 pages of *Regiment of Women* are concerned with relationships between women, and the plot is rather unconvincingly heterosexualized in the final 80 pages. *Regiment of Women* has to be read with the knowledge that no book about lesbians for another fifty years would have a happy ending. Lesbians may have written lesbian love stories but public distaste for lesbianism and publishers' nervousness ensured that they were not published.

The lesbian protagonist Claire Hartill is a complex and in many ways remarkable character. It is Claire's habit of encouraging women's feelings for her, for the sake of idle amusement, that Dane sees as reprehensible, not her lesbianism *per se*. This kind of emotional game-playing was, Clemence Dane believed, common in the intense emotional atmosphere of girls' schools. Dane's object of criticism was the unnaturally cloistered environment in which girls were educated and women teachers spent their lives; this, she believed, was detrimental to their psychological and physical health. *Regiment of Women* should not be read in isolation from Clemence Dane's other writing on the same subject.

In *The Woman's Side*, a collection of essays published by Dane in 1926, an essay is devoted to the subject of the abuse of power in relationships between female pupil and female teacher. 'A Problem In Education' ostensibly takes as its subject the 'problem of emotional attachments between members of the same sex'.[44] Here again, her concern is specifically with the 'hot-house' atmosphere of single-sex schools where teachers have no life (homosexual or heterosexual) outside the school and so devote their time and emotional energy to the intimacies and intrigues within it.

It is precisely the peculiarity of the social isolation of women and girls in single-sex schools and the potential for abuse of power in these circumstances that is the subject of both *Regiment of Women* and of 'A Problem In Education'. The effect of the marriage bar for female teachers, and the importance of respectability, meant that many women teachers spent their lives completely immersed in a small and closed world of school. As Dane said:

> But what opportunity has a woman to mix freely with men and women alike,
> so as to understand her own outlook on these matters, to test her feelings,
> to differentiate between her need of friendship and her need of love? Her
> sole emotional outlet is her fellow-mistresses and her pupils.[45]

Although most well-known for *Regiment of Women* and as a playwright, Clemence Dane was a committed feminist. After World War II, she was one of the four Vice-Presidents of the Six Point Group.[46] *The Woman's Side* was a practical demonstration of her commitment to women, and as her introduction made clear, her aim was to get women to think about matters of political and social policy. She did not necessarily want her audience to agree with her, but to prod them into developing opinions on public matters. Her frank discussion of what she described as the 'un-named affection between women' moved, as *Regiment of Women* also did, lesbianism into centre stage as a subject that could be discussed by ordinary women.

Dane's concern is not lesbian or homosexual relationships *per se*; it is the abuse of power between adult and child, or older and younger women, which can have its most pernicious effects within the closed world of the school.[47] With the position of lesbians in general she is sympathetic:

> It is not pleasant to think of what the more imaginative and passionate among such women must suffer. And the fact that they are rare, that with most women the sex feeling is rather indirect and passive, that their active emotions are more maternal and spiritual than passionate, does not solve the problem either. Women can have an intense longing for attention and affection and comradeship without necessarily or consciously wishing to marry.[48]

Clemence Dane knew a number of lesbians. Michael Baker, Hall's biographer, recounts that Una read *Regiment of Women* aloud to Radclyffe Hall. Hall presumably enjoyed the book and trusted Dane's sympathy towards lesbians, as in the 1930s she asked Clemence whether she would adapt *The Well of Loneliness* for the stage. That Hall made this suggestion is an unequivocal lesbian seal of approval for Dane; Hall was obsessive about protecting the integrity of *The Well of Loneliness*; she had a terror of it being bowdlerized. Sadly, the proposal came to nothing.[49] Clemence Dane was also friendly with Violet Trefusis and Vita Sackville-West from the time of their affair in the early 1920s. Clemence appears to have been Violet's major confidante and a considerable support, as Violet's letters to Vita show.

Dane went to great lengths to keep her private life private, and no biography of her has been written. However, her will shows where her commitments, and her heart, lay. Clemence Dane's last will was made in 1956 and names as her executors Olwen Bowen-Davies and Stanley Gorrie, her accountant. Olwen Bowen-Davies is the major beneficiary of the will, inheriting a house in St John's Wood and all Clemence's other real and personal estate, including her literary assets. The only item not left to Bowen-Davies was an (empty) jewel case that Dane left to her brother. In 1956 Dane, however, was not living in the St John's Wood house but in a rented house in Covent Garden; living in the St John's Wood house was Elsie Arnold.

It seems likely that Elsie Arnold was the 'E.A.' to whom *Regiment of Women* was dedicated: 'To E.A. / Here's Our Book / As it grew. / But it's Your Book! / For, but for you, / Who'd look / At My Book? / C.D.' If *Regiment of Women* was written, as the dedication indicates, for Elsie, by 1956 Clemence Dane and Elsie Arnold would have known each other for over forty years. It appears that the two women had lived together in the house owned by Dane in St John's Wood until 1956. However, as the making of a new will usually indicates, by this date something had changed. Clemence Dane makes the unusual step of acknowledging this in the text of the will itself:

> I DESIRE to place on record the deep and affectionate regard I have always had for the said Elsie Arnold and I wish to state that I have made no provision for her other than as given above as I am satisfied that she is financially able if she so desires to continue to live in the said house for her life and I feel sure that she will understand and sympathise with my desire to share some of the financial results of my life's work with a younger generation of friends as fully as I have shared them in the past with her.[50]

Olwen Bowen-Davies had replaced Elsie Arnold in Clemence Dane's affections. Olwen Bowen-Davies (1890?–1970?) was the author of a number of children's books between 1928 and 1969. The most successful of these, stories about Hepzibah the Hen, were broadcast on Children's Hour in 1934.[51] Clemence and Olwen were probably friends from the late 1920s, when Clemence reviewed Olwen's book *Beetles and Things*; they were certainly friends in 1936 when Clemence wrote the preface to Olwen's *The Hepzibah Omnibus*. Although Dane acknowledged that Elsie Arnold had independent financial resources she obviously felt unable to abandon her completely. Dane stated that she wished her trustees

> to permit my friend Miss Elsie Arnold at present residing therein to have the use and enjoyment of the said house [in St. John's Wood] and my furniture and effects therein so long as she shall live.[52]

What Clemence Dane's will documents is the breakdown of a partnership and the dismembering of a shared life. By the time Clemence Dane died, nine years later, she was living with Olwen Bowen-Davies in Chelsea; both women were described as 'spinsters'. The net value of the estate that Olwen Bowen-Davies inherited from Clemence Dane was £3,614.55.

As well as ordinary executors, Clemence Dane appointed literary executors: Olwen Bowen-Davies and Richard Addinsell (1904–1977).

Addinsell was a composer who had worked with Dane on a number of her plays. The chief duty of her literary executors was to destroy all information on Clemence's private life after her death:

> I DECLARE that the said Olwen Bowen-Davies (or if the said Olwen Bowen-Davies pre-deceases me then the said Richard Addinsell) shall have power to go through my private papers letters and correspondence alone and have power to destroy all those which appear to her (or him as the case may be) to have no bearing on my financial or literary affairs.[53]

Olwen Bowen-Davies did not pre-decease Dane and she apparently did her job well; none of Dane's personal papers appears to have survived.

In the light of Clemence Dane's life it seems that *Regiment of Women* deserves rather more critical scrutiny than it has hitherto received. It might be better to think of *Regiment of Women* as a complex lesbian gothic novel written, at least in part, for a lesbian audience rather than as a lesbian horror story written in order to inculcate homophobia. What it marks is the nightmare of the abuse of power rather than the nightmare of sexual intimacy between women. Whether Clemence Dane was prompted to write *Regiment of Women* as a result of her own experiences as a schoolgirl or as a teacher, a nightmare from which Elsie Arnold saved her, is now lost in the mists of time.

Another novel written by a woman and dealing with homosexuality was published shortly after *Regiment of Women* in 1918. *Despised and Rejected* was written by Rose Laure Allatini (1890?–1980?) and was published under the pseudonym of A.T. Fitzroy. It is the story of a homosexual man and a lesbian trying to make sense of their sexualities and their politics both before and during World War I. *Despised and Rejected* is an overtly political book. The plot focuses as much on the effects of war and the morality of conscientious objection as it does on homosexuality. The radical politics of the first decades of the century, pacifism, women's suffrage and Irish nationalism, are shown at their most intertwined. Rose Allatini clearly had an incisive grasp of the contemporary political scene.

The hero and heroine of *Despised and Rejected* are Dennis Blackwood and Antoinette de Courcy, a name with strong lesbian connotations. 'Antoinette' has been used to invoke lesbianism since the time of Marie-Antoinette, who was popularly known for her lewd behaviour with women.[54] Dennis recognizes that he and Antoinette are united by their homosexuality:

He wanted gently to turn her face toward him, and to look again into her clear grey eyes, and share the dreams that must lurk in their depths. He felt by instinct that they were strange dreams, which for him, however, would hold no strangeness.[55]

The difference between the positions of gay men and lesbians that Allatini wishes to show is that male homosexuality is a named and known entity while lesbianism has been silenced and excluded from public debate. Dennis has to give a name to Antoinette's love and sexual desire:

Rapidly she [Antoinette] cast her mind over those school-girl passions of her early youth – Miss Prescot – Natasha – passing flickers of emotion aroused here and there by the beauty or attraction of women she had met in hotels abroad – finally Hester . . . . This, then, was the taint of which he spoke; the taint that they shared, he and she. Only whereas he had always striven against these tendencies in himself, in herself she had never regarded them as abnormal. It had seemed disappointing, but not in the least unnatural, that all her passionate longing should have been awakened by women, instead of by members of the opposite sex.[56] [ellipses in the text]

Allatini seems ambivalent about whether lesbianism should be known in the same way as male homosexuality, for the knowledge has only made Dennis understand his desires as perverse and unnatural. Antoinette, for all her 'ignorance', would never, without Dennis's help, have seen her love and desire for women as peculiar or indeed in any way remarkable. Dennis proceeds to find a lover, after some emotional and moral turmoil, and the two men are eventually imprisoned as conscientious objectors. Antoinette is left profoundly alone: excluded from both the war and the political rejection of war by her sex, excluded from Dennis's life by his greater love for Alan, and excluded by her new knowledge of her sexuality from loving women.

Despised and Rejected is completely positive about homosexuality; Dennis's lover says, 'For people made such as we are it is natural and it's beautiful to love as we love, and it's perversion in the true sense to try and force ourselves to love differently', and with this Allatini appears to have concurred.[57] Although Rose Allatini did marry and have children, she spent a considerable part of her life in lesbian relationships. According to Bloomsbury gossip, *Despised and Rejected* was the by-product of a lesbian affair; Ottoline Morrell dragged from Rose the story of her 'illicit amour', one day at tea in 1919.[58] Rose was clearly familiar, too, with

Edward Carpenter's writing; *Towards Democracy* is read by the gay men in her novel.[59]

This condoning and normalization of homosexuality was almost certainly a factor in the government decision to prosecute *Despised and Rejected*. However, it was prosecuted not under the obscenity laws but under the Defence Regulations for its espousal of pacifism and support for conscientious objection. It was charged that the book was 'likely to prejudice the recruiting of persons to serve in His Majesty's Forces, and their training and discipline'. Whether the government took this tack because prosecuting a book for pacifism was less problematic and produced less publicity for the book than prosecuting it for obscenity, or because the Director of Public Prosecutions (DPP) genuinely thought that pacifist propaganda was worse than homosexual propaganda, remains unclear. Certainly the effects of the conviction were the same; all remaining copies of *Despised and Rejected* were seized and destroyed, and it was not reprinted for seventy years.

The trial did produce considerable publicity. Although Allatini had used a gender-neutral pseudonym, her previous novels had been published under her own name, and the fact that she was A. T. Fitzroy did become known. The fear of public identification as a lesbian may have been a factor in Allatini's marriage to Cyril Scott in 1921. Whatever the reason for the marriage, by 1941 Rose was living in Rye with her lover Melanie Mills. Both women earned their living by writing romantic novels under a variety of names, such as Eunice Buckley. As Jonathan Cutbill says:

> The thought of these two women, one of them the author of the most important lesbian and gay novel of its time, happily together in E.F. Benson and Radclyffe Hall's Rye and making a living writing for the heterosexual market, is very satisfying.[60]

NOTES

1. The contacts for *Urania* are printed on the back page of each issue.
2. 'Owing to the continued high level of prices', *Urania*, January–April 1922, Nos. 31 and 32.
3. In 1909 a Men's League for Women's Suffrage was established in London by Laurence Houseman, among others. It is probable that Baty was involved in this group.
4. He was Vice-President of the Vegetarian Society (U.K.): *Who Was Who 1951–1960*.

5. See letters from Baty to George Bell (publishers) held at the Publishers' Archive, Reading University.
6. Irene Clyde, *Beatrice the Sixteenth* (London: George Bell & Sons, 1909), p.311.
7. See letters from Baty to George Bell (publishers) held at the Publishers' Archive, Reading University.
8. See letter held at the Fawcett Library, and *The Freewoman*, 22 February 1912.
9. *The Freewoman*, 22 February 1912.
10. From 1916 to 1941, Baty was the Legal Adviser to the Imperial Japanese Foreign Office.
11. *Urania*, January–April 1922.
12. *Urania*, May–August 1929.
13. Xavier Mayne [Edward Stephenson], *The Intersexes* (Italy: published privately, 1908), p.ix.
14. *Ibid.*, p.19. Stephenson uses 'Greek Love', 'Sapphism' and 'lesbianism' to refer to female homosexuality, p.126.
15. *The Freewoman*, January/February 1912.
16. Gifford Lewis, *Eva Gore-Booth and Esther Roper* (London: Pandora, 1988), p.6.
17. I have not been able to trace it as actually being from Sappho, but Gifford Lewis assures me that Esther Roper did believe it to be from her.
18. Esther Roper (ed.), *The Prison Letters of Countess Markievicz* (London: Longman, 1934), p.315.
19. *Ibid.*, p.312.
20. *Ibid.*, p.314.
21. Vera 'Jack' Holme collection, Fawcett Library Archives.
22. Lewis, *Eva Gore-Booth and Esther Roper*, p.182.
23. Diana Hopkinson, *The Incense Tree* (London: Routledge & Kegan Paul, 1968), p.151.
24. Mary Stocks, *Eleanor Rathbone* (London: Victor Gollancz, 1949), p.70.
25. *Ibid.*, p.58.
26. Sheila Jeffreys, *The Spinster and Her Enemies: Feminism and Sexuality 1880–1930* (London: Pandora, 1985), p.152.
27. Carol Dyhouse, *Feminism and the Family in England 1880-1939* (Oxford: Blackwell, 1989), p.101.
28. *Ibid.*, p.102.
29. Suzanne Neild and Rosalind Pearson, *Women Like Us* (London: The Women's Press, 1992), p.33.
30. Mary Stott, *Organisation Woman: The Story of the National Union of Townswomen's Guilds* (London: Heinemann, 1978), pp.13–14.
31. *Ibid.*, p.15.
32. *Ibid.*, p.14.
33. *Ibid.*, p.122.
34. Jeffrey Weeks, *Coming Out: Homosexual Politics in Britain from the Nineteenth Century to the Present* (London: Quartet, 1990, revised edition), p.87.

35. Chambers letter, 19 August 1921, Carpenter collection (Sheffield City Archives).
36. Ibid.
37. Weeks, Coming Out, p.125.
38. See Weeks, Coming Out, pp.124–5, and Timothy d'Arch Smith, Love in Earnest: Some Notes on the Lives and Writings of English 'Uranian' Poets from 1889–1930 (London: Routledge & Kegan Paul, 1970), p.140.
39. The Quorum (1920), p.22.
40. Evelyn Irons, 'Somerville 1918–1921', in Somerville College Report and Supplement (Oxford: Somerville College, 1993), p.63.
41. Janet Hitchman, Such a Strange Lady: A Biography of Dorothy L. Sayers (Sevenoaks: New English Library, 1979), p.44.
42. Ibid., pp.43–4.
43. See, for instance, Annabel Faraday, Social Definitions of Lesbians in Britain 1914–1939: 'Subject to Query' (University of Essex, unpublished Ph.D. thesis, 1985).
44. Clemence Dane, The Woman's Side (London: Herbert Jenkins, 1926), p.53.
45. Ibid., p.74.
46. Dora Russell, The Tamarisk Tree: Vol. 3. Challenge to the Cold War (London: Virago, 1985), p.115.
47. See Alison Oram in Lesbian History Group (ed.), Not a Passing Phase: Reclaiming Lesbians in History 1840–1985 (London: The Women's Press, 1989), for a general discussion of lesbianism in education in this period.
48. Dane, The Woman's Side, p.173.
49. Michael Baker, Our Three Selves: A Life of Radclyffe Hall (London: Hamish Hamilton, 1985), p.118 and pp.259–60.
50. Will of Winifred Ashton (Clemence Dane) of 20 Tavistock Street, Covent Garden, London, 10 September 1956.
51. Clemence Dane, preface to Olwen Bowen-Davies, The Hepzibah Omnibus (London: T. Nelson & Sons, 1936), p.ix.
52. Will of Winifred Ashton (Clemence Dane), p.1.
53. Probate order for the estate of Winifred Ashton (Clemence Dane) of 1 Draycott Place, Chelsea, London, 23 September 1965.
54. Will of Winifred Ashton (Clemence Dane).
55. See, for instance, Terry Castle, The Apparitional Lesbian: Female Homosexuality and Modern Culture (New York: Columbia University Press, 1993).
56. A. T. Fitzroy, Despised and Rejected, 1918 (reprinted London: Gay Men's Press, 1988), p.53.
57. Ibid., p.218.
58. Ibid., p.250.
59. Letter to Vanessa Bell, 27 February 1919, in Nigel Nicolson and Joanne Trautman (eds), The Question of Things Happening: The Letters of Virginia Woolf 1912–1922 (London: Hogarth, 1976), p.336.
60. Fitzroy, Despised and Rejected, p.283.
61. Ibid., Introduction by Jonathan Cutbill.

radclyffe hall

'When I die I shall never be forgotten'
Sappho, Fragment 106

The figure of Radclyffe Hall has been at the centre of the British understanding of lesbianism, both vilified and lauded by lesbians since she became a public figure in the 1920s. The facts of her life are well known. Marguerite Radclyffe Hall was born in 1880. She was to choose to be known publicly, as her books testify, simply as Radclyffe Hall. She was brought up by her mother, step-father and maternal grandmother, and saw her father very infrequently. He died in 1898 and Hall, as his sole heir, inherited a considerable estate on her twenty-first birthday. She received a scant education, although she may have attended lectures at King's College, London.

In her early twenties, when her inheritance had come through, Radclyffe Hall acquired both a country and a town house. The London house was in Campden Hill Terrace, Kensington, and the country house in Worcestershire. As even Una Troubridge was forced to admit, until her early thirties Radclyffe Hall was 'bone idle'. She spent her time

> in pleasure; in hunting; travelling, writing an occasional poem, in entertaining and being entertained. And periodically, from the age of seventeen and onwards, falling in and out of love. She was exceedingly handsome, had plenty of charm, plenty of intelligence, plenty of money, no education to speak of and was out exclusively to enjoy herself and give others a good time.[1]

Between 1901 and 1907 Hall spent considerable time abroad: she travelled extensively in America and Europe with women friends. Her first companion was Jane Randolph, her second Dolly Diehl; both were American relatives. Una Troubridge intimates that both women were Hall's lovers.[2] Certainly both women lived with Hall in England, and were supported by her, for considerable lengths of time. She continued to write the occasional poem and in 1906 her first book of poems, *Twixt Earth and Stars*, was published.

Shortly afterwards, in 1907, she met Mabel Batten while in the German spa town of Homburg. Mabel Batten, née Hatch (1858/9–1916), was married to George Batten, Secretary to the Viceroy of India. Mabel Batten came from a well-connected family, and as a leading 'patroness of music and the arts, mezzo-soprano and composer', was an important woman in the cultural salons of London.[3] Hall was twenty-seven and Mabel Batten, known to her intimates as 'Ladye', was forty-eight when they met. By the summer of 1908 Radclyffe Hall and Mabel Batten had become lovers. When George Batten died they set up home together in Cadogan Square in London.

It was Mabel Batten who first called Hall 'John', the name by which her friends were to know her for the rest of her life. Mabel Batten had encouraged Hall to write, and to apply herself to her work; Una reports that Mabel

> met John's adoring gaze with the brisk remark that people who had loved and been loved by her had always done something, been someone or in any case had used their brains. And so, in her immense desire to make herself worthy of someone she loved, John's real education began.[4]

In 1908 Hall's second collection of poems, *A Sheaf of Verses*, came out. It was followed in 1910 by *Poems of the Past and Present* and by *Songs of Three Counties* in 1913. In these early years the difference in their ages appears to have posed no problems and the two women were happy together, both emotionally and sexually. They travelled, entertained and went to operas, theatres and concerts, and read voraciously.

However, by the Christmas of 1915, Radclyffe Hall had taken a new lover, Una Troubridge. Troubridge and Hall had met briefly in 1912 but their sexual relationship began to develop in August 1915. Una Troubridge, née Taylor (1887–1963), was the daughter of impoverished gentry. She had attended the Royal College of Art in 1907 and subsequently successfully exhibited her sculpture. She was impelled to marry by her father's death and the resulting financial crisis in her family. In 1908 she married Captain Ernest Troubridge.

Ernest Troubridge, as a serving naval officer, had a peripatetic career, and the Troubridges were to spend considerable periods of time abroad. Una seems to have been publicly a successful navy wife and she was popular with Captain Troubridge's colleagues. Although the relationship between Ernest and Una was initially loving, the marriage seems to have been sexually unsuccessful and Una was to seek professional help in overcoming their sexual incompatibility. The marriage was consummated, but with little pleasure on Una's side; their only child, Anthea, was born in 1910.

Una spent considerable periods in England without her husband and daughter; it was on one of these trips that she met Radclyffe Hall. Una was entranced by Hall and they started an affair. By the Christmas of 1915, Mabel Batten had become deeply hurt by Hall's growing attachment to Una Troubridge. While Mabel was in her fifties and had increasingly poor health, Una was in her twenties, pretty and energetic. Radclyffe Hall seems to have been incapacitated by the position she found herself in, unable to leave Batten, whom she loved, or to give up Una, whom she perhaps loved less but certainly desired more. For some time the lives of the three women were rather harrowingly combined, a situation which made none of them happy. Hall lived with Mabel but was sleeping with, and spending a great deal of time with, Una.

The situation was not actually resolved by Mabel's death in 1916. Hall, and apparently Una, felt that they had betrayed Mabel. In an effort to expiate this guilt Hall and Una became very involved in Spiritualism, through which they believed they were able to maintain their relationship with Mabel. Spiritualism enjoyed great popularity and considerable respectability in this period, certainly more than it does today. Mabel Batten's death cast a significant pall over Troubridge and Hall's romance, but by the end of World War I Una, and sometimes Anthea, were living with Radclyffe Hall. The emotional confusion of this time had not stopped Hall writing; *The Forgotten Island*, a book of poetry, was published in 1915. With her private life on a more even keel, Hall went on to write three novels which were published in the mid-1920s: *The Unlit Lamp* (1924), *The Forge* (1924) and *A Saturday Life* (1925). These were well reviewed but she finally struck gold with *Adam's Breed*, published in 1926, which won the Prix Femina Vie Heureuse and the James Tait Black Memorial Prize.

By the late 1920s Radclyffe Hall had established a reputation as a respected novelist. Together Hall and Una Troubridge were a well-known London couple, regularly attending first nights and private views. The combination of Hall's acknowledged success as a novelist, her unusual and well-known domestic arrangements, and her physical appearance all served to focus public attention on her next novel. This was *The Well of Loneliness*, a novel which Hall had been planning for a number of years and which was published in the summer of 1928. It tells the story of the life of

Stephen Gordon, a woman with a natural love of women. It describes how Stephen's lesbianism is an inalienable part of her identity and inexorably informs her experiences.

Within days of the publication of *The Well of Loneliness* it was prosecuted by the DPP on the grounds of obscenity. The very nature of the book was judged obscene because it argued for the naturalness of homosexuality and hence for tolerance of homosexuals. The specific references that Hall makes to the sexual nature of the relationship between Mary and Stephen were obscene in the context of a novel which validated rather than condemned lesbian relationships. Books condemning lesbianism could be as sexually explicit as *The Well of Loneliness* and not face prosecution. The prosecution and subsequent banning of *The Well of Loneliness* shot Radclyffe Hall into history. At the age of forty-eight she became the world's most notorious and unashamed lesbian since Sappho.

Usually the amount of sex in *The Well of Loneliness* is under-reported; 'that night they were not divided' is just the tip of the iceberg. In *The Well of Loneliness* Hall emphasizes that women have autonomous sexual desires and that sexual desire in women is not a sign of moral coarseness. Hall makes it clear that celibacy is not the answer to lesbian desire; unfulfilled sexual desire causes Stephen Gordon profound emotional and physical anguish. In the initial stages of their relationship both Stephen and Mary are tormented by repressed sexual attraction; their relationship is unnatural without sex. Once Mary and Stephen have consummated their love, their world is bathed in the post-coital glow of good sex:

> But beyond the bounds of this turbulent river would lie gentle and most placid harbours of refuge; harbours in which the body could repose with contentment, while the lips spoke low, indolent words, and the eyes beheld a dim, golden haze that blinded the while it revealed all beauty. Then Stephen would stretch out her hand and touch Mary where she lay, happy only to feel her nearness.[5]

For Hall, lesbianism is inalienable from sexual desire for, and sex with, women and lesbian sex is both natural and good.

Hall stresses that men can offer nothing sexually that a lesbian cannot offer as well. Sex between women, Hall is at pains to point out, is no sterile dabbling:

> Like a barrier of fire her [Mary's] passion for the woman [Stephen] flared up to forbid her the love of the man; for as great as the mystery of virginity itself,

is sometimes the power of the one who has destroyed it, and that power still remained in these days, with Stephen.[6]

To give a woman the ability to take another woman's virginity is a blow to the very root of patriarchal society, where female sexuality belongs only to men. When Stephen stops having sex with Mary, Mary is distraught and 'must stand there and plead for what Stephen withheld'.[7]

Hall argues that what all men have, and that lesbians do not have, is social sanction and approval of their relationships with women.

> Men – they were selfish, arrogant, possessive. What could they do for Mary Llewellyn? What could a man give that she could not? A child? But she would give Mary such a love as would be complete in itself without children. Mary would have no room in her heart, in her life, for a child, if she came to Stephen. All things they would be the one to the other, should they stand in that limitless relationship; father, mother, friend, and lover, all things – the amazing completeness of it; and Mary, the child, the friend, the belovèd. With the terrible bonds of her dual nature, she could bind Mary fast, and the pain would be sweetness, so that the girl would cry out for that sweetness, hugging her chains always closer to her. The world would condemn but they would rejoice; glorious outcasts, unashamed, triumphant![8]

Lesbianism is perverted only by social disapproval. The 'terrible bonds' with which lesbians are bound together are terrible only in the eyes of heterosexual and patriarchal society.

Hall refused through *The Well of Loneliness* to accept the popular views of homosexuality; that it was a sickness, a disability, a sad failing or a wilful evil perpetuated by tainted adults. Hall believed that homosexuality was a naturally occurring difference akin to having red hair. Homosexuality was not a sign of illness or evil but a neutral and natural sexual variation. Homosexuality was abnormal only in the sense that the majority of people were not homosexual or did not lead homosexual lives. Hall argues that there is no moral weight attached to the statistical abnormality of homosexuality, it is just an insignificant deviation from the norm.

Because homosexuality is natural, Hall argues that it cannot be *per se* bad. Individual homosexuals might be criminals or delinquents, as might individual redheads, but homosexuality itself has no intrinsic moral or physical flaw. Hall located homosexuality in the natural body, not in the corruption and sophistication of culture. It is on the basis of the naturalness of homosexuality that *The Well of Loneliness* explicitly claims a morally equal ground for homosexuality and homosexuals. The argument that Hall pursues is that lesbians and gay men have been denied their moral equality. Hall sought to shame heterosexual society into just treatment of lesbians and gay men and the abandonment of all prejudice against them.

The Well of Loneliness is written on two levels. It addresses itself to both a heterosexual and a homosexual audience. The message to heterosexuals is that they cause, with no justification, terrible pain to lesbians and gay men. The oppression of lesbians and gay men is morally unjustifiable and hence should cease. The message to lesbians is that lesbians are natural, lesbianism can be morally good and lesbians are everywhere. Most importantly Radclyffe Hall strives to show that lesbians and gay men constitute a people, a definable community. Both by weight of numbers and moral righteousness lesbians and gay men should not be persecuted and condemned forever. These two strands to *The Well of Loneliness* are shown clearly in the double-edged conclusion of the novel.

For the heterosexual audience the novel ends with Stephen relinquishing Mary to a man because she knows that Mary does not have the psychological fortitude to live as a lesbian in a hostile society. Hall works the romantic novel format of *The Well of Loneliness* to its utmost, so that Stephen's sacrifice is seen as noble and tragic. Stephen plays the role of the honourable and decent romantic hero who gives up his true love, or shoots himself when he goes bankrupt. Radclyffe Hall places the full responsibility for the tragedy of Stephen and Mary's love, and that of Barbara and Jamie, onto heterosexual society. Hall works to wring out heterosexual guilt.

For the lesbian audience the tragedy of Stephen's renunciation of Mary is offset partly by Hall's hints that Mary will not recapture the golden happiness of love with a man. Moreover, Hall is equivocal about whether Stephen's renunciation of Mary is a sign of strength or weakness. Most importantly though, through the examination of Stephen's life, Hall shows that lesbians and gay men are everywhere: working as teachers and writers, serving in the trenches and battlefields of the war, flying aeroplanes, going to church, going on holiday, going shopping.

> There were many another exactly like her in this very city, in every city; and they did not all live out crucified lives, denying their bodies, stultifying their brains, becoming the victims of their own frustrations. On the contrary they lived natural lives – lives that to them were perfectly natural. They had their passions like everyone else, and why not? They were surely entitled to their passions?[9]

Hall also showed that lesbians and gay men do have a physical space for their community; it may only be a ghetto, but it is their own. As Stephen moves through the world of Parisian gay bars she comes to see that lesbians and gay men stand as brother and sister, that they are not isolated individuals, and together they can fight the injustice they face. Through Radclyffe Hall and Stephen Gordon, the lost and unarticulated lives of lesbians gained a voice, and were called to arms. Hall's commitment to the idea of lesbian and gay brotherhood was based on her own experience of the lesbian community where she received vital succour and support: in the thirty years they spent together Troubridge and Hall established a large and supportive circle of lesbian friends.

During the 1920s Radclyffe Hall and Una Troubridge saw a good deal of Ida Wylie and her then lover Rachel Barrett.[10] I. A. R. Wylie (1885–1959) was a novelist and journalist. Born in Australia she had led a cosmopolitan life, travelling alone and with her father in Europe, until the age of seventeen when she was sent to Cheltenham Ladies' College. When she was nineteen she went to Germany where she 'stayed with a friend', presumably a close one, for eight years. Ida returned to England in 1911 whereupon she had become 'violently active in the Suffrage Movement'. It was here that she met Rachel Barrett, also a militant suffragette. During World War II Ida undertook war work, of unspecified nature, in France. She eventually settled with her female lover, Dr Joe Baker, in New Jersey, where she collected English bull-terriers. Though now largely forgotten in England, if not America, Wylie published over two hundred short stories and fifteen novels.

Hall and Troubridge were friends of the war hero Toupie Lowther, and of Enid Elliot and her lover, the Hon. Eileen Plunket, who had been drivers in Toupie's ambulance unit.[11] They were also friends with Gabrielle Enthoven (1868–1950). Enthoven's husband had died in 1910, thus apparently releasing her to a life of happy homosexuality. In 1923 they met Teddy Gerard, a lesbian actress and singer who had achieved considerable success during World War I. Hall and Troubridge with other lesbian couples used to go to clubs in London:

> These parties were all girls. Only on some occasions was a man with them. The sight of women dancing together at the Cave of Harmony or the Orange Tree Club or the Hambone aroused neither amusement nor alarm.[12]

They also used to stay in: 'Toupie and Honey and Vere and Budge and the others kept the laughter and the gramophone going until the early hours.'[13]

'Vere and Budge' were Vere Stuart Menteth Hutchinson (1891–1932) and her lover Dorothy Burroughes-Burroughes (1890?–1963).

Vere Hutchinson was the daughter of a general, and a novelist. She had five books published in the 1920s, and although unknown today she merited an entry in Who's Who. Dorothy Burroughes was an artist who trained at the Slade, at Heatherleys and in Paris. She painted, worked in pastels and was a lino-cut artist; she exhibited regularly in England in the 1920s and 1930s. From the 1930s until the end of her life she specialized in illustrating children's books, including Elizabeth Gorrell's Bear Bus series. Burroughes was a member of the Royal Society of British Artists and involved in the Society of Women Artists. Her relationship with Vere was traumatic: Vere developed a virus at thirty-three which progressed to paralysis and insanity, and then to her early death when she was only forty-one.[14]

The publicity that Radclyffe Hall and Una Troubridge received in the late 1920s led to friendships with an ever-increasing number of lesbians. These friends included former suffragette activists like Edy Craig, Chris St John, and Vera Holme. In the 1930s Hall and Troubridge became friends of Lady Maud Warrender, a daughter of the Earl of Shaftesbury, who lived at 'Leasam' in Rye with her lover, the singer Marcia van Dresse.[15] They were also friendly with the former police women Mary Allen, known to them as 'Robert', Miss Tagart and Isabel 'Toto' Goldingham in these years.[16]

Hall and Troubridge did not just know British lesbians. They visited France regularly and became friends with Natalie Barney and through Barney the Parisian-American lesbian community. It was in Paris, for instance, that they met Romaine Brooks, the painter, and Elizabeth de Gramont, Duchess of Clermont Tonnerre, the writer. Elizabeth was a friend of Gertrude Stein, and it was Elizabeth's short haircut in 1926 which persuaded Stein to have her hair cropped by Alice Toklas.[17] Troubridge and Hall were also friendly with Jo Carstairs, the American heiress and speed-boat racer, and Tallulah Bankhead, the American sex goddess.

By situating lesbians and gay men as an international and inter-racial community The Well of Loneliness broke fresh political ground, which has still not been fully explored even today. By placing lesbians and gay men as members of a community, the site of homosexuality is moved away from individual pathology to the public sphere of debate, argument and choice. Homosexuality moves from being a problem for cursed men and women to being a political and social issue which faces everyone.

The Well of Loneliness was a carefully planned polemic against homophobia, and a manifesto to fight, by a known lesbian. A number of memorable books that touched upon lesbians and lesbianism were published in 1927 and 1928 besides *The Well of Loneliness*. None of these other novels was prosecuted, but then none of the others was written by a publicly known lesbian or made any moral-political demands. There was, for instance, Compton Mackenzie's *Extraordinary Women*, which satirized lesbians and the possibility of lesbian community. Set on the island of Capri, it is a bitchy caricature of contemporary famous lesbians, including Hall herself. Some lesbians are very fond of it: 'what a wickedly hilarious tale Sir Compton told: one not to be missed, especially by those who take an earnest or "sacred cow" view of our condition.'[18] It does not take lesbians or lesbianism seriously.

Elizabeth Bowen's *The Hotel* (1927) presents lesbianism as a neurotic option for women unable to handle or attract virile masculinity. Bowen also links lesbianism with the over-education of women, the implication being that lesbianism is similarly unnatural. While Bowen's depiction of lesbians and lesbianism is not particularly appealing, or noticeably positive, it is clearly different from that of Compton Mackenzie. Bowen does not equate 'lesbian' with 'wonderful comic material'. This may have been because Bowen was more involved with lesbianism than Compton Mackenzie could ever be. Bowen was to have, regardless of her marriage, a number of lesbian relationships.

Elizabeth Bowen (1899–1973) had an affair with May Sarton, then a very young woman, during the late 1930s. According to Sarton, Elizabeth had had at least one relationship with a woman before her. Victoria Glendinning, Elizabeth Bowen's biographer, is uncharacteristically reticent about the extent and depth of Bowen's lesbianism. Bowen certainly went on to have, at the very least, erotically charged relationships with both Carson McCullers and Nancy Spain in the 1950s.[19] It seems plausible that the lesbian plot of *The Hotel*, Bowen's first novel written when she was in her early twenties, had some basis in personal experience.

The most critically esteemed 'lesbian' novel perhaps ever written was also published in 1928: Virginia Woolf's *Orlando*. I would query whether *Orlando* counts as a 'lesbian' novel given that it only invokes lesbianism, it does not describe it. Orlando's dynamic life seems to presume s/he is really a man, for no woman through the centuries has had easy access to such a life. In terms of lesbianism, Orlando's indeterminate sex and moments of complete heterosexuality are not particularly appealing to this lesbian reader. Many heterosexual critics disagree, believing that the novel 'has cult status in lesbian and gay culture'.[20]

The lesbianism of *Orlando* lies in the public attention that it drew to the relationship between Virginia Woolf and Vita Sackville-West. The first edition was illustrated with pictures of Knowle, Sackville-West's ancestral home, and with photographs of Vita. In light of what we know now about the lesbianism of Sackville-West and Woolf, these extra-textual clues serve to solidify the gender of Orlando as a woman. Once Orlando the character becomes solidly gendered the lesbianism of the novel comes to the fore. However, given the contemporary public personæ of both Woolf and Sackville-West as wives, and hence not obviously lesbians, Orlando's lesbianism is wilfully hidden from both the lesbian and heterosexual gaze by Woolf.

While these books are not without interest, none of them was written by an author playing Hall's game, even if she may have been batting on her team. None of these books stakes a claim for lesbianism being as sexually and emotionally satisfying and as natural as heterosexuality. None of these books attacks 'normal' society and 'normal' people for daring to enforce the genocide of lesbians and gay men. Perhaps most crucially in the terms of attention from the Director of Public Prosecutions, none of the other 'lesbian' novels of 1927–8 was written by Radclyffe Hall. Radclyffe Hall was a known lesbian who used a man's name, had stolen two men's wives, and who dressed as a butch dyke. The prosecution of *The Well of Loneliness* cannot have been unaffected by the outrageous public spectacle of Radclyffe Hall's life.

In the brief interlude between the publication of *The Well of Loneliness* and its banning it was widely reviewed. What the reviews said depended upon their sympathy with the predicament of lesbians and gay men, and their sympathy with Radclyffe Hall's combative stance. James Douglas in *The Sunday Express* was famously apoplectic with disgust. Douglas was not just against *The Well of Loneliness*, he was against Radclyffe Hall and all of her kind:

> I am well aware that sexual inversion and perversion are horrors which exist among us today. They flaunt themselves in public places with increasing effrontery and more insolently provocative bravado. The decadent apostles of the most hideous and loathsome vices no longer conceal their degeneracy and their degradation.[21]

Douglas wanted *The Well of Loneliness* banned precisely because Hall made her case so well:

The adroitness and cleverness of the book intensifies its moral danger. It is a seductive and insidious special pleading designed to display perverted decadence as a martyrdom inflicted upon these outcasts by a cruel society.

Notoriously, James Douglas stated, 'I would rather give a healthy boy or a healthy girl a phial of prussic acid than this novel.'[22]

I. A. R. Wylie in *The Sunday Times* had much more sympathy with Hall's project. Ida Wylie was undoubtedly influenced here by her own lesbianism and her friendship with Hall. Wylie's review of *The Well of Loneliness* was careful but positive, given the controversy the book was generating. Wylie describes *The Well of Loneliness* and Radclyffe Hall as 'brave', 'courageous' and 'sensitive'. She emphasizes the inevitability of lesbianism and lesbians: 'Not that she is a modern phenomenon. Almost certainly, like her male prototype, she has always existed, but not until late[r] years has she been acknowledged openly.'

What is particularly interesting about the review is Wylie's use of psychoanalysis to *legitimate* the position of the lesbian:

Psychoanalysis if it has done nothing else, has made us deal more gently with abnormality, since it has made us uncertain as to what the norm really is – whether, it is, indeed, more than a conventional mask covering our strangeness.[23]

This suggests that heterosexuality is simply conventional behaviour: heterosexuality as masquerade. This seems to reinforce Hall's position; homosexuality is just as natural as heterosexuality. This lesbian use of psychoanalysis was hardly Freud's plan.

Responses to *The Well of Loneliness* were not limited to reviews. G. Sheila Donisthorpe's *The Loveliest of Friends* (1931) was a vicious, and long, response to *The Well of Loneliness*. *The Loveliest of Friends* told the story of Audrey, lured away from John, her loving and desirable husband, by the lesbian seductress Kim. After Kim and Audrey have revelled in perverse pleasures, Kim leaves Audrey for Honey. John offers to take Audrey back but Audrey knows that it is all too late; her life has been destroyed by the lesbian canker. Donisthorpe's vampiresque prose spells out the curse of lesbianism to lurid effect:

Look at her [Audrey] now: grey flesh pared thin and tear-blistered, starved and hopeless eyes by a flame consumed; a name like a sigh escaping her ever-moving lips, hands whose fingers tear incessantly at some invisible object tortured with the ragged nerves of the invert. Buried when still warm, she writhes and struggles and stretches out hand and heavy limbs towards her destroyers, when she with fastidious weary fingers would have shaken off this clinging musk. This, then, is the product of lesbianism. This the result of dipping the fingers of vice into sex-welter whose deadly force crucifies in a slow, elemental bleeding.

Describing lesbianism as 'dipping the fingers of vice into sex-welter' may sound to our ears queerly post-modern; this was not Donisthorpe's intention.

She continues:

And yet there are those who hug as a martyrdom these sadistic habits, who clamour for the recognition of the sinister groups who practise them, those crooked, twisted freaks of Nature who stagnate in dark and muddy waters . . . .[24]

This last paragraph is an explicit reference to the arguments put forward by Radclyffe Hall in *The Well of Loneliness*. Donisthorpe's reference to 'the ragged nerves of the invert' is also aimed at Hall, who had a fondness for emphasizing how persecution and repression tried the emotional fibre of homosexuals. *Loveliest of Friends* is a warning to those who feel sympathetic to, or justified by, *The Well of Loneliness*; Donisthorpe dedicates the novel 'to all the contemplating Audrey's [sic] of this world'.

Notwithstanding the heterosexual outrage it caused, *The Well of Loneliness* received its greatest response from lesbians. Not all lesbians, then as now, liked *The Well of Loneliness*. Mary Renault, for instance, describes her reaction to it thus:

In 1938, I was staying with a friend [her lover Julie Mullard] in the small hotel of a French fishing village, somewhere near Hardelot. I think it was in Boulogne that we picked up a copy of *The Well of Loneliness*, then still banned in England. It was a thick, pale brown paperback, a collector's edition I expect today, but too bulky to have a chance at customs, so we left it behind. Every morning, before getting up and starting out for the beach, we used to read it with the coffee and croissants, accompanied by what now strikes me as rather heartless laughter. It is a fact however that we both found it irresistibly funny. It had been out ten years, which is a long time in terms of the conventions; but it does, I still think, carry an impermissible allowance of self-pity, and its earnest humourlessness invites irreverence. Solemn, dead-pan earnest descriptions of Mary knitting stockings for Stephen – and when there was real silk! – and mending her 'masculine underwear' (what can it have been? It was long before briefs; perhaps Wolsey combinations) are passages I can still not read with entire gravity.[25]

That all lesbians did not like *The Well of Loneliness* is hardly surprising. The lesbian community was geographically, socially, economically, politically and culturally diverse, and Hall's attempt to speak for all lesbians was doomed to fail. Subsequent books, and other attempts to speak for all lesbians have similarly failed; it is almost impossible for one lesbian to be 'the voice' of the lesbian community. Some commentators seem to think that lesbian disagreement about the book is a simple indication that Radclyffe Hall and *The Well of Loneliness* failed. Michael Baker, for instance, is eager to point out that:

> Violet Trefusis thought the book a 'loathsome example' and longed to write her own novel on the same theme to correct the balance. Vita Sackville-West felt more than ever that 'a really great novel remains to be written on that subject' and itched to try it herself: 'if one may write about [homosexuality], the field of fiction is immediately doubled'. Romaine Brooks dismissed The Well as 'a ridiculous book, trite, superficial, as was to be expected' and labelled John 'a digger-up of worms with the pretension of a distinguished archaeologist'.[26]

Baker's implication is that because these three famous lesbians did not like *The Well of Loneliness*, Hall's project was shown to be unsuccessful. However, that some lesbians disliked, and some lesbians continue to dislike, *The Well of Loneliness* is neither here nor there. It does not detract from Hall's courage, and her success in getting lesbianism discussed. To be fair to Hall, Trefusis, Sackville-West and Brooks cannot be taken as average representatives of the lesbian community. Both Sackville-West and Trefusis were concerned to maintain their respectability and hence the public fiction of their heterosexuality. Hall's public lesbianism and the public opprobrium in which she found herself must have been frightening to them. Romaine Brooks of course was a friend of Hall and Troubridge, and while she liked Una she seems to have had a competitive relationship with Radclyffe. Brooks's comments were based upon a personal animosity to Hall as much as upon objective criticism.

For tens of thousands of lesbians *The Well of Loneliness*, and Hall's visibility as a lesbian, was an empowering boost to their sense of identity.

Una Troubridge estimated that Hall received 5,000 letters from inverts after the publication of *The Well of Loneliness*. Hall had been receiving correspondence from lesbians since the publication of the homoerotic and overtly feminist *The Unlit Lamp* in 1924. Letters from other lesbians served as both a source and a critique to Hall's writing about lesbians and lesbianism. She replied to all the letters.[27] These women, her own people, were keen to see her in action. Cecil Roberts describes attending a Foyle's literary lunch in 1932 where Radclyffe Hall was guest speaker. Roberts, who had the privilege of introducing Hall, cheerfully remarked that:

> Naturally on this occasion Miss Radclyffe Hall drew many kindred spirits, and on rising to speak, [I was] confronted by close cropped feminine heads, some stiff collars and monocles.[28]

An important question for both their contemporaries and for lesbians now is how Hall and Troubridge, the best-known British lesbian couple this century, made sense of the whole of their lives in the light of their lesbianism. Although Hall was the one who wrote *The Well of Loneliness*, Troubridge was as keen as Hall to fight for greater acceptance for lesbians and gay men. When Radclyffe Hall first asked Una what she felt about her writing a book about lesbians, Una told her to go ahead; 'I was sick with ambiguities, and only wished to be known for what I was and to dwell with her in the palace of truth.'[29] Una was keen to expand the range of books available in England which discussed homosexuality, *L'Ersatz d'Amour* by Collette was one of several French novels which she wanted to translate into English.[30]

The political and social beliefs of Hall and Troubridge cannot easily be categorized but it seems clear that their identities as lesbians influenced their entire lives. Both women were, for instance, practising Catholics, but given the Catholic Church's views on the unacceptability of homosexuality, their position as Catholics was problematic. It is surprising that, in Britain, where they were so well-known, they were actually allowed to take communion, given their blatant defiance of the God-given order. It was not only their lesbianism which separated Radclyffe and Una from Catholic orthodoxy; Spiritualism, in which they maintained an active interest, was also strongly disapproved of by the Catholic Church. Their relationship with Catholicism was not conventional.

Religious belief was important to Hall both personally and politically. She believed and argued that lesbians were a creation of God and thus as natural and as morally blessed as all other creatures. The Catholicism that she and Una practised was predicated around this belief which insulated them from the actual homophobia of Papal doctrine. Together Radclyffe Hall and Una Troubridge created a space where they could be Catholics and lesbians. Hall's political writing in *The Well of Loneliness* was infused with spiritual conviction, and used the language of the Bible, a language of authority, to justify her most contentious claims. Adolphe Blanc, Stephen's Jewish mentor, says to her:

> ... this is only the beginning. Many die, many kill their bodies and souls, but they cannot kill the justice of God, even they cannot kill the eternal spirit. From their very degradation that eternal spirit will rise up to demand of the world compassion and justice.[31]

Stephen herself calls on God in the concluding paragraph of the novel:

> 'God,' she gasped, 'we believe; we have told You we believe ... We have not denied You, then rise up and defend us. Acknowledge us, oh God, before the whole world. Give us also the right to our existence!'[32]

Hall and Troubridge were confident that they had reconciled the apparently irreconcilable conflict between their sexual life and their faith:

> Shortly before Una's death, the author Ethel Mannin, long an admirer of Radclyffe Hall, wrote and asked her how she and John had squared their relationship with their religion. What did they do about confession? Una replied simply: 'There was nothing to confess.'[33]

Troubridge is not saying that they did not have sex but that the sex they had was the gift of God.

Hall and Troubridge's political beliefs were similarly informed by the fact that they were women and lesbians. While both tended towards the conservative politics of their class, they held progressive views on issues which affected women; according to Michael Baker, they supported reform of divorce law, and were concerned about the effects of prostitution on women.[34] Radclyffe Hall was in favour of women's suffrage, if not of the means employed by the suffragettes to win it. In the 1920s both Hall and Troubridge were members of the British Sexological Society.[35]

Hall and Troubridge apparently enjoyed breaking the General Strike of 1926, although it is unclear whether this was for political reasons or for the pleasure of driving lorries round London.[36] While Hall was certainly no socialist she was not dogmatic about politics and honoured her debts.

One of the few advocates for *The Well of Loneliness* in 1928 was the Labour *Daily Herald*; its review stated that Hall had 'given to English Literature a profound and moving study of a profound and moving problem'.[37] The *Daily Herald* also organized petitions protesting against the ban on *The Well of Loneliness*, improbable as it may seem, from the National Union of Railwaymen and the South Wales Miners' Federation. In 1929 Hall responded by presenting the striking miners with the £1,000 proceeds of the sale of a Sargent portrait of Mabel Batten to the Glasgow Art Gallery.[38]

Radclyffe Hall's life did not cease with *The Well of Loneliness*. She was to publish two more novels, *Master of the House* (1932) and *The Sixth Beatitude* (1936), and a collection of short stories, *Miss Ogilvy Finds Herself* (1934). It is impossible to estimate how great an effect the public reaction to *The Well of Loneliness* had on the rest of Radclyffe Hall's life. It may well have been a factor in the nomadic way of life that she and Una Troubridge led in the 1930s when they travelled extensively in Europe.

It was during these travels that they employed a Russian nurse, Evguenia Souline, for whom Hall developed a strong infatuation. After considerable persuasion by Hall, Evguenia Souline and Hall became lovers in 1934. For Hall the relationship was charged with an urgent sexuality which is impressive given that her health was already poor:

> Nothing is real but those ten days in Paris when I held you in my arms and taught you to love, when your heart beat close against my heart, and your mouth was on mine, and our arms were round each other straining our bodies closer & more close, until there was agony in our loving.[39]

For the following ten years Evguenia Souline was part of Hall's life, and played fast and loose with Hall's emotions and her money. However, Radclyffe Hall never left Una either physically or emotionally. She died in Una's arms, from cancer, at the age of sixty.

Fifty years after her death it is hard to separate the myth from the reality of Radclyffe Hall, even with the help of three biographies. Una Troubridge's biography is more concerned with the animals that she and Hall had, than with their lesbian milieu or an analysis of what their lesbianism meant to them. Lovat Dickson's biography is, unfortunately, virulently anti-lesbian. He says of Hall and Troubridge's relationship:

> It may have been an unholy love, but it had some element which survived the white heat of passion and the cold deadness, the non-feeling which is so often the consequence of unnatural union.[40]

This was written in 1975; Lovat Dickson obviously must have missed out on gay liberation. Dickson may have felt that Troubridge and Hall should not be reunited in their 'unholy love' even in death; it was his inaction (he was Una's executor) which resulted in Una Troubridge's burial in Italy, where she died, not in the Radclyffe Hall tomb in Highgate with Hall and Batten as she had requested in her will.

The most recent biography, Michael Baker's *Our Three Selves*, is very thorough and impressively detailed, but Baker too appears to be uncomfortable with lesbians and lesbianism. He appears, for instance, to believe that the sexologists invented lesbians:

> True to the lesbian stereotype of Havelock Ellis, Dickie was stout and beefy, with a ruddy alcoholic complexion, while Wilma wore heavy make-up...[41]

Baker also apparently believes that lesbians find the female body unattractive, saying that Una 'positively disliked the softening curves and budding tumescences that signalled the onset of womanhood and awakening sexuality in a girl'.[42] Perhaps most unfortunately Baker seems to believe that Hall was motivated to write *The Well of Loneliness* not by political and moral beliefs but by a psychological neurosis; he includes an index entry for Hall under the heading 'search for martyrdom'. Given that Hall and Troubridge are famous *as lesbians*, this biographical incomprehension of lesbianism is unfortunate.[43]

The Well of Loneliness, and particularly Stephen Gordon, are often treated as transparent mediums through which there is direct and unproblematic access to Radclyffe Hall herself. If there are two standard beliefs about *The Well of Loneliness*, the first is that it is a definitive and complete statement of Hall's beliefs about the nature of homosexuality in general, and lesbianism in particular. Almost all critics, for instance, agree with Michael Baker's view that because Hall asked Havelock Ellis to write the preface to *The Well of Loneliness* she 'took on board without qualification Ellis's distinctive definition of the invert's character and appearance'.[44]

This must surely be to misconstrue what Radclyffe Hall was trying to do with *The Well of Loneliness*. *The Well of Loneliness* was consciously constructed by Hall to argue a case, her discussion of lesbianism and homosexuality within this book being informed by political efficacy. In 1928 Havelock Ellis was the only British sexologist to have written any detailed account of lesbianism at all. By using Ellis, Hall was linking *The Well of Loneliness* to the most sympathetic contemporary medical/psychological position on homosexuality. If Hall wanted to back up *The Well of Loneliness* with *any* academic or objective authority, Ellis was the man to co-opt. The academic gloss that Havelock Ellis supplied meant that *The Well of Loneliness* was treated more seriously because it was claiming to be more than just a novel.

Hall also presumably believed that Ellis's involvement would give a scientific sanction to her own belief that lesbianism was not only natural but morally neutral. As Lis Stanley has commented,

> the idea of inversion offered an essentialist framework of understanding for many women and men whose experience of themselves accorded with it; but even for those who did not, it offered a powerful legitimating rhetoric to compel tolerance if not acceptance.[45]

Hall employed political and rhetorical *strategies* in the writing and presentation of *The Well of Loneliness* in order to make the most persuasive case possible for lesbians and gay men. It is not proven that she herself believed that these strategies corresponded directly with the truth about homosexuality.

Given that Radclyffe Hall was herself a lesbian, knew a great many lesbians, and had thousands of lesbian correspondents, it seems perverse to credit her entire understanding of lesbians and lesbianism to the sexologists. Even in the Ellis-prefaced *The Well of Loneliness*, where it would be counter-productive to attack sexology and sexologists, Radclyffe Hall expressed scepticism about their relevance:

> What doctor can know the entire truth? Many times they meet only the neurasthenics, those of us for whom life has proved too bitter. They are good, these doctors – some of them very good; they work hard trying to solve our problem, but half the time they must work in the dark – the whole truth is known only to the normal invert. The doctors cannot make the ignorant think, cannot hope to bring home the sufferings of millions; only one of ourselves can do that.[46]

Hall's scepticism was presumably based on the awareness of a disparity between sexological descriptions of lesbians and her own knowledge of them. Given that even Havelock Ellis appears to have met only a handful of lesbians in addition to his wife, Edith Lees Ellis, Hall's knowledge of lesbians was bound to be greater than his. While Hall was interested in the genesis of lesbianism it was not for her the chief issue about homosexuality. Her chief concern was winning human rights and civil dignity for lesbians and gay men, not finding a final solution for their 'problem'.

Biographies of Hall and critical studies of *The Well of Loneliness* share a common tendency to confound Stephen Gordon and Radclyffe Hall. The differences between the two women, one a real person, the other a fictional device created by Hall, are routinely blurred. The second belief popularly held about *The Well of Loneliness* is that it is an autobiographical fantasy masquerading as a novel; that Stephen was Hall's fantasy self, the richer, more aristocratic, more noble, more handsome lesbian that she longed to be. However, in writing *The Well of Loneliness* as a romantic novel, Hall was using the most popular and reader-friendly of genres as the vehicle for a contentious political polemic. The genre almost elides the difference between Stephen and the conventional romantic hero. Almost, but not quite, for Stephen remains the heroine, not the hero.

Radclyffe Hall was a highly skilled and creative writer who had won considerable literary acclaim before the publication of *The Well of Loneliness*. Her most critically lauded book, *Adam's Breed*, was about a male Italian waiter; Hall was not a male Italian waiter. To the extent that Radclyffe Hall was a lesbian and so was the heroine she created, *The Well of Loneliness* is autobiographical. There is no reason to think that *The Well of Loneliness* was 'autobiographical' in any stronger sense, unless one believes lesbians congenitally incapable of writing fiction rather than autobiography.

In lesbian and feminist criticism, this inability to separate Stephen Gordon, *The Well of Loneliness* and Radclyffe Hall has been most pronounced round the issues of biological sex, gender and lesbianism. This debate, which includes discussion about the nature of the relationship between lesbian identity and the medico-psychological discipline of sexology, seems to have occupied an extraordinarily large amount of attention. A simple analysis has been made: because Stephen Gordon sometimes articulates her lesbianism in terms of being like a man, then Radclyffe Hall herself believed that lesbians were male souls trapped in female bodies.

Sheila Jeffreys, for instance, believes that Radclyffe Hall's understanding of lesbianism was uncritically drawn from the views of sexologists, and she reproduced this understanding in her writing. Jeffreys for instance states that

> Mary is shown to be not a 'real' congenital lesbian, but a basically heterosexual woman who is temporarily diverted from her path. She falls in love with a woman who is depicted as a substitute man [Stephen]. The book shows how the congenital versus pseudo-lesbian distinction could rigidify in later years into the stereotypical roles of butch and femme.[47]

I would contest two points here: the accuracy of Jeffreys's reading of *The Well of Loneliness*; and the move from the congenital lesbian/pseudo-lesbian distinction to 'butch/femme' manifestations of lesbianism.

There is no suggestion in *The Well of Loneliness* that Mary is less of a lesbian than Stephen. Mary is just as interested in sex as Stephen and desires Stephen because Stephen is a woman. The relationship between Stephen and Mary is explicitly one between two women.

> Seeing Mary in the glass she did not turn round, but just smiled for a moment at their two reflections. Mary sat down in an arm-chair and watched her, noticing the strong, thin line of her thighs; noticing too the curve of her breasts – slight and compact, of a certain beauty.[48]

Jeffreys's reading of *The Well of Loneliness* seems rather insensitive to the actual text. Stephen is not a substitute man and Mary is not a straight girl. Hall has not reproduced the male sexologists' belief that there were two kinds of lesbian; women who were born that way, congenital lesbians, and plain but basically heterosexual women corrupted into it, pseudo-lesbians.

The basis on which Jeffreys matches up the pseudo-lesbian/congenital lesbian distinction with that of 'femme' and 'butch' lesbians is non-sensical. Femme lesbians are not heterosexual women momentarily diverted into a bit of lesbian slap-and-tickle: they are lesbians. Mary and Stephen are clearly not identical twins; they feel and manifest their lesbianism differently. On the whole Stephen is 'butch' and Mary is 'femme', and it is usually Stephen who takes Mary's soft warm body in her strong arms. However, Mary is not a passive victim but an active and desiring partner to Stephen's butch dyke. Jeffreys's analysis presupposes the truth of lesbian-feminist belief that 'butch/femme' identities and relationships are unequal and oppressive.

It should also be noted that in a culture which has only two genders which are together supposed to be exhaustive of all possibilities, if one rejects conventional female heterosexuality one necessarily moves towards masculinity. Sexual desire for women has been 'masculine' in our culture in the sense that it is a desire which is theoretically open only to men. In this sense then, lesbians, however conventionally feminine in all other areas, are 'masculine' in their sexual desire; they enter a realm of desire which is supposed to be male. Hall's contemporary, Ida Wylie, seems to acknowledge this by using 'masculine woman' as well as 'abnormal woman' as neutral synonyms for lesbian. Lesbians are not literally masculine or male; rather they are women who occupy positions between the culturally constructed polar opposites of masculinity and femininity.

The most powerful public statement that Radclyffe Hall and Una Troubridge made about their lesbianism, leaving aside *The Well of Loneliness*, was in how they dressed. Radclyffe Hall dressed like a lesbian as a very public act, designed to show the whole world, gay and straight, that she was a lesbian and that she was not ashamed. Radclyffe Hall and Una Troubridge were both butchish. Troubridge may have played the 'femme' to Hall's 'butch' generally but it was monocled, shingled and trouser-wearing femme. Una, who had always had a penchant for boyish clothes, had her hair cut short early in 1915. Although there are photographs and caricatures that exist of Hall that show her, or seem to show her, dressed as a man, these portraits are deceptive. Hall never wore trousers in public and did not have her hair cut short until 1921 when she was forty-one. When Una first met her in 1915, her hair when loose fell almost to her waist. When Hall posed for portraits she ensured that they were carefully constructed to represent her as more masculine than she actually was.[49]

Michael Baker is very good on Hall's dress and pays it the attention that it deserves, for it was through her dress that Hall positioned herself as a lesbian.

> Throughout 1920 her [Hall's] appearance and habits underwent a conspicuous change. Her clothes became increasingly masculine. To the plain tailored jackets, ties and skirts (she did not adopt trousers until the 1930s, like most women) were added men's socks with garters, heavy, thick-soled shoes with a broad toecap, and (in winter) spats. In August she was fitted for a brocade smoking jacket.[50]

Besides clothes there were other ways in which Hall distanced herself from conventional femininity:

> She bought two pipes at Dunhill's and Una gave her a tobacco jar for Christmas. Pipe-smoking was a purely private indulgence but she soon gave it up when it made her tongue and lips sore and returned to the strong, unfiltered cigarettes she habitually smoked.[51]

Pipe-smoking may have occurred in private, but buying pipe tobacco from Dunhill's, where the records of her tobacco account are still held, was not a private act.

Clothes, pipes and monocles all allowed lesbians, like Hall and Mary Allen, to signal their desire for women, and to distance themselves from women who desired men. This external signalling does not necessarily imply, if at all, that a lesbian wants to be a man; 'masculine' lesbians are not quite such an open book. In an interview Hall gave to The Daily Mail she is quoted thus: 'I think yellow is the best colour for walls,' Miss Radclyffe Hall explained, 'it's so warm and sunshiny' and she adds 'when I feel jarred and disgruntled I work it off in a bout of polishing'.[52] These very feminine preoccupations are juxtaposed without comment with an extremely mannish photograph of Hall.

Hall and Troubridge had strong views on coming out:

> Una made clear their position on the vexed question of 'closet' inverts. She had nothing but contempt for the cowardice of those who refused to declare themselves — if, that is, they possessed independent means. The male homosexual had some excuse because he risked prosecution under the law, and the impecunious female invert stood to lose her livelihood through prejudice. In any other circumstance, though, the invert had a duty, Una maintained, to 'show' herself and by example give courage to her less fortunate sisters.[53]

One of Hall and Troubridge's lesbian friends in the 1920s was Evelyn Irons (1900–), also a friend of Dorothy L. Sayers. Evelyn Irons was Scottish and had graduated from Somerville College, Oxford, in 1921. After working for a couple of years as a bookseller, she gained a place on the Daily Mail editorial staff in 1927, where she worked on the women's page. Hall and Troubridge's relationship with Evelyn Irons cooled after the publication of The Well of Loneliness. Michael Baker, who acknowledges Irons in his book, is presumably correct when he says that this was because Troubridge and Hall were disappointed in her; she had not exerted herself and her contacts enough in support of The Well of Loneliness.

Evelyn Irons was not the only friend that Hall and Troubridge dropped because of a lack of political backbone. They also stopped seeing Toupie Lowther, who as a woman of independent means had much less reason to be closeted than Evelyn Irons, because she refused to come out. According to Una, Toupie

> sought to conceal her homosexuality ... by shunning the company 'of her own ilk' and by wearing 'scarlet silk "confections" in the evenings with accordion pleated skirts and low necks'.[54]

Interestingly it was Toupie's dress, the sign of her masquerade as a heterosexual woman, that was the final straw for Hall and Troubridge.

NOTES

1. Una Troubridge, *The Life and Death of Radclyffe Hall* (London: Hammond & Hammond, 1961), pp.18–19.
2. *Ibid.*, pp.22–7.
3. National Portrait Gallery Archive, Mabel Batten collection, catalogue description.
4. Troubridge, *The Life and Death of Radclyffe Hall*, p.31.
5. Radclyffe Hall, *The Well of Loneliness*, 1928 (London: Virago, 1982, reprinted 1985), p.317.
6. *Ibid.*, p.431.
7. *Ibid.*, p.439.
8. *Ibid.*, pp.302–3.
9. *Ibid.*, p.302.
10. Michael Baker, *Our Three Selves: A Life of Radclyffe Hall* (London: Hamish Hamilton, 1985), p.136.
11. *Ibid.*, p.134.
12. Lovat Dickson, *Radclyffe Hall at the Well of Loneliness: A Sapphic Chronicle* (London: Collins, 1975), p.103.
13. *Ibid.*, p.114.
14. Baker, *Our Three Selves*, p.169.
15. *Ibid.*, p.267.
16. *Ibid.*
17. Diana Souhami, *Gertrude and Alice* (London: Pandora, 1991), p.154.
18. Esmé Langley in *Arena Three*, **4**(3), March 1967.
19. Victorian Glendinning, *Elizabeth Bowen: Portrait of a Writer*, 1977 (London: Phoenix, 1993), pp.188–93.
20. Jane Marcus, 'A tale of two cultures', *The Women's Review of Books*, **11**(4), January 1994, p.10.
21. James Douglas, *Daily Express*, 19 August 1928.
22. *Ibid.*
23. *Sunday Times*, 5 August 1928.
24. Sheila G. Donisthorpe, *Loveliest of Friends* (London: Old Royalty Book Publishers, 1931), pp.254–5.
25. Mary Renault, afterword to *The Friendly Young Ladies* (London: Virago, 1984), p.281.
26. Baker, *Our Three Selves*, p.248.
27. *Ibid.*, pp.248–9.
28. Cecil Roberts, *One Year of Life* (London: Hodder & Stoughton, 1952), p.96.
29. Troubridge, *The Life and Death of Radclyffe Hall*, p.82.

30. Baker, *Our Three Selves*, p.202.
31. Hall, *The Well of Loneliness*, p.396.
32. *Ibid.*, p.447.
33. Baker, *Our Three Selves*, p.357.
34. *Ibid.*, p.48.
35. Jeffrey Weeks, *Coming Out: Homosexual Politics in Britain from the Nineteenth Century to the Present* (London: Quartet, 1990, revised edition), pp.136–7. The British Sexological Society was the new title of the BSSSP.
36. Baker, *Our Three Selves*, p.186.
37. *Daily Herald*, 20 August 1928.
38. Baker, *Our Three Selves*, p.251.
39. Radclyffe Hall to Evguenia Souline, 3 October 1934, quoted in Baker, *Our Three Selves*, p.305.
40. Dickson, *Radclyffe Hall at the Well of Loneliness*, pp.22–3.
41. Baker, *Our Three Selves*, pp.268–9.
42. *Ibid.*, p.259. See also Dickson, *Radclyffe Hall at the Well of Loneliness*.
43. See also Richard Ormrod, *Una Troubridge: The Friend of Radclyffe Hall* (London: Cape, 1984).
44. Baker, *Our Three Selves*, p.218.
45. Liz Stanley, 'Romantic friendship? some issues in researching lesbian history and biography', *Women's History Review*, **1**(2), 1992, p.208.
46. Hall, *The Well of Loneliness*, p.395.
47. Sheila Jeffreys, *The Spinster and Her Enemies: Feminism and Sexuality 1880-1930* (London: Pandora, 1985), p.125.
48. Hall, *The Well of Loneliness*, p.323.
49. Baker, *Our Three Selves*, pp.131–2.
50. *Ibid.*, p.131.
51. *Ibid.*
52. *Daily Mail*, 5 November 1927, credited by Baker to Evelyn Irons (no by-line).
53. Baker, *Our Three Selves*, p.268.
54. *Ibid.*, p.247.

lesbian life in the 1930s

'Aphrodite has honoured you above all others'
Sappho, Fragment 62

In some ways Una Troubridge and Radclyffe Hall were extremely conventional. They lived together as a couple in a relationship which was in theory, if not always in practice, monogamous. Many lesbians lived much more complicated lives than this; for instance, juggling husbands, female lovers and children. The most famous married lesbian is Vita Sackville-West, who had intense and passionate lesbian liaisons throughout her life but showed no overriding desire to leave her husband Harold Nicolson. Today the idea that being a married lesbian could be anything other than nightmare is rare. Stories of married lesbians seem to fall into two categories: then she came out; or then she killed herself/had a breakdown/drowned the baby.

Marriage and lesbianism appear to have been much less incompatible fifty years ago. Vita Sackville-West, and indeed Virginia Woolf, did not feel that their sexual desire for women and affairs with women precluded a satisfying marriage to a man. One reason for this is that these women did not feel that being a lesbian was a possible social identity; for women social identity and economic security existed through marriage. A husband was for a home and children, grand passion did not have to come into it; our contemporary assumption that if the grand passion and the husband are not the same person, the husband has to go, was not so prevalent.

Vita Sackville-West (1892–1962) described her passionate affair with Violet Trefusis (1894–1972) in a manuscript which was found in a locked bag after her death. This manuscript, with additional material stressing the importance of her marriage to Harold Nicolson, supplied by her son Nigel, was subsequently published as *Portrait of a Marriage*. Vita Sackville-West's description of her affair with Trefusis is frank; as she had no intention of the manuscript being published in her own lifetime, she could afford to be. *Portrait of a Marriage* is a popular book that has been marketed over the years as a story of rich, pretty and aristocratic young women in a titillating sex romp. There is, however, a grittier and less glamorous side to Vita Sackville-West's lesbianism.

Nigel Nicolson suggests in his sections of *Portrait of a Marriage* that the sexual relationship between his parents ceased shortly after his birth, and that from this point on his parents were bound together only by their profound love for one another. Certainly there is no indication that they shared many sexual interests: almost all Sackville-West's lovers were women and Harold Nicolson was himself homosexual. In many ways their marriage settled into a convenient arrangement guaranteed to ensure their respectability, protecting them both from the stigma of homosexuality and providing an escape route if their lovers became too demanding. Only Vita's affair with Violet threatened to jeopardize the Nicolsons' marriage.

As Victoria Glendinning's biography *Vita* shows, Vita Sackville-West had her cake and ate it, a position which, while comfortable, was not particularly brave. The most impressive aspects of Sackville-West's life are the large network of lesbian friends and lovers that she amassed, and her honesty in writing about her lesbianism. Vita Sackville-West had, like Radclyffe Hall, read the sexologists:

> Here are the books on the psychology of sex that she had read with Violet, and then with Harold: six volumes of Havelock Ellis, with 'V.N.' written in each. In the volume *Sexual Inversion* Harold had inscribed a quotation from Verlaine, 'On est fier quelquefois quand on se compare.' There is Edward Carpenter's *The Intermediate Sex*, and Otto Weininger's *Sex and Character*, with 'V.N. Polperro 1918' on the flyleaf, and passages about male and female characteristics heavily annotated. 'When [women] marry they give up their own name and assume that of their husband without any sense of loss', wrote Weininger. 'I disagree', scrawled Vita in the margin.[1]

Like Radclyffe Hall, Vita Sackville-West did not credit the sexologists with complete understanding of women's behaviour.

Vita's disagreement with Weininger – she used her own, rather than her husband's, name throughout her life – is a good illustration of her strong and conflicting views on politics. She was deeply conservative; she regularly expressed her hatred of feminists, socialists and the lower classes, yet she was herself a living example of political radicalism. She was more successful than Harold, professionally and financially, she lived in an open marriage, and she was a self-identified lesbian.[2] Of Vita Sackville-West's many female lovers, some were also married, but a number of them were single women who lived their entire lives, often quite publicly, as lesbians.

Hilda Matheson (1888–1940), who had an affair with Vita at the end of the 1920s, was one of these women. She was the daughter of a Scottish Presbyterian minister. Born in London she spent much of her adolescence in Europe where she became fluent in French, German and Italian. She read history at the Oxford Society of Home-Students, now St Anne's College; she then worked at the Ashmolean Museum in Oxford. During World War I Matheson worked for British Intelligence in Rome, and was subsequently employed as Nancy Astor's political secretary. Head-hunted to the fledgling BBC by Lord Reith in 1926, by 1927 she was running the BBC news service as 'Head of Talks'.[3]

In the view of one of her colleagues, R.S. Lambert,

> Hilda Matheson's outlook was that of the typical post-War Liberal, with its idealistic internationalism expressed in a mistaken devotion to the League of Nations, its sympathy with Socialistic experiment, its cultivation of the innovating schools of poetry and art, its enthusiasm for feminism.[4]

Even Lord Reith, initially her supporter, came to describe her as that 'Red woman' – on the basis of her politics rather than her sexual exploits.[5] Sexual attraction works in mysterious ways; on paper nothing could be more antithetical to the conservative Vita Sackville-West than the radical and intellectual Hilda Matheson.

While her relationship with Vita was her first serious sexual relationship, Hilda Matheson had had a 'physical flare-up' with a woman a few years earlier.[6] She did not appear to find being a lesbian problematic; she wrote to Vita:

> Love – all you've given to me – all the physical side of it too – seems to me to be life in its very highest expression – it's mixed up for me with any decent thinking or feeling I've got or ever had – with everything in fact that is true and beautiful and of good report. And yet I suppose some people would regard it as shameful and vicious.[7]

Hilda Matheson was not worried about people knowing about her lesbianism, unlike Vita. Nor was she isolated by it, for she had a supportive and tolerant circle of friends. She lived with two friends, Marjorie Graves and Janet Vaughan (later to become Principal of Somerville), in South Kensington. Both women were aware of her relationship with Vita and were sympathetic towards it. According to Hilda, Marjorie had 'a ribald tongue, enriched by a classical education and a past (I should guess) of her own'.[8] Here again 'knowing the classics' is equated not just with knowing about homosexuality but also with being homosexual.

Hilda Matheson did not seem to find fitting into the Nicolson marriage too difficult. She went as far as arranging for Vita and Harold to give a talk for the BBC on the subject of marriage; where of course they paraded their carefully preserved façade as the exemplary married couple. Harold may even have been the reason Matheson left the BBC; according to Glendinning she resigned in 1932 when her plan for Harold to discuss James Joyce's recently published *Ulysses* on the radio was rejected. After this she spent a number of years living at Sissinghurst, the Nicolsons' home, where she worked as Harold and Vita's secretary, as well as writing for *The Observer* and other newspapers.

In 1936, their affair long over, Matheson left Vita and Sissinghurst, to join the African Survey as Secretary under Sir Malcolm Hailey. By this point Hilda had taken a new lover, another married woman and an old friend and sometime lover of Vita, Dorothy Wellesley. Dottie Wellesley (1889–1956) was a successful poet and was married to Lord Gerald Wellesley, Duke of Wellington. Dottie was a close friend of W.B. Yeats, who admired her poetry, as did Philip Larkin, who included her poetry in his anthology of twentieth-century English verse.

W.B. Yeats seems to have known a surprising number of lesbians, from Eva Gore-Booth in the 1890s to the trio who were at his bedside when he died in 1939:

> His [Yeats's] last passionate affair was with the wealthy feminist journalist Edith Shackleton Heald, who after his death lived for many years with the lesbian painter Hannah Gluckstein. The lesbians Heald, Wellesley, and Matheson were at his deathbed.[9]

Within a year of this dramatic scene Hilda Matheson was herself dead at the early age of fifty-two. Wellesley placed a plaque to Matheson at her home in Sussex, which reads 'Amica Amicorum' (friend above all others).[10]

The painter Hannah Gluckstein (1895–1978), known by the genderless name Gluck, was a lesbian in the Radclyffe Hall mould. It is Gluck's portrait *Medallion*, painted in 1937, of herself and her lover Nesta Obermer which Virago use as the cover illustration for their edition of *The Well of Loneliness*. In terms of popular images of lesbianism Gluck and Obermer, Stephen Gordon and Mary Llewellyn, and Radclyffe Hall and Una Troubridge are confounded in this picture, which has become the archetypal image of British lesbians in the 1930s.

Gluck was the daughter of an extremely wealthy Jewish family who owned the Lyons coffee-house chain. Gluck was never interested in men, and after relationships with the journalist Sybil Cookson and that doyenne of feminine domesticity, Constance Spry, she fell passionately in love with Nesta Obermer in the mid-1930s. Although the relationship between the two was extremely fraught, Nesta Obermer, who never left her husband, appears to have been the love of Gluck's life. Diana Souhami analyses the situation thus:

> Both women moved in social circles where money was the key to the good life. Nesta, along with her works for charity and patronage of the arts, was enmeshed in an extrovert whirl of travel, parties, high fashion, servants, and all the expense of a stylish international social life, financed by her elderly husband. She had no wish to lacerate his feelings. Divorce was none too easy to obtain in the 1930s. Separation would have reduced her income and exposed her to scandal. She kept her marital status perhaps as much for her own sake as for Seymour's. It was one thing to have an intense and secret love affair while seeming to conform to society's rules, another, more unpredictable and isolating, openly to flout those rules and pioneer a different way.[11]

By the mid-1940s Gluck could bear the stress of seeing Nesta on such terms no longer and she became involved with Edith Shackleton Heald. Both Edith Shackleton Heald and her sister Nora, with whom she lived, were journalists, Edith on the *Evening Standard* and Nora at *The Lady*, where she was editor. In the autumn of 1945 Gluck moved into the Heald home. It was not to be a particularly happy arrangement; Gluck was still hopelessly in love with Nesta, while Edith was resentful of Nesta's hold over her, and Nora was jealous of Edith's love of Gluck.

Edith Shackleton Heald was not the only lesbian working on the *Evening Standard*, for in the early 1930s Evelyn Irons moved there, as editor of the Home Page, from the *Daily Mail*. Evelyn Irons was recovering at this point from a tempestuous affair with Vita Sackville-West. The relationship had started in 1931; it was immediately made complicated by the fact that Irons already had a lover, Olive Rinder, with whom she lived in Chelsea, London.[12]

Notwithstanding the demands of married respectability and the aristocratic circles in which she moved, Vita seems to have been happiest wandering around Sissinghurst wearing breeches, jerkins and bits of string. That she saw herself as 'butch' in relation to her women lovers, and perhaps Harold, is borne out by *Portrait of a Marriage* and by her relationship with Evelyn Irons:

> Vita loved Evelyn in the fashionable dresses she wore to Ascot, or to cover the Paris collections for her newspaper. She loved to give Evelyn presents – a new suitcase full of men's silk pyjamas, flowers delivered to her office at the *Daily Mail*, a diamond wrist-watch, Alella wine, a ring – 'your shackle'.[13]

Evelyn, however, unlike Vita, was explicitly feminist. She was a contributor to *Time and Tide*, and she was apparently not so sure that one of them needed to act as a man. She managed to persuade Vita to allow a little more laxity in their erotic arrangements:

> 'Such is our inter-homosexual homosexuality,' wrote Evelyn, 'that we do not take obvious advantage of this arrangement, but choose to appear in similar roles. On Friday, for instance, it will be gardener and water-boy.'[14]

Again the problem of lack of commitment arose in this relationship: while Evelyn did not care if people knew that she was a lesbian, Vita remained dedicated to publicly protecting her perfect marriage. Evelyn Irons eventually left Vita for another woman, a relationship which according to Glendinning was to be life-long. This seems to have been quite a shocking experience for Vita, famous as a *femme fatale*. Vita sent Evelyn a poem, *Valediction*, to mark the moment:

> Do not forget, my Dear, that once we loved.
> Remember only, free of stain or smutch [sic],
> That passion once went naked and ungloved,
> And that your flesh was startled by my touch.
>
> And though the processes of mortal change
> Delude you now to different belief,
> Consider only that the heart's a strange
> Quick turn-coat, undeserving of your grief.
>
> Forget, – regret, – should these two words be brothers?
> If rhyme to rhyme be kith, so let them be!
> Pass from my heart towards the heart of others,
> But in your passing, half-remember me.[15]

The complexities caused by married lesbians were not the only way in which lesbians lived lives which diverged from the prescription of the monogamous couple. Chris St John and Edy Craig had, for instance, formed a *ménage à trois* with Tony Atwood in 1928. This was apparently Edy's idea but seems to have been accepted with relative ease by Chris; together the three women were known as 'the trio'. After Edy's death in 1949, Chris and Tony continued to live together until Chris too died, in 1960.

Clare Atwood (1866–1962), known almost universally as Tony, was a painter of some distinction. She had exhibited her work at the Royal Academy and was one of the first women commissioned as a war artist during the First World War. According to her obituary in *The Times* Tony was a 'versatile painter of interiors with figures, portraits, architectural subjects, landscapes and still lives, including decorative flower compositions'.[16] She was also a Catholic, once giving Radclyffe Hall a piece of the True Cross, the one Jesus was crucified on, for safe-keeping.

The Craig/St John/Atwood trio lived at Smallhythe in Kent and during the 1930s became close friends with Radclyffe Hall and Una Troubridge who had also been based in Kent when they were in England. The two groups shared many common friends, like Micky Jacob and Lady Maud Warrender. The trio spent Christmas with Hall and Troubridge in 1931; Una said of them:

> There is great consolation and gratification to me in the company of these friends who like us & want to be with us because they know us for what we are and respect what John has done for her kind.[17]

Intimacy between the two families became more difficult shortly after this Christmas. In 1932 Chris fell passionately in love with Vita Sackville-West; this caused huge rows between Chris and Edy, with Tony unsuccessfully trying to act as peacemaker. The tension between the women made them, as Una noted, difficult company.

For Vita, her affair with Evelyn Irons and a subsequent brief interlude with the also abandoned Olive Rinder over, Chris must have appeared an amusing dalliance. When they met, Chris was nearly sixty and Vita forty; Vita flirted and Chris succumbed: 'She took Christopher to see Long Barn, she let her hold her hand, she gave her a string of blue beads from Persia and she gave her hope.'[18] It was more than hope. In November Vita 'stretched out her left hand to me and said: "I do love you, for all you give me"' and, a few hours later, 'she gave me a lover's kiss. In all my dreams of her I never dreamed of that. I never knew unalloyed bliss with V. except on that November day.'[19] By Christmas they were lovers.

Victoria Glendinning describes Chris St John as 'very ugly', and implies that she was without charm or great intelligence. Glendinning also minimizes the depth of Chris's relationship with Vita, insisting, for instance, that they had 'one night of love, never to be repeated'.[20] I am unconvinced of the justness of this interpretation of events. Vita was an attractive woman in the prime of life who had few difficulties seducing attractive and desirable women; why would she flirt and sleep with Chris if Chris was physically and in character akin to an ugly old boot? It would seem likely that Vita was attracted to Chris because Chris was actually a desirable woman, even at fifty-nine.

The Nicolson family are not sympathetic to Christopher St John; this is unsurprising. Chris's relationship with Vita is extremely problematic for them. The image of Vita and her lesbianism which they have worked to promote is a glossy, smoothed-over and media-friendly version of the reality. Chris was certainly not a pretty young women in a short skirt; it is with Vita's relationship with her that the glamorous, aristocratic and titillating version of Vita crashes against real lesbianism. Chris St John and her lesbian circle are shaven-haired dykes in boiler suits to the 'lipstick lesbian' version of Vita that has been promoted, for instance, in the television series of *Portrait of a Marriage*. It is hard to explain why Vita, erotic legend, would sleep with Chris if Vita's lesbianism is conceptualized simply as a straight boy's wet dream.

The affair dragged on into 1934; Chris was in love and demanding, and Vita was unable to deal with the situation. Many of their lesbian contemporaries felt that Vita had behaved very badly and was playing games with Chris. Ethel Smyth, who was very fond of Chris, was particularly angry with Vita and stopped talking to her. The affair upset Virginia Woolf, who was angry and jealous with what she felt as Vita's betrayal of her with Chris; normally so articulate, she was reduced to referring to Chris as 'that mule-faced harridan of yours'.[21] Eventually of course Chris came to terms with the situation and, with Edy and Tony for support, carried on her life. She and Vita managed to remain friends.

Fortunately Chris had other activities with which to distract herself from Vita. In 1932 she started to write the biography of Dr Christine Murrell (1874–1932). Chris St John was invited to write the biography by one of Murrell's lovers, Honor Bone. The choice of St John can have hardly been arbitrary. Although there is no evidence that Murrell and St John knew each other well, they were almost certainly acquainted from their days of suffragette militancy: Murrell was one of the doctors who attended the suffragettes when they were released from Holloway, where Chris herself had been a prisoner.[22]

The strongest link between Chris Murrell and Chris St John, however, was their domestic arrangements. By the time of her death in 1932 Chris Murrell was living with two women: Honor Bone and Marie Lawson. The arrangement was very similar to the Chris St John / Tony Atwood / Edy Craig *ménage à trois*. Vera Holme was a close friend of both groups, and they must have known of the similarity of their erotic arrangements.[23] *The Times* recounts in St John's obituary that George Bernard Shaw once said to her, 'You must write of your *ménage à trois*. I know of nothing quite like it.'[24] Shaw obviously did not move in the right circles.

It seems likely then that St John was asked to write Christine Murrell's biography because she had a unique understanding of what Murrell's life had been about: as a feminist, and a lesbian, and as part of a *ménage à trois*. Chris St John was the obvious, indeed almost the only possible, biographer. St John had a fine line to tread in the writing of Murrell's life. Her objective was to honour Murrell's achievements as a doctor and to record her personal and political commitments. However, Murrell's personal commitments were potentially rather scandalous; St John had to acknowledge, but simultaneously obscure, the exact nature of Murrell's private life.

Christine Murrell, like St John herself, used the male name Christopher, although Murrell had rather more nicknames than St John: Chris, Chrissie, Chri'fer and CMM.[25] Given the striking number of similarities between Murrell and St John, trying to strike the right authorial note must have caused St John to wonder what would be made of her own life. There was also the delicate question of ensuring that both Honor Bone and Marie Lawson felt that their individual relationships with Murrell were accorded due weight. St John's dedication of the book to Honor Bone *and* Marie Lawson is perhaps the final balancing of these scales.

The public aspects of Chris Murrell's life are straightforward. She was one of the first women doctors to achieve recognition by the institutions of British medicine: the wish to mark her importance for women by commissioning a biography of her is perfectly understandable. She was the first woman elected to the General Medical Council of Great Britain, in 1933, having been the first woman elected to the Council of the BMA in 1924. She had been a supporter of women's suffrage and was subsequently a member of the Open Door Council, one of the feminist groups lobbying for equal employment rights. As well as giving medical attention to the suffragettes, Murrell had also been the official doctor to Mary Allen's women's police force; Allen was presumably also an old ally from the suffragettes.[26]

Once St John starts to talk about Murrell as a woman the difficulty of writing a sensible biography becomes clear. St John describes Murrell as a 'woman of massive frame, a virile woman, whose irreproachably feminine clothes seemed incongruous'.[27] She then explains why Murrell never married and 'never even had a love affair'. This was because

> she was not the kind of woman who has a natural chemical affinity with a man. It was possible that she was sexually underdeveloped or as I prefer to put it, too highly developed as a human being with a nice balance of male and female attributes and qualities, to be strongly sexed. But I think that this was rather a fortuitous help to a celibacy that she felt incumbent on her than its curse.[28]

The choice of explanations that St John offers for Murrell's 'virile unfeminineness' here is wide: a chemical or hormonal imbalance; a stunted physical or psychological development; a transcendence of the sexual through the achievement of an intellectual and emotional androgyny; and a chosen renunciation of sex in order to dedicate herself to her work. This passage is illuminating as an example of the variety of explanations that women could offer, in 1933, for not being interested in men and, indeed, for being homosexual.

The contention that Murrell might have been 'too highly developed as a human being with a nice balance of male and female attributes and qualities, to be strongly sexed' is carefully nonspecific. To describe a woman as not strongly sexed can mean that she is not very womanly or it can mean that she does not have strong sexual desires. St John's description is strongly reminiscent of Edward Carpenter who wrote:

> The chief difference in the case of homosexual persons is that in them the male and female elements are more equalised; so that when, in addition, the general development is of a higher grade, we find among this class the most perfect type of humanity.[29]

Carpenter certainly does not imply that people who are the 'most perfect type' do not have sex.

Chris St John's resolute non-description of Christine Murrell's relationship to femininity and sexual desire has similarities with the love letter that she wrote to Vita Sackville-West a year later:

> I can never think of your sex, only of your humanity. I could love you in breeches, or in skirts, or in any other garments, or in none. I know you must be a woman – evidence your husband and your sons. But I don't think of you as a woman, or as a man either. Perhaps as someone who is both, the complete human being who transcends both.[30]

Chris St John describes both Chris Murrell and Vita Sackville-West in similar terms as women who transcend gender by uniting aspects of both male and female within themselves. The underlying link between Sackville-West and Murrell's transcendent perfection, the great unsaid in the case of Murrell, is their lesbianism.

The net effect of offering so many competing explanations for Murrell's disinterest in male lovers and lack of conventional femininity is that Murrell's actual sexual identity and sexual practice is hidden from the prurient (heterosexual) onlooker. By explicitly discussing Murrell in relation to gender and accepting that she was not like the mass of women, St John is honest while remaining committedly obscurantist. St John's heterosexualizing PR job can of course only go so far, for Christine Murrell did have women lovers. Chris's brief was not to make Murrell look heterosexual but to protect her memory from homophobic sneers.

St John initially contextualizes Murrell's relationships with women within a feminist framework:

> A stable friendship between two women which often leads to their setting up house together is now quite common, and accepted as an alternative to marriage. The theory that the greater economic independence of women is largely responsible for the increase in such partnerships seems to me quite sound. They are, as a rule, most successful when the partners are busy women, engaged in some professional work. If in the same work all the better, for they have an enviable community of interests.
>
> Christine Murrell and Honor Bone were in this happy situation. Their friendship which lasted for over thirty years was cemented by their professional partnership as doctors.[31]

However, Chris St John cannot leave it here. What she has just described, the happy situation of friendship with an enviable community of shared interests, is not only Murrell's chosen life but her own. The only alternative element in this 'marriage' is that it is two women, not a man and a woman, who are the partners. St John continues lyrically:

> Friendship originates in many different ways. There may be an irresistible mutual attraction at the very first meeting of two people whose lives in the future are to be closely associated The bond is formed in a twinkling of an eye. There may be nothing of the kind. The future friends, like some future lovers, may be unconscious of their destiny.[32]

Having explained the romantic nature of the love that exists between women 'friends' St John then returns to the events of Murrell's life. Her dead-pan style is very successful in diverting attention away from the actual substance of what she is recounting.

> Honor Bone was hindered from supplying all that Christine Murrell needed in the companion of her rare hours of leisure by her disinclination for strenuous activity, and by reasons of health which, apart from this temperamental disinclination, prohibited it. She had to rest during the hours when she was not engaged in medical work. Fully conscious that this created a problem as Christine Murrell's idea of recreation was to find some outlet for her energy, she was glad when she was no longer called upon to solve it. The solution, the formation of a new friendship with someone younger, stronger and more energetic than herself, might have been unwelcome to Honor Bone if she had been a selfish, jealous and possessive woman. As she was not, was sensible enough to recognise that the new friendship was to her advantage as well as to Christine Murrell's, she adapted herself to the change it brought about in their domestic life together with something more than good grace. That the transformation of ménage à deux into a ménage à trois should have been effected without any friction was creditable to everyone concerned.[33]

A close reading of this passage raises the question of exactly what this energetic thing was that Chris Murrell liked to do in her free time which required a female partner? More generally, change the names and this could be the story of Tony Atwood's move into the relationship and home of Edy Craig and Chris St John.

Christine Murrell and Honor Bone lived in London during the week and went to their house in Surrey at weekends and for holidays. When Murrell became involved with Marie Lawson, 'CMM expressed to me [Marie] the belief that to get the best out of our friendship we must give it the background of a common life.'[34] As an initial move, and presumably to ensure that Honor took things calmly, Marie bought a house in Surrey, very close to theirs, in 1922. By 1925, however, all three women were able to move into a house which Christine Murrell had herself designed, The Four Winds, Frimley Green, near Aldershot. Here the three women 'shared a common life'.[35] Finally, in 1930, Marie reported that 'our triple domestic partnership was extended to London'.[36] Shortly after this the idyll was destroyed with Murrell's death at the age of fifty-eight. It is unclear what happened to Honor Bone and Marie Lawson after Chris Murrell's death. Honor was certainly still living at Four Winds in 1941, but Marie Lawson although in regular and fond contact with her, was no longer living with her.[37]

Some lesbians did not feel as worried as others that their lesbianism would come out. Valentine Ackland (1906–1969) left a record of her life, *For Sylvia: An Honest Account*, written in 1949 to explain herself more completely to Sylvia Townsend Warner, her lover. It is impossible to know how much Valentine might have cleaned up her history if she had been writing for publication. Ackland and Townsend Warner did not hide their relationship, and Ackland's dress was, certainly by the 1930s, clearly identifiable as lesbian. However, there are different degrees of public recognition, and a reputation as public as Radclyffe Hall's may well not have appealed to either Townsend Warner or Ackland. *For Sylvia* was eventually published posthumously.

In *For Sylvia* Ackland is candid about the women that she has loved, and her love for Sylvia. When she was fifteen, in 1922, Valentine was sent to school in Paris. She fell in love with Lana almost immediately:

> I was swept into a wild confusion of ecstasy and shyness; I clasped her in my arms and she kissed me again and again. I had no idea of what had happened; my blood burned me, my heart-beat stifled me; I felt as though something had exploded beside me and I had been blown to atoms – [38]

Happiness and delight ensued. However, on returning to England, her father discovered their relationship and questioned Valentine 'severely and furiously' on its nature.

> I did not understand at all what he was trying to find out. I told him that we were in love.
> I remember very vividly the expression of disgust on his face. He became

very angry indeed – much angrier than I had ever seen him before. He asked if I knew what a filthy thing I had been doing? I answered, No, it had not been at all filthy. It was something very strange, but not at all wrong. I thought one or other of us must have been wrongly made – He asked furiously what I meant? I said that Lana ought to have been a man; I thought she must have been one in a previous incarnation – He muttered something and rushed out of the room. My mother came in and began to question me more gently. I patiently explained that we had fallen in love; no one could help that, could they? It was wonderful. We were very, very happy. We would love each other for ever. What could be wrong in that?[39]

As Valentine makes clear, at fifteen she had no conception that she was doing something out of the ordinary. Her lack of knowledge was not confined to ignorance about lesbianism being a taboo, she was also, to start with, unaware of what having sex entailed, what you did:

We were both totally ignorant (innocent is the better word) and all we knew of love-making was to lie close together and kiss; but no two have ever loved more or been more completely, passionately fulfilled.[40]

Her parents sent Ackland to a domestic training college in Eastbourne in order to have feminine normality drilled into her. However, this strategy failed: 'The place was (by an ironical stroke on the part of God) given over to unnatural vice' and 'I never moved from my conviction that what we had done was right, inevitable and in the circumstances perfectly natural'.[41]

In 1925 Valentine Ackland married partly in order to be able to leave home and her mother, with whom she had a difficult relationship. An indication of her ambivalence was that she had her hair Eton-cropped on the morning of her wedding day. Nearly twenty-five years later she seems still unsure about why she got married:

Perhaps because my body was wholly given over to X [her current female lover] whose love excited and satisfied me, profoundly and superficially too, I did not even think whether I felt desire for Richard.[42]

Neither apparently did Richard. He was also homosexual, and the marriage was never consummated and eventually annulled.

At the beginning of the 1930s Valentine met Sylvia Townsend Warner (1893–1978), the poet and novelist. Sylvia and Valentine were members of a bohemian and radical set, and their lesbianism seems to have caused little comment in their own circle. The only publicly available edition of Townsend Warner's diaries, edited by Clare Harman, seems to show that she never thought about her lesbianism at all; Valentine, however, certainly did. She summarized her experience thus:

> I was naturally more inclined to love women than men; I found deep pleasure, true pleasure and complete satisfaction from making love with women, and less complete pleasure, but still good pleasure, from being made love to by men. I did not ever really and completely make love with men: but with women I was released and happy, and I gave happiness and pleasure.[43]

Ackland's life was not without its difficulties; she struggled with Catholicism, alcohol, and genteel poverty. Although her relationship with Townsend Warner was absolutely essential to her happiness, it made her feel a failure as a poet and writer when she measured her success (minimal) against Sylvia's (great). However, tortured as she undoubtedly was about her self-worth, she did not view her lesbianism as any sort of trial:

> I have never thought (do not now, and do not expect to think) homosexuality wrong; that it is still considered to be a social offence makes it dangerous to a certain type of mind – offences against Society often intoxicate the offender, and the righteous who condemn them very often become intoxicated, too.[44]

While lesbian networks were both complex and strong in the 1930s and 1940s, there were still few physical venues which the lesbian community could occupy; throughout the country lesbians continued to use what women-only spaces there were. However, from the mid-1930s the lesbian scene seems to have been much improved by the establishment of the Forum Club by Alice Williams. The Forum Club provided the same kind of social space as traditional men's clubs did, but for a female membership. Although it did not advertise itself as a lesbian club, a significant proportion of its members were lesbians.

Alice Williams (1863–1957) lived with Fanny Mowbray Laming (187?–1941).[45] Williams was a bardic poet and one of the instigators of the Women's Institute; Fanny Mowbray Laming was a singer. The two women kept one diary which Fanny wrote unless she was ill. She died in 1941 from one of the vicious and quick strains of influenza which swept Britain during the war. Alice continued the diary on the next day, apparently loath to be separated even here from Fanny. Alice Williams and Fanny Mowbray

Lamming went on holiday together and were publicly recognized as a couple.

The Forum Club Record shows how within this institution love between women had a place:

> Finally a toast was raised to a lady who was so bound up with Miss Williams' life in the club, and we raised our glasses to Miss Mowbray Laming, and paid a tribute in our hearts to friendship.[46]

On a separate occasion, as part of a speech, Alice Williams said to her assembled peers

> that during so many years of office she had naturally been often disheartened, disappointed and even furious, but that she had the great fortune to have a dear friend with her always to whom she could pour out her troubles, certain of a ready sympathy – after which worries seemed less black and she was able to smile again, and she was very grateful for the help Miss Laming had been to her ever since the club started.[47]

The Forum Club was at Hyde Park Corner in Knightsbridge; it provided somewhere for its members to stay, to eat and to meet friends. The Forum Club seems to have been truly luxurious, a far cry from the poor and depressing female institutions that Virginia Woolf described in *A Room of One's Own*. Lilian Barker was a member and she used to take her niece there for lunch in the late 1930s:

> Lily always ordered extravagantly: first a sidecar cocktail then perhaps tomato soup with cream (she always added a spoonful of sugar), a tender Tournedos steak, or cold salmon in the summer, meringues with cream, and coffee in the beautiful upstairs drawing room.[48]

Lilian Barker retired from the Prison Service in 1943; she was awarded the DBE in 1944. She spent the last ten years of her life with Florence Francis in their small country bungalow occupying herself by 'reading, knitting and tending the garden'. Lilian Barker appeared to maintain her Eton crop until her death.[49]

Membership of the Forum Club cannot have been cheap; it must have been a refuge only for the professional woman and women with private incomes. However, for women with enough money the club provided a certain kind of forum, presumably the origin of the name, where they could meet and discuss cultural and political issues with like-minded women. There were numerous committees, such as the music committee and the international committee, which met frequently for debates, talks, trips and performances.

Mary Allen was a member, and as she tended to wear her police uniform of breeches, jackboots and a peaked cap, the membership was obviously broad-minded. Ethel Smyth and Eleanor Rathbone were also members of the Forum Club. It must have provided a unique meeting-point for many women who superficially led very varied and separate lives. Apparently now defunct, the Forum Club was still in existence in 1966, when it was cited as an exemplary women's club in *The New London Spy*.

NOTES

1. Victoria Glendinning, *Vita: The Life of* V. *Sackville-West* (London: Penguin, 1984), p.405.
2. See Suzanne Raitt, *Vita and Virginia: The Work and Friendship of Vita Sackville-West and Virginia Woolf* (Oxford: Oxford University Press, 1993) for a detailed discussion of Sackville-West, femininity and politics.
3. Fred Hunter, 'Hilda Matheson and the BBC, 1926–1940', in Sybil Oldfield (ed.), *This Working-Day World: Women's Lives and Culture(s) in Britain 1914–45* (London: Taylor & Francis, 1994), pp.169–70.
4. R. S. Lambert, *Ariel and All His Quality: An Impression of the* BBC *from Within* (London: Gollancz, 1940), p.64, quoted by Fred Hunter in Oldfield, *This Working-Day World*, pp.171–2.
5. Hunter, quoted in Oldfield, *This Working-Day World*, p.172.
6. Hilda Matheson, quoted by Glendinning, *Vita: The Life of* V. *Sackville-West*, p.210.
7. *Ibid.*
8. *Ibid.*
9. Elizabeth Cullingford, *Gender and History in Yeats's Love Poetry* (Cambridge: Cambridge University Press, 1993), p.269.
10. Hunter, quoted in Oldfield, *This Working-Day World*, p.174.
11. Diana Souhami, *Gluck: Her Biography* (London: Pandora, 1988), p.138.
12. Glendinning, *Vita: The Life of* V. *Sackville-West*, pp.238–41.
13. *Ibid.*, pp.242–3.
14. *Ibid.*, p.242.
15. *Ibid.*, pp.249–50.
16. *The Times*, 4 August 1962.
17. Michael Baker, *Our Three Selves: A Life of Radclyffe Hall* (London: Hamish Hamilton, 1985), p.271.
18. Glendinning, *Vita: The Life of* V. *Sackville-West*, p.252.

19. Christopher St John quoted *ibid.*, p.253. Christopher St John's journal in which she recorded her affair with Vita Sackville-West is owned by Nigel Nicolson and held at Sissinghurst.
20. *Ibid.*, p.253.
21. *Ibid.*, pp.270–1.
22. Christopher St John, *Christine Murrell*, M.D. (London: Williams and Norgate, 1935).
23. Vera 'Jack' Holme collection. 1941 letter from Honor Bone to Holme which mentions both Christine Murrell and Marie Lawson. The letter starts with 'Dear Jack' and ends with 'Much love, I wish I could see you'.
24. *The Times*, 25 August 1960.
25. St John, *Christine Murrell*, M.D., p.3.
26. Sophia Mary Allen, *The Pioneer Policewoman* (London: Chatto & Windus, 1925), p.158.
27. St John, *Christine Murrell*, M.D., p.xvii.
28. *Ibid.*, pp.99–100.
29. Edward Carpenter, *The Intermediate Sex* (London, 1908), appendix.
30. Quoted in Glendinning, *Vita: The Life of* V. *Sackville-West*, p.253.
31. St John, *Christine Murrell*, M.D., p.35.
32. *Ibid.*, pp.35–6.
33. *Ibid.*, p.100.
34. *Ibid.*, p.103.
35. *Ibid.*, p.104.
36. *Ibid.*
37. Vera 'Jack' Holme collection. 1941 letter from Honor Bone to Holme.
38. Valentine Ackland, *For Sylvia: An Honest Account* (London: Chatto & Windus, 1985), p.62.
39. *Ibid.*, p.67.
40. *Ibid.*, p.64.
41. *Ibid.*, pp.68–9.
42. *Ibid.*, p.79.
43. *Ibid.*, p.119.
44. *Ibid.*, p.88.
45. Alice Williams collection, Fawcett Library Archives, London.
46. *The Forum Club Record*, April 1937, p.26.
47. *The Forum Club Record*, May 1938, pp.11–12.
48. Elizabeth Gore, *The Better Fight: The Story of Dame Lilian Barker* (London: G. Bles, 1965), p.248.
49. *Ibid.*, p.x.

the second world war

Economically and politically the 1930s was a confusing and frightening decade. There was the Wall Street Crash of 1929, which halved Radclyffe Hall's income, followed by the Depression and high unemployment. The Spanish Civil War polarized political opinion in England between the new doctrines of fascism and communism. Now pacifism was not the only internationalist cause. While many people buried their heads in the sand and refused to deal with the new realities, others threw themselves wholeheartedly into the new politics which had opened up.

Valentine Ackland and Sylvia Townsend Warner joined the Communist Party in the 1930s. As well as being involved in Communist activism in Dorset and London they travelled to Spain with an international party of writers to see the reality of war and to give intellectual succour to the Spanish left. The Spanish Civil War emphasized again how women were not equal with men. While many of their male friends joined the International Brigade to fight for the Communists, Valentine, butch as she was, was disbarred by virtue of her sex.

Mary Allen became during the 1930s a fascist sympathizer. She visited Italy where she met Mussolini; as a public figure, her trip and her resulting support for Mussolini was widely reported in the press. In the early 1930s, of course, it was not clear where fascism, which so famously got the Italian trains running on time and stood for discipline, Christian values and an end to Communism, would lead. When England eventually entered the war there were calls in Parliament for Allen to be interned for the duration because of her pro-fascist views. Mary Allen was not interned; she was by this point in her sixties, but she forfeited the public esteem in which she had been held as a result of her unpatriotic views.

Radclyffe Hall admired 'Il Duce' for the same reasons as Mary Allen in the 1930s, although she did not seek to publicize her views. Hall's letters to

Souline in this period make shameful reading. Hall's crusade to end the persecution of homosexuals did not lead her to sympathize with other persecuted peoples:

> Jews. Yes, I am beginning to be really afraid of them; not of the one or two really dear Jewish friends that I have in England, no, but of Jews as a whole. I believe that they hate us and want to bring about a European War and then a World Revolution in order to destroy us utterly.[1]

Hall wrote this in 1939. By 1942 Hall's views had become slightly more humane; she did not see genocide as an appropriate response to the threat that the Jews posed and she reacted to news of the gas chambers with horror.[2]

Hall may have been overstating her views in order to endear herself to Souline, who was rabidly anti-Semitic. Naomi (Micky) Jacob, who was proudly Jewish, recounts how she had a cataclysmic row with Hall, Troubridge and Souline when they were staying with her in Italy in 1934. The row was caused by Souline making some anti-Semitic comments. Micky Jacob, terribly upset and angry, literally threw the Hall *ménage* out of her villa. Eventually Radclyffe and Una managed to convince Jacob that Souline's anti-semitism was not shared by them.[3] The extent of Hall and Allen's fascist sympathies was not enough to terminally damage their friendships with Micky Jacob. Either their fascism was relatively muted or the bonds of lesbian friendship were just too strong. Micky wrote appreciative accounts of both women in one of her last books, Me – and the Swans, published in 1963.

As Germany geared up to war in the 1930s, pacifist organizations re-emerged. While they enjoyed considerable public support before 1939, from the time of the Munich Appeasement many pacifists came to believe that Hitler posed a greater threat to freedom and civilization than war did. Micky Jacob was a pacifist in the 1930s, but by 1939 she was well aware of the terrible threat that Hitler posed, particularly to the Jews. As she said in 1940:

> There comes a time when you do your best to combat the powers of evil, or you are automatically subscribing to them. I believe, have believed for a very long time, that Nazism is evil, that it is the death of all that is best and highest in human nature. I believe that it stultifies, limits, cramps everything except cruelty, greed, and hate.[4]

For many pacifists the evil of Hitler made pacifism during this war untenable.

Peace activism was seen as almost womanly and it engaged the political energies of a considerable number of women, both women who saw pacifism as a maternal duty to their children and women who viewed it as a form of international feminism. Sybil Morrison (about 1894–1983) was educated at Wycombe Abbey and had been, in her own words, 'a member of the militant Women's Suffrage Movement from 1912'. She was on the Equal Pay Committee and involved with the Howard League for Penal Reform. Her only non-political work appears to have been when she was briefly an interior decorator in the 1930s.

Morrison's main commitment was to feminist and pacifist politics; she was an active member of the Six Point Group and Women for Westminster, a group campaigning for more women MPs, and in 1936 she was one of the first members of the Peace Pledge Union, which was founded in the same year. As a pacifist Sybil Morrison was a speaker, organizer, pamphleteer, *Peace News* contributor and twice Chairman of the Peace Pledge Union; she was also Chairman of the British Section of the Women's International League for Peace.[5] The Peace Pledge Union had a high proportion of active Christians, and of feminists and radicals, such as Laurence Houseman, Ethel Mannin, Vera Brittain, Storm Jameson and Sybil Thorndike, among its membership.

While the PPU grew quickly to begin with, during 1938 and 1939 roughly half the membership resigned. This pattern was repeated in most pacifist groups of the period. However, Sybil Morrison and Vera Brittain, among others, remained committed to the peace movement. Even during the war, pacifist papers had a circulation of around 30,000 and had over a thousand street sellers. Those pacifists who did not renounce their beliefs received rough treatment during World War II. Morrison was arrested in 1940 while speaking from a soapbox:

> I had been giving the gist of an appeal to the British people from Gandhi which had just been published when I was arrested. I was charged with using 'insulting words and behaviour' liable to cause a breach of the 'peace', which caused many people to believe that I had been involved in a brawl.[6]

She was sentenced to one month in Holloway gaol.

> The Governor told me that I had committed a worse offence than any other prisoner and the Officers frequently told me that if there was an invasion I at

least would never be released. I knew a chill of helplessness and fear that I hope not to experience again.[7]

She was not alone: there were hundreds of female pacifists who were arrested and charged under the Defence of the Realm Regulations during the War.[8]

World War II was very different from the 1914–1918 war in terms of British experience. In World War I, fighting was concentrated in two geographical areas, and British civilians were able to lead relatively normal lives. World War II was a total war, with fighting over much of the globe. At home the British population was affected not only by shortages and rationing but by bombing and evacuation. For women more than ever before, the war involved not only their fathers, brothers, friends and sons as previous wars had done, but it also involved them.

It particularly involved lesbians, as in January 1942 the government instituted limited female mobilization aimed primarily at single women and childless widows. Women were required by law to register their availability for war work; once registered, the government 'directed' their labour.[9] Though many married women and mothers did work, in the eyes of the government this was voluntary, although it was usually necessary for the economic survival of the women and their families. The great brunt of governmental and popular feeling was directed towards the mobilization of single women. Although the regulations initially only targeted women within a small age group, by August 1942 single women up to the age of forty-five were required to register for war work.

Women were not literally conscripted; this was believed to be too potentially damaging to public morale. However, even a partial and quasi-conscription of women was a vast social and political change. It gave women an involvement in war, and a duty to their country, that they had never before had. The fact that women were not paid equal rates with men for comparable or similar work showed the extent to which this change was resisted and downplayed by the government. Women's role in World War II so radically undercut many preconceived ideas about femininity, gender, patriotism and citizenship that it could hardly be mentioned.

While the conscription of women was not total it was real:

> Women who refused to register and take Government approved employment, or who left vital war work, found that 'direction' and compulsion amounted to one and the same thing. They could be fined up to five pounds a day and even imprisoned.[10]

The effect of the mobilization of women as an army did have a politicizing effect upon the women involved. Myrtle Soloman, who worked in a factory during the war, said, 'I had developed my feminist consciousness through my experience in the factory, which I would never have had without the war.'[11]

While women could still not be soldiers, they could now be conscientious objectors. As in World War I, many pacifists refused to undertake any work which made them part of the machinery of war. Sybil Morrison said:

> When fire-watching became compulsory there were many PPU members who refused on the grounds that conscription to this duty made them part of the war machine, although they had been completely willing to share the dangers and the duties in a voluntary capacity.[12]

Women who refused to fire-watch because of such pacifist beliefs could be, and were, imprisoned.

Women may have had mixed feelings about being drafted into essential occupations but they liked the money and the company. Although the working life was tough, 55-hour working weeks being unexceptional, the general level of women's health improved during the war. For women in the services this was a result of regular exercise, increased medical attention and regular and balanced, if not necessarily particularly nice, meals. Women working in industry benefited from canteens; there were over 17,000 industrial canteens by the end of the war. Domestic pressures on working women were also reduced by the establishment of over 2,000 government-supported 'British Restaurants', which served millions of nutritious meals at low prices.

The women's services were all mobilized in 1939. The number of women actually in the services was not vast but it was significant. By 1944 there were 207,000 women in the Auxiliary Territorial Service, 176,000 in the Women's Auxiliary Air Force, 75,000 in the Women's Royal Naval Service, and tens of thousands of these women had served abroad. There were also 80,000 women in the Women's Land Army by the end of the war; one of their patrons was Vita Sackville-West. Importantly in 1939 the 'camp follower' status of women in the ATS and the WAAF was dropped; servicewomen could now serve on more equal terms with their male counterparts.

War did not destroy all the social fabric of Britain and women's war work had widely recognized class connotations. Usual hierarchies did not disappear: work in factories or as cleaners was largely done by working-class women. Of the women's services the smartest branch was the WRNS, the least smart the ATS, although they did have Princess Elizabeth, who served as a mechanic. Women who had been to university or had the right connections usually sought better-paid and higher-status jobs in the government or the intelligence services.

Women in the services did many more of the jobs of regular soldiers in World War II than they had in World War I. Women in the WAAF, for example, worked as regular mechanics, flight mechanics, electricians and transport pilots. This, however, was not received with complete equanimity, as this government book celebrating the WAAF illustrates:

> Neither a war nor a uniform nor an era of emancipation has destroyed their charm. They still have an eye for a young man, they still demand time to dance, to knit, to sew, to curl their hair and go courting. The recent exhibition of WAAF handicrafts and arts in London was a very revealing thing. Its hundreds of paintings, embroideries and toys, its craft in silk and satin, were more than the result of a sideline. They showed better than any words how intensively, among all the grease and oil and masculinity and mechanisation of modern war, a women's army had struggled to cherish its feminine identity.[13]

The message from the government here is a warning to women: 'Don't think you can abandon your femininity just because you have the vote and you are fighting for your country'. Women in uniform had been incorporated back into heterosexuality by 1944.

There is a clear sense here of anxiety about how the destruction of some conventional distinctions between men and women might lead to the collapse of the known gendered world. While Britain needed women's work and women's skills for the war effort there was conscious nervousness in the government that this might all lead to trouble in the future. Presumably it was due to such mixed feelings about the extent of women's involvement in the war, and what it might presage, that some institutions remained bastions of masculinity. Women, for instance, were barred from the Home Guard until 1943; the Home Guard might well have been more worried about its own masculinity than most organizations.

Anxieties about women's sexuality, and lesbianism was one of them, in conjunction with the licence of war, persisted. While the government did not publicize lesbianism in the ranks it did not deny its existence. As had happened in World War I, a government Commission, the Markham

Committee, was established in 1941, to look into sexual immorality in the women's services. In one War Office-backed report on the ATS, lesbianism was discussed under issues of social and moral welfare. It stated that lesbianism was rare but that

> as cases arose they were usually dealt with by posting [one woman to a different location from the other] and only a very few promiscuous lesbians had to be discharged from the service.[14]

Lesbians concurred with this. Esmé Langley, for instance, commented, 'As all of us who been in one of the women's services well know, homosexuality is a commonplace and very few discharges result.'[15] The discharges which were made appear to have been on medical, rather than criminal, grounds.[16]

Obviously lesbians were involved in the British war effort. Many lesbians served in the forces during World War II and after, as the women recalling the 1950s in *Daring Hearts* make clear:

> It was very easy to be gay. It wasn't a hassle or a problem, certainly not at the age of sixteen and a half going into the WRAC, where practically everybody was gay. I mean, all the women were gay.[17]

However, it is harder to detect lesbians in the 1939–1945 war than in that of 1914–1918.

One reason for this is that women's involvement in World War II was far more formal than in World War I. It was no longer possible to nip over the Channel to check out the action. Women who wanted to participate in the war effort had to join official organizations, and subsequently accept, or not obviously break, official rules about sexual conduct. Many women made careers from their war-time service in the armed forces and were in no position to subsequently come out.

It is ironic that many lesbians enjoyed service life precisely because it sanctioned a lack of femininity, positively encouraged them not to marry, and allowed them to live in a women-only environment. As one commentator benignly put it, 'A large number of women in the ATS had become so attuned to service life that they could not envisage any other type of work.'[18] However, records of the lives of many of these service lesbians have not yet appeared. It is only recently that the issue of lesbians and gay men in the armed services has begun to come out at all; fifty years ago the sanctions against publicly admitting one's homosexuality were far more severe. Often the only indication that women who made their careers in the services were lesbians is their obituaries, which occasionally refer to a close friendship with a fellow officer.

For some lesbians the war was, professionally at least, business as usual. Evelyn Irons continued working as journalist, working as a war correspondent mainly in France; she won the Croix de Guerre. Irons settled in New York in the early 1950s, where she worked for *The Sunday Times* and *The Telegraph* as a foreign correspondent. She remained a friend of Vita's until the latter's death.[19] Micky Jacob served in ENSA, the Entertainments National Service Association, which toured army camps, military hospitals and factories producing essential supplies, providing entertainment.

Since leaving her munitions factory in 1919, Jacob had been seriously and recurrently ill with tuberculosis. In 1927 she moved on a permanent basis to Italy, with her then lover Sadie Robinson, in the hope that the climate would be better for her lungs. During the phoney war phase of World War II she remained in Italy, which was at that point still neutral, accompanied by her lover Marjorie Zamble and Zamble's two daughters. Zamble was married and appears to have spent half her time with Micky in Italy and half her time in England with her husband.

When Italy came out on the side of the Axis powers, Jacob and her family moved to Southern France to await developments. Within weeks of arriving they were evacuated with other British nationals on cargo ships from Cannes. It took seven days to reach Gibraltar and the ship was ill-equipped for its rescue mission; many people, including Micky, Marjorie and the children, slept in the hold, and there were no washing facilities. The ship was attacked by German submarines but reached Gibraltar unscathed; the last leg of the voyage home was on a passenger ship and was less eventful. However, all Micky's possessions and money were in Italy and she arrived in England in the autumn of 1940 with only the clothes she was wearing.[20]

NOTES

1. Quoted in Michael Baker, *Our Three Selves: A Life of Radclyffe Hall* (London: Hamish Hamilton, 1985), p.329; 22 March 1939 to Evguenia Souline.
2. *Ibid.*, p.337, 20 December 1942.
3. Naomi Jacob, *Me – and the Swans* (London: William Kimber, 1940), p.76.
4. Naomi Jacob, *Me in War-Time* (London: Hutchinson, 1940), p.76.
5. Sybil Morrison, *I Renounce War: The Story of the Peace Pledge Union* (London: Sheppard Press, 1962), p.vi.
6. *Ibid.*, p.52.

7. *Ibid.*, p.53.
8. John Costello, *Love, Sex and War: Changing Values 1939–45* (London: Collins, 1985), p.211.
9. This was the result of the National Service Number 2 Act, December 1941.
10. Costello, *Love, Sex and War*, p.211.
11. Hall Carpenter Lesbian Oral History Group (ed.), *Inventing Ourselves* (London: Routledge, 1989), p.19.
12. Morrison, *I Renounce War*, p.54.
13. *The WAAF in Action* (London: A. & C. Black, 1944), p.11.
14. J. M. Cowper (ed.), *The Auxiliary Territorial Service* (London, 1949), p.227.
15. *Arena Three*, **4**(9), September 1967.
16. *Arena Three*, **8**(1), January 1971; see also *Arena Three*, **8**(7–12), July–December 1971.
17. Brighton Ourstory Project, *Daring Hearts: Lesbian and Gay Lives of 50s and 60s Brighton* (Brighton: QueenSpark Books, 1992), p.19; see also p.57.
18. Roy Terry, *Women in Khaki: The Story of the British Woman Soldier* (London: Columbus, 1988).
19. Victoria Glendinning, *Vita: The Life of V. Sackville-West* (London: Penguin, 1984).
20. Jacob, *Me in War-Time*.

8 lesbians in the 1950s

'I want to tell you something but shame prevents me'
Sappho, Fragment 39

The post-war period in Britain is generally agreed to have been a time of increased conservatism on many fronts, although there is no consensus about why this was so. It is possible that the end of a war which had brought Britain to its knees produced a cultural yearning for certainty, stability and order. The conditions of war itself, the bureaucracy and regulations of the British war machine, had created a new climate where uniformity and conformity began to be perceived not as means to an end, but as ends in themselves. Certainly the cultural ferment and debate of the 1930s ceased. From politics to women's dress (maybe not so very far apart) what had been *risqué* but possible thirty years before was now unacceptable; women with short hair and trousers were again pointed out on the streets by the beginning of the 1950s.[1] Radical politics, feminism, pacifism and communism were to be perceived in the 1950s not as intellectual debates but as social diseases.

One paradigmatic development of the 1950s was the rise of the Anglo-American sociological theory of functionalism. Functionalism was a theory which equated human social structures and societies with simple biological organisms. Functionalists argued that if one could explain all the features, attributes and behaviours of an amœba in terms of the maintenance of its life, one could explain all the features, attributes and behaviours of human beings in terms of the maintenance of the life of the society in which they lived. Functionalism hence provided a justification for the maintenance of the political, social and economic status quo on the grounds that such a status quo would not have evolved unless it was functional for society. In this context what was morally and politically good became elided with the maintenance of society in its current state.

Within functionalism the model of 'deviancy analysis' was developed to examine the dysfunctional elements within a social system. Anyone who did not conform to generally held social mores was described as 'deviant'; child abusers, speeding drivers, murderers, Communists, pacifists, and homosexuals were all lumped together under this label. Deviancy from the norm was perceived by functionalists as a social problem which required curing. Political debates about whether particular forms of 'deviancy' had any moral weight did not occur within functionalism. All deviants were problems for society because they did not conform; for functionalism the non-conformity itself was the problem. The influence of functionalist thought was not limited to academic sociology: it affected social policy and psychology, and was a tacit influence on much understanding of human behaviour though the 1950s and 1960s.

It was not incidental that one of the major sites of functional analysis was the family.[2] The relationships between men and women, biological sex and gender, and female emancipation and child care, caused much anxiety in this period. This can be seen as a wish to return to a time without anxiety, when men were men and women were women and their place was in the home. The first generation of women who had always had the vote had come of age, and there seems to have been some nervousness that along with their political emancipation they would emancipate themselves from traditional patterns of female behaviour. Luckily, functionalism offered a serious academic explanation of why this would be a bad thing. As Elizabeth Wilson has noted:

> After the Second World War the debate [about women and their role] continued but was recast. Popular manuals on sex and marriage openly rejected the period of women's 'false' emancipation, the Jazz Age of the twenties. Then a boyish appearance and a wish to ape men by swearing, drinking, and demanding too much independence had led women away from true democratic equality within marriage.[3]

Marriage was reconceptualized, at least in public, in the 1950s. The nuclear family living in the suburbs was represented as all that was best in Western society.

The women's institutions, such as the WI and the Townswomen's Guilds became much more focused on conventional femininity, the home and the heterosexual family. Their original mission to educate women in civic responsibility and on political issues was greatly diluted, and they now stuck largely to women's issues, child health, education and religion. Ann Morley and Liz Stanley argue that even this attenuated feminism was better than nothing, saying, for instance, that

> the history of the WI in this country is that of active, vocal and politically aware women, who not only met together *as women* during the 1940s and 1950s, when no other local 'women's groups' existed, but also organised together to act, to reform, to change.[4]

Certainly lesbians continued to use these organizations; in 1949 Edy Craig, as Vera Holme's guest, gave a talk on 'How to trim hats' to the local WI.

Feminism as a challenging and aggressive threat to the established order virtually disappeared; as a potentially destabilizing force it was under attack. The Six Point Group and the Women's Freedom League managed to hang on through the 1950s but membership and radicalism was sharply down. The links between subversive pacifism and subversive feminism were maintained: in 1949 the Six Point Group re-established itself in the offices of the Peace Pledge Union in Bloomsbury.[5] Peace campaigning continued in the 1950s around the Korean war, fighting in Cyprus and CND, and it continued to attract lesbians. Sybil Morrison, for instance, remained actively involved and was joined by a younger generation of lesbians, the best known of whom were Pat Arrowsmith and Myrtle Soloman.

Myrtle Soloman (1929–1987) was Jewish and became involved in pacifism and feminism in the 1950s. She was involved in the Peace Pledge Union, CND and then War Resisters International, and was elected the Chairperson of War Resisters International in 1975. She had met Sybil Morrison in the lobbying group for women MPs, Women for Westminster, after World War II. Soloman reported that Women for Westminster was 'full of lesbians'[6]. Sybil Morrison was apparently positive about her lesbianism. Soloman remembers that 'Sybil, having made this fantastic discovery at the age of forty, went wild about it.'[7]

Pat Arrowsmith (1930–) was expelled from a number of schools including Cheltenham Ladies' College and then went to Newnham College, Cambridge. Her subsequent career has been remarkably varied: although she trained in social work she has been best known for her peace campaigning. She was imprisoned on eleven separate occasions between 1958 and 1985 as a result of her campaigning and has been involved with War Resisters International, CND and Amnesty International. Her novel *Somewhere Like This* (1970) draws upon some of this prison experience. Today Arrowsmith is one of the few lesbians who, having merited an entry in *Who's Who*, lists a lesbian partnership in her entry.

Homosexuality generally came to be considered not as an issue of invariant biology or of rational choice but as a curable defect of psychological and moral health.

In the political climate of the fifties to suggest that homosexuality might be a matter of moral indifference was heretical. Both in the United States and in Britain homosexuality came to be associated with moral unreliability, and, like Communism, with treason.[8]

This view of homosexuality was exacerbated by the lumping together of homosexuals and Communists by Senator Joseph McCarthy in the USA; McCarthy declared that both communists and homosexuals were subversives dedicated to destroying the American Way. This view obviously influenced Britain, united with America in fighting the Cold War, although there were of course home-grown scandals which confirmed it, most famously the defection of the homosexuals, Burgess and Maclean, to the USSR in 1951.

By 1945 the pre-war sexological groups had ceased to exist, although Norman Haire was able to revive the Sex Education Society in 1947. The relationship of the Sex Education Society to homosexuality was largely through Haire himself, although Jeffrey Weeks argues that:

Homosexual reform was clearly part of its programme. Point 8 called for 'the establishment of a rational attitude towards sexually abnormal persons', and Point 9 for the reform of the law relating to sexual offences.[9]

Norman Haire's death in 1952 led to the collapse of both the Sex Education Society and the associated *Journal of Sex Education*. As with earlier sexological groups there appears to have been little discussion of lesbianism and few lesbian members. The period between 1952 and 1958 appears to have been one of the few times in this century when there was no forum for the discussion of male homosexuality or a meeting place for homosexual men under the umbrella of sexology.

For lesbians the effects of the conformist 1950s were subtle: lesbians were not publicly exposed on the same scale as gay men. However, lesbianism was perceived, like male homosexuality, to be a problem and lesbians were seen by psychiatrists, who sought to cure their homosexuality.[10] The Maudsley Hospital in London certainly used aversion therapy on lesbians to cure them in the 1950s. In 1956 lesbianism was included in the Sexual Offences Act; this did not criminalize lesbianism, but it made it possible for a woman to be charged with the sexual assault of another woman.[11] Whether this was a simple tidying-up exercise, an attempt to increase the jurisdiction of women over their bodies or a way of marking the threat that lesbians posed to heterosexual women is open to discussion.

The Well of Loneliness remained the major introduction for lesbians to their sexuality as a public phenomenon rather than a private desire. Women continued to have complex feelings about it. Diana Chapman read The Well of Loneliness when it was reissued in 1949 by the Falcon Press. This was the first British edition since the 1928 ban; it was priced, expensively, at thirty shillings, when many novels sold for ten. Diana Chapman said that when she read it

> it swept me off my feet. I identified with Stephen Gordon, and I thought it was tragic and I wept buckets and went around in a daze, for days. I didn't think of it in any literary or critical way, it was far too emotionally powerful for me. It had far too many resonances. I felt a bit religious about it I think, as though it was something rather wonderful and noble to be. Again, I suppose identifying with Stephen in the Well of Loneliness, I didn't think it was anything terrible, although I realised, of course, that there were enormous disadvantages.[12]

Diana Chapman, however, has also said, à propos The Well of Loneliness, 'I thought to myself well if that's what lesbianism is all about, it's not really homosexuality, it's a form of heterosexuality.'[13]

The most obvious manifestation of lesbianism remained dress, and the same style of lesbian dress as in previous decades. Francis King describes Kay Dick looking like a dyke about 1950:

> Above a narrow black skirt, reaching to below her knees, she was wearing a white silk shirt, with a black bow tie, and a dinner jacket. A monocle was screwed into one eye. Her sleek blonde hair was closely cropped.[14]

Jewellery had also become a recognized indicator of lesbianism. By the 1950s pinky rings were the Masonic symbol of lesbianism:

> You would always have a little finger ring on your left hand, that was another sign . . . . You always had a little finger ring if you were butch or femme.[15]

The 1950s is often seen as the decade where 'butch-femme' lesbianism was at its most widespread. However, it is hard to judge how many lesbians identified as 'butch' or 'femme', and how rigid butch and femme roles were in this period. Many older lesbians came out in the 1950s; it is thus this decade which has been relatively well-covered in terms of oral history. Certainly the Gateways, a lesbian club in Chelsea, appears to have been split into 'butch' and 'femme' camps in the 1950s:

> There was role-playing and that was the way it was. If you weren't one way or the other, if you didn't conform, they derided you for it and said that you didn't know what you were.[16]

Here it seems that 'butch' women were expected to have 'femme' women as their partners: once a 'butch' or 'femme' always a 'butch' or 'femme'.

It is hard, however, to extrapolate such information generally from the mores of a particular club. While there have always been mannish lesbians who made their lesbianism clear through a rejection of femininity, there is little indication before the 1950s that the mannish lesbian needed a 'femme' partner. If there was a real change during the 1950s, so that only 'butch-femme' partnerships were perceived as possible, what caused this? The relationship between masculine dress and public style and private behaviour including sexual behaviour in the 1950s is not transparently clear. For instance were lesbians 'butch' on the streets and 'femme' in the sheets, and *vice versa*, in the 1950s? Did butches never cook the dinner?

Butch-femme relationships and identities came under considerable attack from certain lesbians and certain feminists in the 1970s and 1980s. This created a climate which may have discouraged older lesbians, who had been in happy butch-femme relationships in the 1950s, from telling their stories. Given the diversity of lesbian experience generally, it would seem unlikely that in the 1950s butch-femme was the totality of lesbian experience. It does not seem to have been an element in all lesbians' lives.

Being semi-publicly known as a lesbian was still fraught with difficulties for many women. Kay Dick (1915–198?) was a novelist and lived with Kathleen Farrell, 'petite, sharp, reserved, very beautiful', from the middle of the 1930s to the end of the 1950s. Although Dick dressed like a lesbian, at least occasionally, this was aimed at other lesbians, not the straight world:

> Everybody knew from the Snows, Orwell, everybody: there was no attempt to disguise our relationship, there was no need. Everybody in the world knows that it was quite a relationship but one didn't go around with a sweatshirt saying so.[17]

Kay Dick came out publicly in 1984 when her last novel, *The Shelf*, a story of a lesbian relationship, was published.

Some older women remained unselfconscious and apparently unanxious about their relationships with women; perhaps their identities as lesbians had been fully forged in a more liberal climate. Dr Louisa Martindale (1873–1966) published her unusually vivid autobiography, *A Woman Surgeon*, in 1951. *A Woman Surgeon* belongs to that category of biographical writings about women which came out of the suffrage movement. These feminists felt that it was important to record and mark women's achievements in fields which had traditionally been closed to them. The motivation behind Louisa Martindale's autobiography was similar to that which led Honor Bone and Marie Lawson to commission a biography of Dr Chris Murrell twenty years earlier. Dr Martindale felt that it was genuinely important to describe how she made a life in a male field and as a feminist. Her private life was not irrelevant to the success of her professional life, as she makes clear.

Louisa Martindale had the luxury of a truly exceptional mother. Louisa Martindale Senior was passionately interested in women's education, women's suffrage and politics generally; interests that she passed on to her daughters. Widowed when her two daughters were still small, Mrs Martindale left England with the girls and established a nomadic and apparently idyllic life in Europe. On their return to England Mrs Martindale became famous for her attempts to communalize cooking in the domestic home. Both Louisa and her sister Hilda were to establish successful professional careers, and never married.

Louisa Martindale Junior studied at Royal Holloway College, before going on to the London (Royal Free Hospital) School of Medicine for Women when she was nineteen. Upon qualifying, Martindale became a house surgeon; soon, however, she decided to move into general practice, although she specialized in obstetrics and gynaecology. She pioneered the use of radiotherapy in the post-operative treatment of breast and cervical cancer. Throughout her working life she travelled widely, studying and teaching in America and Europe. She was very successful; in 1931 she was made a CBE and in 1933 she was made a Fellow of the Royal College of Obstetricians and Gynaecologists. She was also President of the Medical Women's International Association. Louisa Martindale was clearly seen to be a pillar of the non-medical community too; she was the first woman Justice of the Peace to be appointed in Brighton.

Louisa Martindale was involved in the pre-war suffrage campaigning, although her interest was less in doing battle with the police than with elucidating the nature of women's relationship to the world. Louisa was particularly interested in the relationships between women's health, sex and the position of women. *Under the Surface* (1910), her history of prostitution, was so sexually explicit that questions were raised in Parliament about its morality. Martindale deplored the lack of knowledge women had about the sexual functioning of their bodies; she used to take pleasure in removing their ignorance and hence ensuring more enjoyable honeymoons.

During World War I she was part of the suffrage medical team organized by the Scottish Women's Hospital working at Royaumont Abbey in France. Leaving England must have been hard, for it meant separation from the woman with whom she lived, Ismay Fitzgerald. Louisa had met the Hon. Ismay Fitzgerald, daughter of Lord Fitzgerald of Kilmarnock, at a dinner party in 1910. Louisa wrote 'She was, I thought, very unusual looking and beautiful.' The relationship came to fruit with some speed:

> A few weeks later she came to me on a visit. This was a success, so from then on, and indeed for the rest of her life she lived with me.[18]

When Ismay Fitzgerald died in 1945 they had lived together for thirty-five years. With Ismay, Louisa Martindale wrote, she had found her 'full share of love and friendship'.

In the same year that Dr Martindale published her autobiography, Margaret Jourdain died. Margaret Jourdain (1876–1951) was the daughter of a clergyman with little money and a large family. She read Classics at Lady Margaret Hall, Oxford, and after she left in 1897 she supported herself through journalism, translating and writing on the history of furniture, textiles and decoration. Her first book on lace was published in 1908; by the time she died she was regarded as one of Britain's leading experts on the history of interior decoration. Margaret Jourdain never made much money from this work; probably the most lucrative period in her life was during World War I, when she was employed on 'war work' by the government.

Margaret Jourdain had many talents: one was for poetry, and the first poem she had published was entitled 'Seleucis of Lesbos'.[19] In 1911 Jourdain published a collection of poems, with the unfussy title, *Poems*, under the gender-neutral name 'M. Jourdain'. *Poems* was dedicated to Janette Rankin, an intimate friend of Jourdain, and Rankin apparently paid for them to be published. It was, according to Hilary Spurling, these poems that Jourdain was referring to when she wrote to Rankin, 'Here are a few last desperate violets laid at your feet.'[20] Janette Rankin was eventually to marry the actor Ernest Thesiger, well-known to be homosexual.[21] Thesiger was famous as the man who took his embroidery to the Front, and when asked about his experiences of war replied, 'Oh, my dear, the people!' Thesiger, a long-standing friend of Radclyffe Hall's, may well have been the model for Jonathan Brockett, the effeminate homosexual in *The Well of Loneliness*.

In 1919, shortly after Janette's marriage, Margaret Jourdain set up home with the novelist Ivy Compton-Burnett (1884–1969). Ivy Compton-Burnett was educated at Royal Holloway College in Surrey where she too read Classics. She almost immediately began writing the novels which were to win her a damehood in 1937. Compton-Burnett's novels are concerned with the daily minutiae of the emotional interaction within families and familial institutions. Her novels deal with incest, illegitimacy, hatred, love, desire and homosexuality.

Compton-Burnett's novels are famously dialogue-heavy with few descriptive passages; she traded on the weight of conversation and left the drama largely understated. In her novel *More Women than Men* (1933), the complicated family drama is concluded by the matriarchal headmistress of a girls' school, Mrs Josephine Napier, taking as her new professional partner the 'masculine' Miss Rosetti:

> 'Then you are my partner, and I am yours; and we will live our partnership in our lives, observing it in thought and word and deed.' Miss Rosetti knew that on some things there would be silence. 'We begin our new life from this moment.'
>
> 'It will easily cease to be new to me; it is my natural life; my happiness depends on women.'
>
> 'I think with me it has been the other way round,' said Josephine, causing the other to give her low, deep laugh before she knew it.
>
> The two women seemed to be easy with one another, with their permanent ease.[22]

After further dramatic developments Miss Rosetti approaches Josephine again:

> 'Do you still want me as a partner?' she said in a blunt, rather ruthless voice.
>
> 'Why, what a question! I want you more than ever. And you are already my partner; so the question cannot arise. With yet another vacancy on the staff

to fill, we shall indeed be dependent on each other. I cannot have you talking so out of the spirit of your place. And you know Miss Keats better than I do, and will be able to tell me her youthful desires. She may hesitate to impart them to me: I make no claims to your gifts with young women.' Josephine's tones seemed to fail through some lack in the feeling behind them. She caught the eyes of her companion, and, starting forward, fell into her arms, and the two women stood locked in their first embrace.[23]

The kind of partnership which Miss Rosetti and the widowed Josephine Napier are about to enter seems fairly clear.

There is a well-known apocryphal story that Ivy once described herself and Margaret as 'neuter'. This is usually interpreted to mean that not only were they not lovers but that both women were wholly without sexual desire. Even Jane Rule appears happy to describe Ivy as 'standing at the asexual extreme of lesbian sensibility'. Rule places Margaret and Ivy in the category of women 'who have no taste for heterosexual politics and are limited by morality or convention or lack of experience to relationships of deep emotional commitment to other women which do not involve sexual expression'.[24] The evidence for this assertion appears to be questionable.

As I have stressed before, there was a strong homosexual tradition, based in the classics, of describing men and women who felt themselves to be between genders as sexless. In grammar of course 'neuter' means sexless, the third gender. Being without gender does not mean that one is without sexual desire. It is perhaps salient to note that Miss Luke, who appears to have been Miss Rosetti's lover at the beginning of *More Women than Men*, describes herself as 'neuter'.[25] Miss Luke's relationship with Miss Rosetti is destroyed by the arrival of the young and pretty Miss Keats. In a highly charged scene where Miss Rosetti pushes Miss Luke against a wall, Miss Luke says:

> 'Ah, you have come to the end of us. But Miss Keats is fresh ground for you to plough, until you can approach your ultimate goal. I believe you have an unconscious affection for our head.'[26]

Certainly Miss Luke is not sexually disinterested; to 'plough' is widely known, and long-established, slang for 'to fuck'.

Ivy and Margaret lived together for thirty-one years, and in that time their domestic life became well-organized. Ivy, for instance, looked after the housekeeping and Margaret chose the wine. Socially they spent much time with gay men:

> Ivy's regular guests were like the young novelist Francis King, from the literary milieu, but many of Margaret Jourdain's guests were homosexual young men of the world of art and interior design.[27]

As Francis King is a gay man, it appears that both Ivy and Margaret's guests were gay men. They were also friendly with women like Vita Sackville-West and Kay Dick. Ivy rather mischievously left Kay Dick and Kathleen Farrell identical mirrors in her will, in a symbolic reiteration of her belief that they should not have split up. Francis King recounts that Ivy said of their split that it was 'so sad, I do wish they'd get together once more'.[28]

Compton-Burnett and Jourdain were, famously, extremely reserved women. However, in the shock of Jourdain's death, Ivy's composure did crack; she wrote:

> I am trying to get over the shock and strain of Margaret Jourdain's death. It is the loss itself that I cannot get over, and I find it hard to look forward.

It was, she said, 'my great trouble – the greatest that I could have had'.[29] Lesbian friends and acquaintances felt considerable sympathy for Ivy; Victoria Glendinning notes how Vita Sackville-West was moved by Ivy's sadness and loss.[30] Margaret Jourdain left her estate and royalties to Ivy; as Ivy had significantly more money than Margaret this was a symbolic, rather than practically necessary, final commitment. Ivy's life after Margaret's death was not a completely barren affair. Francis King says 'Ivy all too plainly had her crushes, the last of these being on Madge [Gartland]'.[31]

The famous reserve of Jourdain and Compton-Burnett may well have stemmed from the disastrous effect public attention had on the life of Margaret's sister, Eleanor. Eleanor Jourdain (1864–1924) was from 1902 Vice-Principal of St Hugh's College, Oxford, where her close friend Charlotte Moberly (1846–1937) was Principal. Eleanor Jourdain and Charlotte Moberly were, like many of their contemporaries in women's education, keen supporters of women's suffrage and they were unmarried.[32] In 1911 they published, pseudonymously, An Adventure, which described a vision of Marie-Antoinette that they had seen at Versailles.

An Adventure spawned many criticisms and much popular debate. This focused as much on the characters of Jourdain and Moberly as on the veracity of their psychic experience. To understand the nature of the publicity which these women received, we can turn to Lucille Iremonger's *The Ghosts of Versailles* (1957), the definitive study of *An Adventure*. Iremonger's book is divided in two: the first half describes Eleanor Jourdain and Charlotte Moberly; the second is an incredibly detailed critique of their putative vision. Popular psychology of the 1950s runs wild in *The Ghosts of Versailles*; educated women, suffragists, unmarried women, women without children and lesbianism are all stirred together to produce an exotic evil.

Charlotte Moberly was the daughter of the Bishop of Salisbury. Iremonger describes her as 'short and ungainly', 'the plain, lonely one, the ugly duckling', and 'so shy and tongue-tied in social conversation, [and] so cold and austere in the habits of her daily life'.[33] While Moberly was cast as the unloved and unlovable dupe, Eleanor Jourdain was the manipulative and perverse villain. She is described by Iremonger as 'passionate', 'tyrannical', 'ambitious'; and 'in sum, a sneak and a spy, with uncanny powers to boot'.[34] Eleanor Jourdain's academic work was, Iremonger states, an 'uninspired, savourless and pedestrian collection of the rubbish of scholarship'.[35] The relationship between the two women is characterized as one of exotic and erotic power abused:

> The clumsy Miss Moberly fell for the airs and graces of 'French' Miss Jourdain. . . . The older woman in short fell a victim to the younger one. It was not the first time Miss Moberly had been enchanted by a more feminine creature than herself. She had had a brief, but surprising, admiration for Marie Corelli, once . . . . Others did not find Miss Jourdain as attractive a personality as Miss Moberly did – even heartily disliked her.[36]

The reference to Marie Corelli is not without interest: Corelli, a romantic novelist, had lived quite openly with her lover, Bertha Vyver, from the late nineteenth century until her death in 1924.

Iremonger notes that the Jourdain family viewed Eleanor's entrance into the public arena via the publication of *An Adventure* with some trepidation: 'Miss Jourdain's family too disliked the whole affair and dreaded the publicity which its publication would entail.'[37] Given what happened after the publication of *The Ghosts of Versailles* – the antecedent gossip and snideness, and the complete denigration of Eleanor's character which resulted – their dread would seem wholly vindicated. While Margaret Jourdain may not have been particularly close to her sister, there was a clear lesson in what happened to Eleanor that she could not have failed to absorb.

Women who become public figures, and Ivy and Margaret were public figures, risked having their characters and reputations destroyed if they behaved in any way that was perceived to be out of the ordinary. Neither Margaret nor Ivy, nor indeed many other women, would have wished for their life together and their love for each other to be portrayed in the way that Eleanor Jourdain's relationship with Charlotte Moberly was portrayed. Ivy's family was not without its share of lesbian nightmares; two of her sisters committed suicide, while in bed together, in their late teens. By masquerading publicly as fusty old maids and refusing to discuss their relationship, Ivy and Margaret managed to avoid malicious and damaging gossip.

Fortuitously, there were women in the 1950s who were publicly available as lesbian icons, and the lesbian gaze of the 1950s was fixed most firmly on Nancy Spain. Spain was viewed as a comrade in arms: 'We used to say, "Nancy Spain went to Roedean." You felt a connection, you see, because you knew she was gay.'[38] And with lust: one woman interviewed at the age of eighty said with longing, 'She was gay . . . that's a woman I could have fallen for.'[39] The knowledge of Spain's homosexuality was apparently widespread outside the lesbian community:

> I once asked Nancy Spain . . . if she had ever been blackmailed.
> 'As everybody in creation knows I'm queer,' she said, 'Only a moron would try it on.'[40]

Nancy Spain (1917–1964) was born in Newcastle-upon-Tyne. She was educated at Roedean, where her health was safeguarded by Louisa Martindale, who was the school's doctor. During World War II she served in the WRNS, initially driving lorries, which she very much enjoyed, and subsequently working in the Press Office and in recruitment. Her service in the forces was again a point of recognition for other lesbians. After the war she supported herself through journalism, acting, and writing a biography of her relative Mrs Beeton and an account of her time in the WRNS.

By the end of the 1950s Nancy Spain was a successful novelist, book and film critic, and ultimately radio and television star. She was one of the first generation of personalities made extremely famous by the combined power of press, radio and television. Spain was by no means universally liked; her resolutely middle-brow writing irritated many. The literary establishment and those who thought her too populist disdained her work as noisy and knock-about journalism. She got into serious trouble by attacking certain literary sacred cows; she was sued for libel by Evelyn Waugh in the late 1950s. Waugh's friend and biographer, Christopher Sykes, is emphatic in his dislike of Nancy Spain; 'She was an iconoclast who hoped to reduce certain reputations which in her crude opinion were over-valued.'[41]

Spain lived with her lover and business partner Joan Werner Laurie, known as Jonnie. Spain played her cards carefully in public, neither denying the importance of her relationship with Jonnie nor explicitly stating its erotic basis. She wrote of Jonnie regularly:

> What a difficult thing to write objectively of a relationship in which I have been happily bound up for five years, and which is still going on! Jonnie is, I think, one of the most remarkable people I have ever met: remarkable in her potential greatness and past achievement, but even more remarkable in being the only person I have ever met (except Lord Beaverbrook) who has never bored me. She is certainly the only person who has ever let me be myself . . . therefore the only person with whom I can cheerfully live in close disharmony.[42]

Spain cheerfully and without self-consciousness described Jonnie as 'a girl four years younger than me, very good looking with rather a long nose and a very small waist'.[43]

Jonnie was divorced with a young son, and in 1952 she adopted a second child. Nancy Spain and Jonnie Werner Laurie, with Jonnie's children, were a family. Spain dared to represent them as such:

> I only wished that Jonnie and Nicky and Tommy could have been there. For what use is a peaceful day unless you can say, 'Look, darling,' to your family around you?[44]

Spain managed to acknowledge her lesbianism but avoided coming out. She played a complicated game of bluff and double-bluff about her private life: on the one hand she was candid, and on the other she dissembled. Nancy Spain overtly emphasized her heterosexuality by publicly mourning her lack of success with men, and indulging in some well-publicized but ridiculous flirtation with Gilbert Harding.

Nancy Spain partnered Gilbert Harding on *What's My Line*; Harding was also gay and widely known to be so.[45] Harding and Spain spent many years engaged in a tongue-in-cheek 'romance' which Spain reported cheerfully to the public. She first knew that he cared, she announced, when 'he gave me a gramophone record called, significantly, *Mon Homme*'.[46] However, even when writing of her fantasy of marriage to Harding, Spain re-inscribes the centrality of Jonnie in her life:

> For one mad moment we even discussed the possibility of a full-dress wedding from the Governor's House, Jamaica, with Jonnie (by now radiantly pretty and in the best brown of health) as matron of honour.[47]

All this fairly transparent play-acting did not seem to cause offence; Nancy Spain sailed closest to the wind when she said, in a serious tone, on the radio, 'that a wise woman wouldn't marry'.[48]

The stories about Nancy Spain and Jonnie Werner Laurie are numerous. Jonnie was the founder and editor of *She* magazine, which according to Esmé Langley was once memorably slashed with the line 'Britain's Gayest Magazine for Women'. Laurie had a passionate love for motor-racing. Nancy Spain was famous for many years for her preference for trousers, a blatant declaration of homosexuality particularly as modelled by Spain, and her fondness for pints of beer.[49] When Laurie and Spain were killed in 1964, in a plane crash on their way to the Grand National, they had been living together for thirteen years.[50] Nancy Spain's death was front-page news.

Unsurprisingly, Jonnie was not the first woman in Nancy Spain's life. Around 1950 Nancy Spain had a run-in with Elizabeth Bowen. Victoria Glendinning writes that:

> Nancy Spain's cultivation of Elizabeth had been intense .... They [Bowen's husband and a friend] complained to Elizabeth about her apparently endless visits to Clarence Terrace. Suddenly Nancy's visits stopped. Why was that? asked Eric. The answer was, that she had made a pass at Elizabeth: and that, in her case, was the end of that as far as Elizabeth was concerned.[51]

Bowen's objection was based on her feelings for Nancy, rather than a more general lack of erotic interest in women. It is possible that Nancy was just too blatant a lesbian for Elizabeth to handle.

Nancy Spain wrote three autobiographical books: *Thank You – Nelson* about the WRNS, *Why I'm Not a Millionaire*, which was mainly about her life as a struggling journalist and actress, and A *Funny Thing Happened on the Way*, which describes her travels and her house in Greece. A *Funny Thing Happened on the Way* was published posthumously; the foreword notes that given the circumstances of her death the title is no longer apposite. These comic autobiographies were written as an adjunct to her public personality, as unsuccessful heterosexual and hopeless incompetent, and they make no pretension to describe the real life and loves of Nancy Spain.

Among Spain's friends, though they are not the ones she dwells on in her autobiographies, were Naomi Jacob and Angela du Maurier. Spain's comic mystery *Poison for Teacher* (1949) was set in a school called Radclyffe Hall. It was dedicated to Angela du Maurier, presumably with the belief that she would get the joke. *Poison for Teacher* was reissued in Virago's *Lesbian Landmarks* series in 1994. Angela du Maurier (1904–) was the sister of Daphne du Maurier, a relationship which she clearly felt defined her public *persona*. One of her books of reminiscences is called *It's Only the Sister*. Daphne du Maurier's lesbianism has recently been examined with considerable care in Margaret Forster's biography.

Angela du Maurier led a quieter life than that of her more famous sister though she too wrote novels. She recalls:

> As for myself [about 1931] I had written a book! it had taken me many long weary months, and I had poured heart and soul into it . . . The curious thing is that I cannot remember showing it to my family. It went the rounds of many an unknown author's first MS. and returned always with the same kind message: I could write, but the subject was considered too unpleasant. I called it *The Little Less* and it dealt – but only in part – with a girl's love for another woman, and after the hullabaloo created by *The Well of Loneliness* no publisher was ready to take on another battle for the same cause . . . *The Little Less* was finally published as my third novel, somewhat whittled down, in 1940 or '41.[52]

What prompted du Maurier to write *The Little Less* is not indicated. Du Maurier does mention, albeit fleetingly, 'my "crush" on a notorious figure with supposedly ancient Greek ideas [which] was doomed from the start'. Angela, however, makes clear that there was nothing untoward in this relationship:

> She [the Greek] must obviously remain nameless, but in all the weeks and months I knew her I never met anyone kinder, more generous, more amusing and so utterly uncontaminating in influencing the impressionable girl I was. She had every opportunity under the sun and never said a word on any subject that could not have been shouted from the rooftops.[53]

The precise form that the 'whittling down' of *The Little Less* took is nowhere elucidated by Angela du Maurier. To the contemporary reader it appears very positive and open about lesbianism; arguing that love between women is just as deep as heterosexual love, and that lesbianism is not perverse and should be tolerated. One can only wonder what was cut.

Angela du Maurier's views on relationships between those of the same sex, as she has explored them in her memoirs, are complex:

> I would remind you that two of the greatest stories of love in the Bible deal with love in friendship; that of David for Jonathan (passing the love of women, so it says), and of Ruth for Naomi. So do not argue that because possibly you've never had a friendship that covers many emotions that such does not exist, or that if it does it must be homosexual or 'unhealthy' and unnatural to say the least of it.[54]

This could be described as slightly defensive equivocation.
In a further point Angela du Maurier states that

> far too much is talked about homosexuality nowadays, and when it comes to discussions about it on the radio and television I despair, because anything new is interesting to youth, and an innocent-minded boy or girl may learn by these means of homosexual friendships and, prompted by curiosity, set out to discover for himself or herself what it is all about ... How sad it is that in these days no relationships seem to be safe from slander and unjustified attack. All sorts of exotic vicious interpretations are levelled at the most innocuous friendship.[55]

However, in the middle of this passage she says:

> I do not know much about school-boys, I admit, but I am pretty sure that 'crushes' on head girls and mistresses would lead to fewer pregnancies in the girls' schools!

The effect of the publicization of lesbianism was obviously double-edged, for Ceri Ager too describes the days of lesbian invisibility, about 1925, as in some sense halcyon:

> I was so lucky, I didn't have any sort of hassle or embarrassment. There was no interference from the media, nothing on radio, there wasn't even television, then. And life went on beautifully.[56]

The third in this trio was Micky Jacob (1889–1964), whom I have already discussed: suffragette, actress, munitions supervisor and writer. From the 1930s Jacob concentrated on writing her quasi-autobiographical 'Me' series of books and novels; The Times described her as 'a lively, sympathetic and deservedly popular novelist'.[57] By the 1950s she too was a media star, if not on the same scale as Nancy Spain. H. Montgomery Hyde sums up her life at breakneck speed:

> One of the original suffragettes, Naomi Jacob had been in charge of an ammunitions factory during the First World War before she emigrated to Italy, where she spent her time writing two novels a year, 'telling people how to cook', lecturing on the theatre and literature, 'working for the animals' cause', and never taking exercise.[58]

Angela du Maurier is more revealing: 'She was wise, and she was amusing. She was courageous and she was good.'[59]

Naomi and du Maurier had been friends since 1926 and Jacob's last book, *Me – and the Stags*, was dedicated to Angela.[60] Angela du Maurier remarks that when she first met Micky Jacob she was struck by her appearance. Jacob was an 'extraordinary woman . . . wearing a velvet dinner jacket, and with a head like Beethoven'.[61] Photographs of Micky Jacob show a short stocky woman with small round glasses and short hair; she habitually wore trousers and shirts, and she famously smoked small green cigars. However, Angela du Maurier was quick to point out that 'In spite of her masculine appearance, Micky was extremely feminine in many things; she was a very good cook . . .'[62]

Jacob was claimed by the lesbian Minorities Research Group in the 1960s: 'We have had many supporters in the senior age group – e.g. the late Miss Naomi Jacob who was nearly eighty.'[63] Micky Jacob apparently corresponded with the lesbian magazine *Arena Three* in the spring of 1964; the following extracts from her letters were subsequently printed in *Arena Three*:

> One saying of Radclyffe Hall's often comes back to me: 'A great many women can feel and behave like men. Very few of them can behave like gentlemen'. Unfortunately this is only too true.

And:

> I only wish that Radclyffe Hall and Una Troubridge were here that they might read your magazine with me. I thought the last number was exceedingly good and most interesting.[64]

Jacob was to die shortly after writing these letters and this seems to have been her only interaction with the new lesbian communities and politics which had begun to develop in the 1960s. Jacob had always been supportive of other lesbians. Writing in one of her last books of *The Well of Loneliness*, she said that 'The main theme is naturally a delicate one, and John treated it with a delicacy which only a mind as fine and clear as hers could possibly have done.'[65]

By the end of the 1950s the cultural climate in Britain appeared to be growing more tolerant of homosexuals. In 1957 the Wolfenden Report on the problem of homosexuality was published. Although the Report was not positive about homosexuality it argued that there should be more tolerance of homosexual practices if they occurred between consenting adults in private. The Wolfenden Report argued that the liberal doctrine that there was a private sphere, within which the individual could make his own choices without interference from the state, applied to homosexual preferences.

Spurred on by the pro-decriminalization stance of the Wolfenden Report, the Homosexual Law Reform Society (HLRS) was founded in the spring of 1958 with a view to encouraging the enactment of its recommendations; the Albany Trust, its welfare/charity arm, was set up in the same year. Neither the HLRS nor the Albany Trust was an openly gay organization; both groups were, at least nominally, established by and run by socially principled heterosexuals. Nor were they mass-membership organizations; they did not have members but rather supporters, many of whom were gay men and lesbians.

Those gay men and lesbians who were involved with the HLRS and Albany Trust had to accept that publicly, and often within the organization itself, they must pass as straight. The most well-known gay man involved with the HLRS was 'Anthony Grey', the pseudonym of A.E.G. Wright, who has since written widely on gay politics. In 1958 it was too potentially dangerous for Wright to be involved in the HLRS under his own name. While the establishment of the Homosexual Law Reform Society was a positive step towards the partial decriminalization of gay male sex, it did not offer a space where gay men could publicly fight for their own rights.

The approach of the HLRS and the Albany Society was cautious, and the emphasis was on decriminalization; there was no public suggestion that gay men or lesbians could hope for or demand equal rights with heterosexuals. The two newsletters published by the HLRS and the Albany Trust, *Spectrum* and *Man and Society*, were not particularly positive about homosexuality although obviously much of their readership consisted of gay men and lesbians. Lesbians not only supported the HLRS but some, like Myrtle Soloman, also worked as volunteers at the London office.

Even in the late 1960s Anthony Grey stressed the inadvisability of trying to establish any kind of homosexual organization:

> Because even this desire, for innocent social gatherings, can appear to the over-anxious, non-homosexual person as a 'drive for recruits', the passport to the 'nameless orgies', which so inflame some people's rather lurid imaginations.[66]

The oppressive culture of the 1950s cast a long shadow over lesbian and gay politics. While the 1950s was not much fun for lesbians or gay men it was perhaps particularly hard on lesbians, as cultural pressures re-emphasized the importance of heterosexual normality and conventional femininity.

NOTES

1. Diana Chapman, C456/015, Hall Carpenter Oral History Collection, about 1985.
2. See, for instance, Talcott Parsons, The Social System (New York: Free Press, 1951).
3. Elizabeth Wilson, Only Halfway to Paradise: Women in Postwar Britain: 1945–1968 (London: Tavistock, 1980), pp.82–3.
4. Ann Morley, The Life and Death of Emily Wilding Davison (London: The Women's Press, 1988), p. 145.
5. Dora Russell, The Tamarisk Tree: Vol. 3. Challenge to the Cold War (London: Virago, 1985), p.114.
6. Hall Carpenter Lesbian Oral History Group (eds), Inventing Ourselves (London: Routledge, 1989), p.20.
7. Ibid.
8. Wilson, Only Halfway to Paradise, p.101.
9. Jeffrey Weeks, Coming Out: Homosexual Politics in Britain from the Nineteenth Century to the Present (London: Quartet, 1990, revised edition), p.151.
10. See Suzanne Neild and Rosalind Pearson, Women Like Us (London: The Women's Press, 1992), p.63, and Hall Carpenter Lesbian Oral History Group (eds), Inventing Ourselves.
11. Susan Edwards, Female Sexuality and the Law (Oxford: Martin Robertson, 1981), p.45.
12. Neild and Pearson, Women Like Us, p.97.
13. Diana Chapman, loc. cit.
14. Francis King, Yesterday Came Suddenly (London: Constable, 1993), p.263.

15. Brighton Ourstory Project, *Daring Hearts: Lesbian and Gay Lives of 50s and 60s Brighton* (Brighton: QueenSpark Books, 1992), p.51.
16. Neild and Pearson, *Women Like Us*, p.60.
17. Brighton Ourstory Project, *Daring Hearts*, pp.42–3; see also p.14.
18. Louisa Martindale, *A Woman Surgeon* (London: Gollancz, 1951), p.228.
19. *Academy*, 16 May 1908.
20. Hilary Spurling, *Secrets of a Woman's Heart: The Later Life of I. Compton-Burnett, 1920–1969* (London: Hodder & Stoughton, 1984), p.93.
21. Elizabeth Sprigge, *The Life of Ivy Compton-Burnett* (London: Gollancz, 1973), pp.61–3, and Douglas Plummer, *Queer People: The Truth about Homosexuals* (London: W. H. Allen, 1963).
22. Ivy Compton-Burnett, *More Women than Men* (London: Alison & Busby, 1983), pp.198–9 (first published 1933).
23. *Ibid.*, pp.201–2.
24. Jane Rule, *Lesbian Images* (London: Pluto Press, 1989), p.105.
25. Compton-Burnett, *More Women than Men*, p.211.
26. *Ibid.*, p.18.
27. Jane Emery, *Rose Macaulay: A Writer's Wife* (London: Murray, 1991), p.222.
28. Francis King, *Yesterday Came Suddenly* (London: Constable, 1993), p.228.
29. Sprigge, *The Life of Ivy Compton-Burnett*, p.131.
30. Victoria Glendinning, *Vita: The Life of V. Sackville-West* (London: Penguin, 1984), p.272 and p.369.
31. King, *Yesterday Came Suddenly*, p.229.
32. A. J. R. (ed.), *The Suffrage Annual and Women's Who's Who* (London: Hutchinson, 1913).
33. Lucille Iremonger, *Ghosts of Versailles: Miss Moberly and Miss Jourdain and Their Adventure* (London: Faber, 1957), pp.27–8 and p.54.
34. *Ibid.*, p.104.
35. *Ibid.*, p.94.
36. *Ibid.*
37. *Ibid.*
38. Brighton Ourstory Project, *Daring Hearts*, pp.42–3; see also p.60.
39. M. H., C456/014, Hall Carpenter Oral History Collection.
40. *Arena Three*, **3**(6), July 1966.
41. Christopher Sykes, *Evelyn Waugh: A Biography* (Harmondsworth: Penguin, 1977), p.499.
42. Nancy Spain, *Why I'm Not a Millionaire* (London: Hutchinson, 1956), p.134.
43. *Ibid.*, p.133.
44. *Ibid.*, p.203.
45. See, for instance, Plummer, *Queer People*.
46. Spain, *Why I'm Not a Millionaire*, p.214.
47. *Ibid.*, p.213.
48. *Ibid.*, p.243.
49. *Arena Three*, **1**(3), March 1964.

50. Nancy Spain, A *Funny Thing Happened on the Way* (London: Hutchinson, 1964), p.46.
51. Victoria Glendinning, *Elizabeth Bowen: Portrait of a Writer*, 1977 (London: Phoenix, 1993), p.189 and pp.192–3, and Spain, *Why I'm Not a Millionaire*.
52. Angela du Maurier, *It's Only the Sister* (London: Peter Davies, 1951), pp.155–6.
53. *Ibid.*, p.75.
54. Angela du Maurier, *Old Maids Remember* (London: Peter Davis, 1966), p.108.
55. *Ibid.*, p. 55.
56. Neild and Pearson, *Women Like Us*, p.38.
57. *The Times*, 28 August 1964.
58. H. Montgomery Hyde, *The Other Love: A Historical and Contemporary Survey of Homosexuality in Britain* (London: Heinemann, 1970), pp.184–5.
59. du Maurier, *It's Only the Sister*, p.113.
60. *Ibid.*, pp.112–13.
61. du Maurier, *Old Maids Remember*, p.52.
62. *Ibid.*, p.53.
63. *Arena Three*, **3**(4), April/May 1965.
64. *Arena Three*, **4**(9), September 1967.
65. Naomi Jacob, *Me – and the Swans* (London: William Kimber, 1940), p.122.
66. *Arena Three*, **4**(2 and 3), February and March 1967.

esmé langley and arena three

'Come to me now free from this aching pain'
Sappho, Fragment 78

In the 1960s life for British lesbians began to change. While the fabled sexual revolution of the time did have some influence on how lesbians lived, and thought about their lives, the crucial date was not 1968 but 1963, when two lesbians founded the first explicitly and dedicatedly lesbian social and political organization in Britain. The importance of the Minorities Research Group and its magazine *Arena Three* cannot be overstated. Even lesbians who did not support the MRG were affected by its existence – shades of *The Well of Loneliness*. The letters in *Arena Three* provide a detailed view of how ordinary lesbians in the early 1960s conceived of their lesbianism. For these reasons I will examine British lesbianism in the 1960s through the medium of *Arena Three*.

When Esmé Langley and Diana Chapman started the MRG they stated that its aims would be:

> to conduct and to collaborate in research into the homosexual condition, especially as it concerns women; and to disseminate information and items of interest to universities, institutes, social and educational workers, writers, poets, editors, employers and, in short, all those genuinely in quest of enlightenment about what has been called 'the misty, unmapped world of feminine homosexuality'.[1]

Later, the objectives of the MRG were to be expressed in more prosaic terms: offering counselling to lesbians, publishing a magazine for lesbians, informing public opinion about lesbianism, contacting isolated lesbians, reducing the salaciousness with which lesbianism was discussed, and initiating and assisting in unprejudiced research on lesbianism.

The name 'Minorities Research Group' was chosen partly on the grounds of discretion; if 'lesbian' was in the title the organization might receive more police or media attention than it really wanted. Langley and Chapman were also worried that a name in the 'Dykes' Delight' vein might attract male soft-porn *aficionados* rather than the lesbians whom they were trying to reach. Langley and Chapman wanted the MRG to be taken seriously by the straight world and to be trusted by lesbians, and for that reason it needed a serious name. The nature of the MRG's mission was underlined by a quote from Freud which headed their stationery: 'Homosexuality is no advantage, but it is nothing to be ashamed of, no vice, no degradation; it cannot be classified as an illness.'

In practice, however, the MRG was a more cheerful and shambolic affair than any of this implies. Its primary audience was lesbians and Esmé Langley was dedicated to her mission to encourage lesbians to come out and build successful lives. Given the discretion and low expectations of contemporary homosexual lobbying organizations, the emergence of Esmé Langley must have been literally stunning. Langley was a journalist and a writer; she appears to have used the pseudonyms Lee Langley and Ann Bruce.[2] *Why Should I Be Dismayed?* by 'Ann Bruce' was published in 1958. An apparently autobiographical piece, it describes what it was like to be a single parent in the 1950s. Esmé Langley had one son; the experience seems to have been mixed. She later commented: 'My own opinion and experience is that for a Lesbian *having* children could quite easily set up severe emotional disturbance.'[3]

By the early 1960s, if not before, Esmé Langley looked like a lesbian. Rachel Pinney describes how when Esmé first mooted the idea of a group for lesbians, she tried to dissuade her, saying 'Anyway if something's going to be done, it shouldn't be done by somebody like you – dressed like that, looking like that.' With the benefit of hindsight Rachel Pinney said:

> An ordinary butch les, not all that butch . . . [but] I was absolutely horrified that she didn't look like someone straight out of *Vogue*. If you're going to sell a thing like lesbian, you've got to look like *Vogue*.[4]

Diana Chapman describes Esmé Langley during this same period as 'a rather strange figure kitted out in motorcycle gear'.[5]

Esmé Langley may have had her eccentricities but this seems irrelevant, given the zest for lesbianism that she had. Langley not only liked women but she was consistently upbeat about the possibility of lesbian heritage. In an unpublished essay written in the early 1960s, Langley attacked with considerable force the belief that lesbian history did not exist or had been ignored. She cites books, which are certainly now obscure, such as

Margaret Goldsmith's biographies of Sappho and Queen Christina, and Edith Olivier Faber's *Four Victorian Ladies of Wiltshire*, which discusses the Ladies of Llangollen, as examples of the lesbian history that we already have.[6]

By March 1964 the MRG had only thirty-six paid-up members. This was largely because few mainstream newspapers would accept their advertisements so they had to rely on word of mouth, not a very effective form of advertising. Moreover, for women outside London, the MRG apparently had little to offer. The need for a magazine for lesbians which would encourage nationwide membership of the MRG was clear. It was with this in mind that *Arena Three* was set up by five of these early members. Esmé Langley was the editor, and working with her on the magazine were Diana Chapman, Cynthia Reid, Julie Switsur and a P. Dunkley. Of these women most were in their thirties and most were middle-class, certainly by occupation. They included a dentist, an engineer and a librarian.[7]

The first issue of *Arena Three* was published in the spring of 1964, somewhat later than the date line of January. While *Arena Three* and the MRG were supposed to be separate entities, in practice little distinction was subsequently drawn between the activities of the MRG and those of *Arena Three*, or between the membership of the MRG and the readership of *Arena Three*. *Arena Three* quickly became the very life-blood of the MRG. It was not a glossy magazine. It consisted of approximately twelve sheets of roneoed typing secured with a staple at one corner.

Although the focus of MRG concern was lesbians and not gay men, membership was open to both men and women regardless of their sexuality. From the letters pages of *Arena Three* it is clear that a number of gay men were members. In this period of course it was seen as far too dangerous, if not actually illegal, to establish a social magazine for gay men. *Spectrum* and *Man and Society* were acceptable because the Homosexual Law Reform Group and the Albany Trust maintained that they were campaigning for the decriminalization of some gay sex, not encouraging further sexual contact between gay men. The possibility that even a magazine for lesbians might incur the unwelcome attention of the Crown Prosecution Service was recognized by Esmé Langley. She was aware that there was a risk that *Arena Three* could be charged with 'corrupting public morals'. It was to reduce this risk that *Arena Three* was set up as a private circulation magazine and not sold to the general public.[8]

The MRG and *Arena Three* were not founded in an international lesbian and gay desert. The American lesbian organization the Daughters of Bilitis had been producing *The Ladder*, their lesbian magazine, the first in the world, since 1956. Esmé Langley had obviously been in touch with *The Ladder*; it carried adverts for the MRG and *Arena Three*, and consequently many of the first paid-up members of the MRG were American lesbians. The Dutch homosexual organizations also provided a model for the MRG; the success of Dutch homosexuals in creating a social sphere for lesbians and gay men was deeply envied. The lesbian and gay Cultural and Recreational Centre (Cultuur en Ontspannings-Centrum) was established in 1946, and was able to buy the building in which it was housed in 1965.

Arena Three consisted of features about the moral and social position of lesbians, book reviews, autobiographical articles, short stories and poetry, and pages of letters from subscribers. Articles on lesbians in the press and on television were noted and commented on. There were also some articles which were feminist rather than specifically lesbian, for instance, on the work of a computer engineer, and on how to buy a car.[9] The majority of articles were written by a relatively small circle of lesbians: Esmé Langley, Diana Chapman, and later Lorna Gulston and Carol Potter. Readers, although encouraged to send in articles, seemed keener to contribute their views via letters.

In the first couple of issues, keen interest was expressed in establishing a club in London for lesbians and gay men, seemingly along the lines of the now defunct London Lesbian and Gay Centre. It was quickly realized, by the start of 1965, that this was beyond the financial resources of the MRG and the idea was dropped, but not forgotten.[10] There was an article by 'Hilary Benno', one of Esmé's numerous pseudonyms, on the myriad and contradictory ways that lesbians are stereotyped by heterosexuals. 'Benno' concludes that most heterosexuals probably wouldn't know a lesbian if one hit them in the face. 'Benno' followed this up by an article on the possibility of a 'cure' for homosexuality. She cheerfully concluded that there was, sadly, no known cure.

Poems and short stories about the reality of lesbian life, coming out, falling in love and losing one's lover, also appeared regularly, and there were some particularly good short stories by Sandy Horn.[11] Biographical sketches of famous lesbians from history were also a strong and popular feature. Given the almost complete dearth of explicitly lesbian history or biography, the women identified match up surprisingly closely to our 1990s canon of lesbians in history: Katherine Mansfield, the explorer Lady Hester Stanhope, James Barry the doctor, and Colonel Barker, the lesbian bigamist, were all featured.[12]

Theatre reviews occurred infrequently, although in 1965 Rosemary Manning reviewed *The Killing of Sister George*, which was running in London with Beryl Reid as Sister George and Eileen Atkins as Childie. Manning could not get over the fact that it was being performed, let alone to acclaim, given its subject-matter.[13] Book reviews and lesbian reading lists were, however, a regular feature of *Arena Three*, ensuring that even those lesbians who had never met another lesbian had some sense of being part of a community. Many of the books mentioned are familiar: Valerie Taylor's *Journey to Fulfilment*, Violette Leduc's *La Bâtarde*, Jane Bowles's *Two Serious Ladies*, Jane Rule's *Desert Hearts*, Gale Wilhelm's *We Too Are Drifting* and *Torchlight to Valhalla*, and Claire Morgan's *The Price of Salt*, to name but a few.[14]

Other titles have since vanished from the lesbian canon. Most of the books which are unfamiliar to us now as lesbian novels are British, such as: Shirley Verel's *The Dark Side of Venus*, Louise King's *The Velocipede Handicap*, Tereska Torress's *Women's Barracks* and *The Golden Cage*, Iris Murdoch's *The Unofficial Rose*, Helen Foley's *Handful of Time*, Elizabeth Mavor's *Temple of Flora*, Vera Randall's *Inner Room* and Garet Rogers's *The Jumping Off Place*. The MRG did set up a library of lesbian fiction which was taken to meetings so that members could borrow books, but, as so often happens, many of the books 'disappeared'.

For the first eighteen months the book round-up was edited by 'Clare Barringer', purportedly the pseudonym of 'the assistant editor of a World-famous magazine'. Barringer's reviews were sophisticated. In one (queerly and post-structurally) entitled 'Fringe Benefits of Marginal Reading' she points out that a great deal of women's writing not usually dubbed lesbian is interesting to the lesbian reader. She cites Muriel Spark, Elizabeth Taylor, Antonia White, Brigid Brophy, Elizabeth Bowen, Rosamund Lehmann, Katherine Mansfield and Virginia Woolf, among others. This article foreshadows much feminist and lesbian work in the 1980s.[15]

There were few reviews of non-fiction, simply because there was much less non-fiction which had a specifically lesbian appeal. Betty Friedan's *The Feminine Mystique* was reviewed in 1964. The reviewer liked the book but had one, familiar, criticism: why are lesbians ignored? Simone de Beauvoir was cited by Diana Chapman in an article in the spring of 1964. De Beauvoir's *The Second Sex* had been translated into English in 1953; it was the first sophisticated feminist analysis of the position of women in society, and one of the first interesting examinations of lesbianism. It was, however, never reviewed in *Arena Three*.

By the standards of the mid-1960s, *Arena Three* was clearly feminist. This was in large part due to Esmé Langley. As early as 1964 Langley expressed her objection in the pages of *Arena Three* to the way that women were viewed as 'sex objects' by straight men. Langley's indignation was because even lesbians could not create a space where they were free from male sexual harassment. She was angry that any woman should be demeaned by being treated merely as a potential sexual receptacle by men. The women's symbol, ♀, which was to be taken up by straight feminists some years later, adorned the cover of *Arena Three* from this date.

In practical terms the establishment and success of the MRG and *Arena Three* depended upon being able to advertise for members and being able to hire rooms for MRG meetings. *Arena Three* was involved in a perennial struggle to get its advertisements accepted by regional and national newspapers. The adverts, 'homosexual women read *Arena Three*', were refused by the advertising departments of newspapers even when the papers featured the MRG and *Arena Three* in articles. Even at the end of 1967 *The Sunday Times* and *The Observer* were still refusing to carry advertisements although *The Sunday Telegraph* had finally agreed to accept them.[16]

There was more success in finding a venue for MRG meetings; in June 1964 they had established an arrangement to hire an upstairs room one Thursday evening every month at the Shakespeare's Head in Carnaby Street, Soho. From the winter of 1964 monthly meetings were moved to the Bull's Head, Clapham. The Shakespeare's Head could no longer accommodate the hoards of lesbians which attended, whereas the Bull's Head could hold 150 people. Men, even those who were members of the MRG, were not usually admitted to social meetings or talks. This was not because of fear of the police: mixed gay groups were much safer than single-sex ones. A MRG questionnaire distributed to members in the winter of 1964 showed that 74 per cent of the membership did not want men to attend MRG meetings.[17] However, lesbians in the MRG were not uninterested in the situation of gay men, and there were regular reports in *Arena Three* on the progress of the decriminalization campaigns.

Membership of the MRG was wide. Colonel H. Montgomery Hyde, who subsequently wrote *The Other Love* about homosexuality in Britain, was a member, as were Iris Murdoch and the MP Dr David Kerr.[18] Presumably their membership was the result of a benevolent commitment to civil liberties and sociological interest. These members were generous with both public support and money; in 1965 Iris Murdoch donated £30 to the MRG.[19] Some organizations concerned with psychological welfare were also members, such as the National Association for Mental Health. Annual membership initially cost thirty shillings, and eventually rose to £3.

Many MRG/*Arena Three* projects were mooted but never successfully established. A sound library, which was to hold recordings of plays, lectures, autobiography, oral history, poems and stories of lesbian interest, either recorded from the radio or by members, was set up in 1965. It never really took off; it was reported after a year that less than five hours of recordings had been made. Given the technology available it was an ambitious scheme; tape-recorders were still very rare, and there were constant pleas in *Arena Three* for women who owned them to come forward.

A constant topic at MRG meetings and in *Arena Three* was the nature of lesbians and lesbianism. While lesbians in the MRG and *Arena Three* certainly questioned, and usually demolished, spurious academic and popular beliefs about lesbianism, they were not necessarily confident about what to put in their place.[20] In the first issue of *Arena Three* Diana Chapman wrote an article on the pros and cons of explaining lesbianism as either an innate or an environmental condition. Mary McIntosh responded to it with some acerbity, saying that 'considering herself as the moral equivalent of a thalidomide baby is surely not the only way for a lesbian to remain at peace with herself'.[21]

The readers' letters published in *Arena Three* show an interesting set of reactions to the MRG and the magazine itself. Some readers of *Arena Three* were unhappy with its composition:

> It was misrepresented to me that your magazine sought to solve the emotional problems which some people feel about 'life'. Having read two issues I now realise you actually seek to perpetuate these problems – but in greater comfort.
>
> I would ask you therefore to remove my name from your mailing list.[22]

Other women thought that the very success of the MRG in attracting publicity and bringing light to the murky world of the lesbian was a mixed blessing:

> We think that too much publicity about your club's activities in the popular press is making it very difficult for two women to live together unnoticed, without being viewed with suspicion.[23]

A number of issues reappear regularly, most noticeably discussions about dress, and about married lesbians. The issue of dress generated strong feelings. In the June 1964 issue of *Arena Three* an editorial note remarks:

> A good many members who attended the first two MRG meetings have been somewhat piqued by the exhibitionist tendency of one or two others, and want to know if it is really absolutely *necessary* to turn up to these meetings dressed in what is popularly known as 'full drag'. As the majority of women homosexuals are not 'transvestites' we shall be glad if at further meetings there will be no further cause for wounded sensibilities.[24]

'Full drag' meant wearing men's clothes from head to toe, or in Langley's words, 'natty gent's suiting'. However, many lesbians thought that women who wore trousers, or shirts rather than blouses, were risking public exposure. Lesbians who wore just a couple of items of male clothing or masculine women's clothing received criticism, and were occasionally referred to as transvestites.

Those lesbians who dressed as lesbians had done for fifty years did not take this criticism lying down. One woman, who said that she habitually wore trousers and tie, wrote to *Arena Three* in response:

> I most vehemently object to this harsh criticism and find it extremely difficult to believe that my dress could have 'wounded' anybody; on the contrary I have been wounded by certain members of a Group, that was to be my hopes and dreams. Also I disagree that the majority of female homosexuals are not 'transvestites'. *At least fifty percent are or would like to be.*[25]

There is a clear anger here that lesbians were being criticized by other lesbians within an openly lesbian space. This woman's contention that 'at least fifty per cent' of lesbians wanted to wear 'male' clothes, even if they did not actually do so, is interesting. It may have been predicated on the belief that the lesbian community was, equally, divided into 'butches' and 'femmes'. Alternatively, it could be suggesting more generally that masculine dress was an important part of manifesting a lesbian identity.

While wearing men's clothes was a subject upon which lesbians disagreed, there was considerable lesbian agreement about when mannishness became problematic. In the summer of 1967 two *Man Alive* documentaries were broadcast which examined male and female homosexuality. The one on lesbianism included controversially, as far as the readership of *Arena Three* was concerned, an interview with a lesbian called Steve Rogers. Esmé Langley described Rogers as

> a youthful 'Colonel Barker' whose over-riding compulsion is to pass as a man, even to the point of 'courting' and getting engaged to another girl and using an artificial penis.

Rogers was, Langley believed, an inappropriate lesbian to feature because she was a 'rare and way-out case of transvestism (if not indeed of transexuality [sic])'.[26] Nobody spoke in support of Steve Rogers's lesbianism. It seems that by the 1960s lesbian identity did not allow denying or hiding the fact that one was woman, lesbian butchness not being equated simply with wanting to be a man.

Some lesbians could not understand the appeal of lesbian butchness either for the 'butch' lesbian or her potential lesbian audience:

> Nearly all the lesbians I have come across have been the exhibitionist full drag types, and I was beginning to wonder if intelligent honest lesbians really existed. Why some have to dress in this fashion is beyond me. A lesbian is a woman attracted to another woman, surely, so why this male impersonation?[27]

It is not irrelevant that this letter was from a 'Miss G.H., Kensington': 'butch' lesbians were publicly displaying a sexualized identity as lesbians, and this behaviour resonated in terms of intellectual ability and social class. Middle-class and professional women had a

> dread of the entrance of the so-called 'roughs' – full drag females with undertones of hidden violence and blackmailing instincts – [which] developed into a myth out of all proportion to reality.[28]

There was, and perhaps still is, a tacit assumption that butch or mannish lesbians were working-class women with nothing to lose, while lesbians who passed as straight were middle-class women who were not 'lesbian enough' to come out.

'Butch' working-class lesbians were blatantly sexual and dangerously stupid because they did not care what straight society thought of them. Straight-acting middle-class lesbians were 'decent people', i.e. not 'butch', not working-class and not dangerous. They could not afford to be recognized as lesbians, and did not wish to be seen as sharing a common identity with 'butch dykes'. 'Decent' lesbians wanted to distance themselves from 'women who only wish to satisfy their sexual desires'.[29] Respectability and class were intertwined. Rachel Pinney (1909–) describes her experience of being a middle-class lesbian doctor in the 1950s thus:

> When I set up in medical practice in Chelsea I tried to be respectable – that was in 1949 – I put on lipstick and I wore a skirt, for the first six months until I got established. One of the things I was terrified of, was that one of them [a lesbian from 'a non-U, sub-threshold gang'] would turn up in the waiting

room. So I put on respectability, for six months. And being respectable meant not fraternising with your lesbian friends.

I had a series of girlfriends, they were all either my secretary in the practice, or attached to the practice in some way or other. But no word would be spoken, and I denied it fiercely if anyone mentioned it. You've no idea how strong this thing was. Like if I'd committed murder, I wouldn't admit it, ever, to anybody.[30]

Butch lesbians were visible as lesbians, both to other lesbians and to the straight world, and much criticism of them seems to have been a result of other lesbians' anxiety about this visibility. Debates about the risks of lesbian visibility, but the need for lesbians to be recognizable to each other, were to continue. In 1968 there was, for instance, some discussion about adopting the seahorse, which was on the cover of *Arena Three* and in its PO Box address, as a lesbian badge. Seahorse jewellery (cuff links and badges) was acquired and advertised in *Arena Three* but some women remained nervous that this sign of lesbianism would not remain a lesbian secret; as one woman said, 'I wouldn't wish to tell the "World" that I was homosexual'.[31] This nervousness about being identified as a lesbian was understandable: known lesbians did catch public attention, and attract public anger.

While arguments about dress were heated, when it came down to numbers the readership of *Arena Three* was clearly for tolerance rather than a lesbian style police. An MRG questionnaire in 1964 showed that 61 per cent of lesbians questioned thought that lesbian 'drag' was OK compared to 36 per cent who did not: the legacy of Mary Allen and Radclyffe Hall had not been rebuffed.[32] The issue of class remained a hot one for the MRG and *Arena Three*. The 1964 questionnaire also showed, according to Langley, that the membership was socially broad. However, there was a middle-class slant; teaching and nursing were the predominant occupations.

Esmé Langley objected vehemently when the MRG was described by Brian Magee as a middle-class organization in an article in *The Statesman* in 1965.[33] It is an indication of how radical Langley's politics were that she saw a problem in the MRG being, or being perceived to be, a middle-class organization. Some working-class women wrote to *Arena Three* saying that they were being ignored:

nobody seems to want to know the ordinary working-class homosexual. As soon as I write to say I am employed as a car worker I have not heard from them again.[34]

Letters were subsequently published which contested this allegation. However, it seems that the MRG was to remain predominantly middle-class: in 1971, for instance, 40 per cent of the readership identified as 'professional' and significant further minorities as 'executive' and 'clerical'.[35]

Married lesbians were also the subject of a number of discussions in *Arena Three*.[36] This may have been because a large proportion of *Arena Three* readers had been involved in significant heterosexual relationships: 40 per cent of them were, or had been, married.[37] It was keenly debated whether it was worse to be a married lesbian or to be having a homosexual relationship with a married lesbian, and why lesbians stayed married to men if they were really lesbian. In pubs and clubs used by lesbians, married lesbians had a low level of visibility and this led to some lesbians asking if married lesbians really existed; if they did, where were they?

This brought some sharp responses:

> Where are they all? They are in mental hospitals: in neat little semis yelling at their children: sitting at desks writing poetry and novels: queuing in doctors' waiting rooms with imaginary ailments: visiting psychiatrists in search of a 'cure'; loving their children and crippling them with guilt: searching — via the bottle, the pills, the occasional friend, for peace: weeping in their living-rooms: striving to live an impossible role: shrivelling with every possible device their great capacity for love: fighting with their husbands: fighting with themselves: battling, within the normal framework of permissible housewifely friendships, against impossible desires: shocking intimates: all this in the name of decency.[38]

What acts or desires made women lesbians remained largely undiscussed. It was agreed that a lesbian was a woman who was attracted to women but the sexual nature of that attraction continued to be delicately and diplomatically put to one side. *Arena Three* had been published for two years before the word 'orgasm' or any of its synonyms appeared in the magazine.[39] It was presumably because of this sexual silence that H. Montgomery Hyde, who used *Arena Three* as a research resource, felt justified in stating that lesbians 'while they indulge plentifully in kisses and caresses are often apt to stop short of full physical expression'.[40] In 1968 as a response to a rather salacious letter from the husband of a lesbian, Langley said that *Arena Three* had never received demands for more sexually explicit material from their lesbian readers.[41]

That perennial favourite 'why are we homosexual?' was also the subject of debate. Two views were aired in *Arena Three*. One was that homosexuality was an innate or genetic imperfection. The second was that homosexuality was the result of environmental influences which turned children away from the natural heterosexual path. One became homosexual if one had suffered some trauma in childhood, such as poor quality parenting, divorce, or the death of a parent. Statements such as 'We have long known that divorce, or having only one parent alive, has been the childhood pattern of many homosexuals' were regularly made by lesbians in *Arena Three*.[42]

In January 1965, a middle-aged social worker recounted her coming-out story in *Arena Three*. She felt that a childhood bisexuality in conjunction with lack of heterosexual advice, presumably counting as poor parenting, had unfortunately resulted in her lesbianism:

> Had someone encouraged me to do some serious dieting in my early twenties, and introduced me to some suitable men, the bisexuality of my childhood would not have developed into homosexuality.

As the decade progressed, lesbians became less accepting of this commonplace belief that homosexuality was somebody's fault. In 1967 one woman wrote a long and angry letter about the 'bad mothering' school of lesbianism:

> My mother is the sweetest gentlest woman in the world, and I very deeply resent any suggestion that it might be her fault I am what I am, that she singled me out for some kind of 'special' mismanagement and not my sisters.

This produced notable agreement with other readers.[43]

That homosexuality was, or could be, a matter of choice is not suggested. Connections between being a lesbian and rejecting the traditional, and second-rate, female rôle were touched upon, but it was not suggested that lesbians chose to be lesbians in order to escape the limitations of conventional femininity. It was rather that future lesbians were particularly conscious of conventional femininity and perceived it as an unpleasant constraint. Lesbianism was antecedent to the rejection of the female rôle. There was a strong perception that even the most well-balanced lesbian leading a happy and profitable life was still fatally flawed by her homosexuality.

A second coming-out story was given by a nineteen-year-old painter torn between marrying a homosexual man for respectability or going to live with her female lover in London. The difficulty she feels in being a lesbian is that 'Even with all my love, I can't give her children, or the respect of other people, or the security that she deserves'.[44] It is not clear whether this woman felt that the unhappiness which lesbianism entailed was contingent on prevailing negative attitudes to lesbianism or an inevitable result of lesbianism. The biological inability of a woman to give another woman a child is currently certain; however, this does not necessarily imply that lesbianism is a less tenable way of life than heterosexuality.

The question of how good a life could be had if you were a lesbian received much more debate than the cause of homosexuality in *Arena Three*. There were several long-running discussions on whether homosexuals had the capacity to have good relationships just like heterosexuals. There is a strong belief that heterosexuals did have good relationships, and that they provided a model for married happiness that lesbians wanted to emulate.

The beliefs expressed within *Arena Three* and the MRG are not uniform. Some lesbians saw themselves as flawed heterosexuals who would inevitably long for an impossible lesbian 'heterosexuality'. Other lesbians believed that it was the pressure of being homosexual, in a society which denigrates and abuses homosexuals, which produced stresses which caused homosexuals to be less happy than heterosexuals. If the social stresses suffered by lesbians could be eased then lesbians would be able to lead lives that were as complete and as satisfying as those of heterosexuals. Often these two beliefs were confused, as they had been earlier in the work of Radclyffe Hall.

What is startling about this discussion in *Arena Three* is that at no point does anyone question the 'factual' basis of the debate that lesbians are less mature and less successful at relationships than heterosexuals. One letter from an American lesbian, who asked 'what's so great about monogamy?', was published. Apart from this there appears to have been little cynicism about the joys of heterosexuality or dissension from the belief that straight people have lovely lives. There was one small, and surprising, voice of calm from a 'M[ary] R[enault], Cape Town'.[45]

Mary Renault (1905–1983) was born in Britain and educated at St Hugh's College, Oxford. She trained as a nurse and published several mildly successful novels focusing on hospitals and lesbians in between the wars. These featured homoerotic liaisons, the most interesting being *The Friendly Young Ladies*. In her later books Mary Renault switched her attention to the ancient world. She wrote a series of highly successful novels set in a scrupulously researched antiquity and dealing in a forthright manner with male homoeroticism. In 1947, she had emigrated with her lover Julie Mullard to South Africa.

Mary Renault always had quite a tart approach to lesbian and gay anxiety:

> I thought it becoming in people whose only problem was a slight deviation of the sex urge – not necessarily an unmixed tribulation – to refrain from needless bellyaching and fuss.[46]

She did not greet the rise of a lesbian and gay rights movement in the 1970s with much more sympathy: 'Conventions change; but defensive stridency is not, on the whole, much more attractive than self-pity.'[47] Mary Renault was noticeable in the context of Arena Three for her bracingly unproblematic conception of lesbianism.

Arena Three was concerned with analysing, through many different genres, what being a lesbian was, and what it meant. Women wanted a framework in which to understand their lesbianism, to make sense of what they felt. Presumably it was for this reason, and for the accompanying commission, that the MRG became involved in selling Jess Stearn's The Grapevine in the autumn of 1965. Jess Stearn was a male American journalist, and The Grapevine: A Report on the Secret World of the Lesbian was a documentary-like examination of the real lives of American lesbians in the early 1960s. The book was important in that it told lesbians how other lesbians managed their lives, but its style and tone were that of complete incomprehension. The Lesbian is described as though she was a Martian, the near-obligatory capital 'L' of the period re-enforcing the gulf between normality and lesbianism.

Esmé Langley had seen one of the aims of the MRG as raising the public profile of lesbians, and she certainly succeeded. Between 1963 and 1965 alone, articles appeared in the Guardian, Spectator, Scotsman, Sunday Times Magazine, Daily Mail and News of the World. Langley was particularly pleased with the News of the World article, which appeared in December 1964 and included several photographs of her.[48] She said that it 'proved once again that in matters of genuine social importance this huge-circulation Sunday "family" newspaper is of serious and responsible outlook'.[49] This was followed within weeks by the television screening of a report about lesbians; Brian Magee had received extensive help and advice from the MRG for this item.[50] It was estimated that the edition of This Week which included Magee's report was seen by one-quarter of the adult population of England and Wales, approximately 11,000,000 people.[51]

In the first months of 1965, following this huge burst of publicity, the MRG received hundreds of letters from lesbians and enquiries from the media. Some letters also arrived from helpful men:

> Dear Madam,
> I was sorry to hear of the problems of your members, particularly as I feel that their main need is a man, therefore if you have any members residing in the North Staffs area I would be delighted to help them all I can if they would get in touch with me.[52]

Mad but polite responses such as this were the norm, and Langley reported that only one really offensive letter was received.

Much of the media coverage of lesbianism and the MRG focused on Esmé Langley. At a time when many lesbians used pseudonyms even in the privately circulated *Arena Three*, the extent to which Langley was prepared to be publicly identified as a lesbian was remarkable. Not since Radclyffe Hall had a woman willingly given her name and photograph to the press and declared that she was a lesbian. One result of the press attention was requests for Langley to talk about lesbians and lesbianism at various meetings. In 1965 she spoke to the Wimbledon Young Conservatives, and groups at Oxford University and Royal Holloway College. In 1966 she spoke to the Young Liberals of Putney and 'Surbiton Housewives' [*sic*].[53] Other lesbians in the hierarchy of the MRG and *Arena Three* were also open about their lesbianism, like Ceri (Olive) Ager, Julie Switsur and Cynthia Reid.[54] Reid's mother was interviewed by the press and on television as 'the mother of a lesbian' and Cynthia Reid gave a talk on 'The Changing Face of Lesbianism' to Mensa in Birmingham.

From the beginning of 1965 Ceri Ager, on behalf of the MRG, tried to set up a system of regional organizers to facilitate social activities and meetings for those who lived far from the legendary bars of London such as the Gateways.[55] Ironically but unsurprisingly, the organization of social activities was most successful in London where there was the highest incidence of lesbians and a pre-existing network of pubs used by lesbians. London MRG activity, known as the London Volunteer Committee, was organized by Cynthia Reid; by the summer of 1965 there were lesbian groups in London for outdoor sports, indoor games, musicians, classical records, and metaphysics, and there was a lesbian reading group.[56]

The success of the London Volunteer Committee in establishing itself as an a largely autonomous organization led to warfare within the MRG and on the pages of *Arena Three*. It appears that the London Volunteer Committee felt that Langley was autocratic and shamelessly intent on becoming the face of British lesbianism, representing herself as the bodily incarnation of *Arena Three* and the MRG to both lesbians and the straight press. Diana Chapman had left the MRG, *Arena Three*, Esmé Langley and the country in May 1965 and from this point Esmé Langley appears to have lost important support from lesbians.[57]

For the rest of the year the MRG and *Arena Three* and a significant number of lesbians were locked in a power struggle: Esmé Langley and her supporters versus Cynthia Reid, Julie Switsur, and their supporters. It was Langley who held the most powerful weapons, the membership and mailing lists for the MRG and *Arena Three*. At the MRG meeting in July 1965 at the Bull's Head, Reid and Switsur circulated a petition calling for the establishment of a committee to manage the finances and decide policy for the MRG and *Arena Three*. This petition was subsequently mailed to those MRG members and *Arena Three* subscribers who lived outside London.

This petition was clearly seen by Esmé Langley as a declaration of all-out war against her and she fought to keep control of the MRG and *Arena Three*. Langley used the forum of *Arena Three* to denigrate her opponents and to state her side of the story.[58] On one occasion she published a letter which referred to the London lesbians as 'a collection of morons, dyed blonde hard-faced "Tarts" and betrousered fat tough guys'; this misuse of editorial control backfired, and a number of members objected to such 'vicious attacks on our community'.[59] Langley successfully resisted the attempted coup but ultimately lost the battle; in the autumn of 1965, Reid and Switsur and their supporters left the MRG and founded KENRIC.

KENRIC, so named because many of the members lived in the boroughs of Kensington and Richmond, differed from the MRG and *Arena Three* in that its aim was solely to provide a social forum for lesbians. Since then it has always maintained a distance from lesbian and gay rights issues and political campaigning, and from feminist activism. Julie Switsur has made clear in subsequent interviews that she dislikes anything that makes 'homosexuals look like a disadvantaged group', and within this falls state support for homosexual organizations and other such initiatives.[60] KENRIC has certainly been seen as élitist by some lesbians. One woman described it as being, in the late 1970s, 'middle-class and full of frightened and closeted women'.[61]

KENRIC, however, was operating to an agenda of its own, providing social activities and contacts for a relatively middle-class lesbian constituency; it is hardly fair to charge KENRIC with a lack of radicalism when it never set out to be politically radical. KENRIC has now existed for thirty years so the women who founded it obviously knew their market: it is the longest-established lesbian organization in Britain. It does seem that it should have been possible for KENRIC and the MRG/Arena Three to co-exist peacefully: two lesbian organizations in London was hardly a glut. However, Esmé Langley was to bear a grudge against KENRIC and its founders, who were always referred to snidely in Arena Three, and for the rest of the decade the two organizations were to remain at loggerheads.

As the suggestion that a committee should be set up to manage the MRG's finances indicates, the MRG was perennially on the point of collapse through lack of money. The MRG only had an office for the first couple of years, and there was a high turnover among MRG volunteers.[62] The length of their commitment to the MRG appears to have directly related to their commitment to Esmé Langley; Langley makes enough arch comments in Arena Three for it to be possible to list her sexual partners. In a financial sense the MRG was Esmé Langley: the practical basis of the MRG and Arena Three was a personal bank loan from her. The most intractable problem faced by the MRG, and other groups subsequently, was that the women who came to it for counselling and support while coming to terms with their homosexuality used precious resources free of charge. Theoretically the cost of helping non-members was subsidized by members. However, once a member had established a network of friends, a lover and a lesbian identity, her financial support for the MRG would often lapse. In Arena Three there were constant requests for members to renew their subscriptions and not to share subscriptions with friends and partners.

In many ways the aims of the MRG had been achieved by the end of the 1960s. There were a number of well-established, if small, regional lesbian groups in Norfolk and Suffolk, the Midlands, Hampshire and Dorset which had been sired by the MRG and facilitated through the publicity of Arena Three. The Lancashire and Cheshire group was established in 1965 and it eventually developed into the Manchester-based 'New Group'. The New Group was the largest lesbian organization outside London although it still had only sixty members in 1968.[63] There was an MRG-backed SM group running in London from the mid-1960s; 'shy members', I eventually discovered.

The actual impact of the MRG and *Arena Three* on lesbians generally is hard to determine. By July 1965 it had over 600 members, with more people subscribing to *Arena Three*, but it never had more than 1000 members.[64] In 1968 Esmé Langley said that the average print-run of *Arena Three* was 350 to 500 copies per month to subscribers, with 100 copies being distributed in the form of one-offs and complimentary copies. It should be borne in mind, however, that a significant minority of subscribers were not lesbians, but gay men, social workers, psychiatrists and so on.[65] The circulation of *Arena Three* is hard to judge, but even if every copy was seen by ten women that means that no more than 12,000 lesbians in any month saw it.[66] Moreover, *Arena Three* was distributed internationally: there were subscribers in North and South America, throughout Europe, Africa and Australia. The British-based lesbian community linked by *Arena Three* probably consisted of less than 9000 women.

Certainly there were lesbians during the 1960s who had never seen *Arena Three*.[67] *Arena Three* was not racy, and for lesbians who had a lively social network and moved in the fledgling commercial scene, it may well have appeared worthy and slightly dull. The readership of *Arena Three* tended to see their lesbianism as a cause of anxiety; they worried that because they were lesbians they were perceived to be less decent and respectable than heterosexual women. They were in a difficult position with this, as the active sexuality which is linked to coming out as a lesbian is not really compatible with traditional ideas of female respectability.

Hip lesbians, who were not perturbed by the idea of being tainted women, derided the readership of *Arena Three* for the impossibility of this hope: it has to be said that respectability and decency on the one hand and lesbianism on the other remain profoundly contradictory. Among an earlier generation of lesbians, who perhaps avoided guilt through the cultural silence about lesbianism, it had been possible to be a lesbian pillar of the orthodox community without feeling at risk of exposure. By the 1960s the possibilities of going privately about one's private business but without shame, as Louisa Martindale and Lilian Barker had done, appear to have been reduced.

Younger lesbians, and those who enjoyed the romantic status of lesbian outlaws, were quick to point out that lesbianism cannot in the circumstances of our society be respectable, because the common bond that lesbians share is an unrespectable sexual desire for women. In 1966 Maureen Duffy argued that those lesbians who desired to be respectable were women who had not really realized the transgressiveness of their lesbianism:

> Not having fully come to terms with their own condition they still want to keep it in some way separate from themselves. 'Just because I'm like this it doesn't mean I have to mix with a lot of layabouts I've nothing in common with.'[68]

Duffy concluded that the MRG and *Arena Three* provided the illusion of a safe and separate space for these women, who could not accept the actual bonds of the lesbian community.

Some letters to *Arena Three* do seem to support this view:

> Please accept this donation of £1 which I hope may do a little in lessening your estimated 1967 deficit. As a rather unhappy and unwilling lesbian, I, personally, see no point in my subscribing to Arena 3 but would like to help a little in this way to support the work of those mature enough to face their difficulties.[69]

However, the membership of the MRG and *Arena Three* were by no means a homogenous group; they were among the best-known ways into the lesbian community in the 1960s and there was not much room to be picky. *Arena Three* and the MRG attracted lesbians, as I have tried to show, with a broad range of views and from a wide age range, although the vast majority of subscribers were under forty-five.[70] The younger membership do appear to have been more inquisitive about their homosexuality; the mean average age of lesbians recruited by Dr Kenyon for a research project in the mid-1960s was 36·38 years.[71]

In the late 1960s *Arena Three* began to receive notably more correspondence from much younger lesbians, sixteen- and seventeen-year-olds. These younger lesbians appear to be very enthusiastic about being lesbians; they were also unworried by giving their full names and addresses. Jane Marshall, for instance, infused by the spirit of 1968 wrote 'I could hardly believe my eyes when reading through the apologetic mush written in *Arena Three*. At 18 I am a lesbian and proud to feel different.'[72] She may not have liked it but she still read it. A 'Mrs R. F., Kent' wrote a reply to this which highlights the differences that existed between the lesbians who communicated via *Arena Three*:

> I would point out to Jane Marshall that we do not feel guilt about being lesbians; indeed, I would not change even if it was possible. I think when she is

older she will realise several things –

That her private life is of no interest to anyone else.

That people who feel really deeply are reticent about their private affairs.

That the happiest relationships can be destroyed by public ridicule, and

That exhibitionism is a sign of immaturity.

Surely there are other people whose feelings she has to consider besides her own.[73]

Certainly debates about coming out were regular and heated in the pages of Arena Three by the end of 1960s.[74]

To many heterosexuals the MRG and Arena Three appeared frighteningly radical. The contemporary non-lesbian point of view is perhaps best shown by H. Montgomery Hyde's description of Arena Three in The Other Love. Hyde was a member of the MRG so he was not speaking from a position of complete ignorance, and he was presumably sympathetic to the agenda of the MRG; homophobes do not usually pay to join pro-gay organizations. Hyde criticized Arena Three, saying that

[it has a] tendency to overemphasise the merits of being a lesbian in a crusading spirit, occasionally going so far as to indicate antipathy towards the opposite sex.[75]

The lesbian alternatives to the MRG and Arena Three were the lesbian-friendly clubs and pubs of London, the most famous of which was the Gateways. The Gateways, which was a straight but bohemian club in the 1930s, had 'acquired its present exclusive flavour during the war' as Maureen Duffy phrased it.[76] It was certainly frequented by lesbians right through the 1950s when it opened sociably early at three in the afternoon.[77] It was a members-only club with literally thousands of members, the membership fee in 1966 being only ten shillings (50p).

The Gateways consisted of one large room and a bar, and with space for only about two hundred people it was extremely busy. Men were allowed in, although only homosexual men ever turned up. At the weekends it was packed to the rafters with lesbians in frocks and front-fastening trousers, the 1960s equivalent to button-fly 501s, drinking and dancing. Latterly it was run by a lesbian couple, Gina and Smithy, who had speaking parts in the Gateways scene in the film version of The Killing of Sister George. Whether lesbians congregated there because it was run by lesbians, or whether Gina took a female lover as a result of running a lesbian bar is hard to establish.

There were a number of other options: the Robin Hood on Inverness Terrace was a popular lesbian pub and Cynthia Reid mentions that there was a coffee bar in Notting Hill where lesbians hung out about 1960.[78] Maureen Duffy also refers to a lesbian club in Westbourne Park but here, she says:

> The clientele is slightly different: there are more tourists and more of the extreme transvestites, many of them from the women's barracks. There are also one or two after hours drinking and coffee clubs in this district mostly patronised by prostitutes and their girl friends, who live on the fringes of the criminal world and are therefore more likely to be involved in fights and drug taking.[79]

Maureen Duffy (1933–) became a publicly known lesbian following the publication of her novel *The Microcosm*, concerning a group of lesbians and set largely in a lesbian club, in 1966. As her contemporary, Elizabeth Wilson, has said:

> It was in a way a breakthrough for Maureen Duffy even to have described the social world of lesbianism and not to have confined it to the level of a unique and very private experience.[80]

Maureen Duffy was one of the guests on a panel discussion about lesbianism screened on BBC 2 in the summer of 1967.[81]

An interesting legacy of 1960s lesbian organizations is the rôle they played in scientific research on lesbians and lesbianism; both KENRIC and the MRG provided subjects for such research.[82] This participation was not motivated by a selfless commitment to knowledge; lesbians wanted to know if there was anything special about lesbians. Lesbians were recruited via KENRIC and the MRG to assist the work of Mrs Hopkins, Charlotte Wolff, Eva Bene, and Dr F.E. Kenyon.[83] While these were among the first empirical studies of lesbians in Britain, none of them involved large enough groups of lesbians to *prove* anything. The researchers also operated with certain preconceptions about lesbians and lesbianism. That said, the published results are not without interest.

In two papers presented back-to-back in the *British Journal of Psychiatry*, Dr Kenyon gives his results from a comparison of 123 lesbians with a control group of 123 married heterosexual women. His results indicated that the lesbians were better educated than the heterosexual women, and tended to be more middle-class. His results also indicated that fewer lesbians were members of the Women's Institute (8.1 per cent) than heterosexual women (30.1 per cent). Kenyon also showed that of the women studied far more lesbians had served in the armed forces than had women in the control group: 26.8 per cent to 3.3 per cent. These are the most concrete results because they are most amenable to the methodology employed; it seems safe to assume that membership of the WI is a 'yes/no' question.

On the emotional and psychological issues Kenyon's results match psychological orthodoxy: he proved that lesbians came from unhappy families or broken homes, that their relationships with their mothers were significantly worse than normal, and often their mothers were mad. They also hated babies. Kenyon gives a number of possible explanations for lesbianism, such as: the parents wanted a boy, the parents treated their daughter like a boy, and the lesbian was sexually abused by a man. A simple and unproblematic attraction to women is omitted from this list. He concludes that

> the evidence from the present study points towards long-standing personality problems and neurotic manifestations which, no doubt, can be exacerbated by social and cultural factors.[84]

Kenyon's questions on sexual practice are interesting because there is still little information on the sexual experience of lesbians. His results showed that more than 90 per cent of the lesbian respondents had had full sexual contact with a female partner. This contrasts pleasingly with Montgomery Hyde's contention that lesbians did not do it very much. It also suggests that lesbianism was a highly sexualized identity even among the respectable and decent lesbians of the MRG and KENRIC. This is further underlined by Kenyon's finding that more than 10 per cent of the lesbians in the group had had more than 13 female sexual partners.

The most obvious flaw with Kenyon's work is his use of only married heterosexual women as a control group; a more appropriate control group would have included single heterosexual women too. Kenyon's work is also problematic because it takes women's statements as transparent reports of their feelings rather than culturally mediated responses. In the 1960s, for instance, it was unlikely that one would find many married women who would admit even to themselves that they did not like children; married women were expected to like children. Similarly, far more lesbians said that they masturbated than married women. Given that masturbation was a stigmatized sexual practice and, moreover, one that was even less acceptable in married women who had access to a penis, it is unsurprising that these women said that they did not do it.

Mrs June Hopkins's 'The Lesbian Personality' is rather more positive, although again, as it is based upon interviews with only forty-eight lesbians, not statistically significant. Mrs Hopkins's thesis was that there were no significant neurotic or abnormal personality characteristics that lesbians had as lesbians *per se*. She concludes, gratifyingly, that lesbians are more independent, Bohemian, self-sufficient, dominant, composed and resilient than heterosexual women.[85] The only difficulty with this is that it is hard to comprehend that there might be an accurate scientific test for 'Bohemian-ness'.

NOTES

1. *Arena Three*, **1**(1), January 1963, Editorial note, p.2.
2. Re Lee Langley: she claimed as her own a *Guardian* profile by Lee Langley of George Axelrood, 29 December 1965. She certainly was not George Axelrood. Re Bruce: see *Arena Three*, **2**(4), April 1965.
3. *Arena Three*, **2**(4), April 1965, in response to Bryan Magee's article in *The Statesman*, 26 March 1965.
4. Suzanne Neild and Rosalind Pearson, *Women Like Us* (London: The Women's Press, 1992), p.26.
5. *Ibid.*, p.100.
6. About 1963, held at the Hall Carpenter Archives.
7. *Arena Three*, **1**(12), December 1964.
8. *Arena Three*, **5**(1), January 1968.
9. Cynthia Reid, *Arena Three*, **1**(1), January 1964, and Godfrey [Diana Chapman], *Arena Three*, **2**(2), February 1965.
10. *Arena Three*, **1**(1, 2 and 3), January, February and March 1964, and *Arena Three*, **2**(1), January 1965.
11. For example, *Arena Three*, **3**(3), March 1966.
12. See, for instance, *Arena Three*, **1**(3 and 4), March and April 1964; **2**(3), March 1965; and **3**(4), April/May, 1966.
13. *Arena Three*, **2**(7), July 1965.
14. Subsequently re-issued as *Carol* by Patricia Highsmith.
15. *Arena Three*, **2**(2), February 1965.
16. *Arena Three*, **4**(12), December 1967.
17. Interestingly, Langley said that the anti-male attendance feeling increased with age.
18. *Arena Three*, **2**(6), June 1965, and **2**(5), May 1965.
19. *Arena Three*, **2**(6), June 1965, p.12.

20. For instance, Anthony Storr's view of lesbians as manifested in *Sexual Deviation* (1964) was rejected. *Arena Three*, **1**(5), May 1964.

21. Mary McIntosh, response in *Arena Three*, **1**(6), June 1964.

22. *Arena Three*, **1**(6), June 1964, p.12.

23. *Arena Three*, **2**(6), June 1965.

24. *Arena Three*, **1**(6), June 1964.

25. *Arena Three*, **1**(7), July 1964.

26. *Arena Three*, **4**(7), July 1967, re *Man Alive* programme on lesbians screened on BBC2, 14 June 1967.

27. *Arena Three*, **2**(1), January 1965.

28. As described in an article by The New Group in 1966. *Arena Three*, **5**(5), May 1968.

29. *Arena Three*, **2**(10), October 1965, p.15.

30. Neild and Pearson, *Women Like Us*, p.25.

31. *Arena Three*, **6**(5), May 1969.

32. *Arena Three*, **2**(2), February 1965.

33. *The Statesman*, 26 March 1965.

34. *Arena Three*, **6**(6), June, and (7), July 1969.

35. *Arena Three*, **8**(3), March 1971: total response was only 50 subscribers.

36. For example, *Arena Three*, **4**(1), January 1967.

37. *Arena Three*, **2**(6), June 1965, estimate by Esmé Langley. (This proportion was unchanged by 1971. *Arena Three*, **8**(3), March 1971: total response was only 50 subscribers.)

38. *Arena Three*, **4**(6), June 1967.

39. *Arena Three*, **3**(6), June 1966.

40. H. Montgomery Hyde, *The Other Love: A Historical and Contemporary Survey of Homosexuality in Britain* (London: Heinemann, 1970), p.282.

41. *Arena Three*, **5**(9), September 1968.

42. *Arena Three*, **3**(4), April/May 1965.

43. *Arena Three*, **4**(4), April 1967; *Arena Three*, **4**(6), June 1967.

44. *Arena Three*, **2**(1), January 1965.

45. *Arena Three*, **3**(3), March 1966, second letter published in **7**(6), July 1970.

46. Mary Renault, *The Friendly Young Ladies* (London: Virago, 1984), p.282.

47. *Ibid.*, p.283.

48. *News of the World*, 13 December 1964. Article was written by Ron Mount.

49. *Arena Three*, **2**(1), January 1965.

50. *This Week*, 7 January 1965.

51. TAM (Television Audience Measurement); *Arena Three*, **2**(1), January 1965.

52. *Arena Three*, **2**(1), January 1965.

53. *Arena Three*, **3**(3), March 1966.

54. Cynthia Reid, C456/033 and Julie Switsur, C456/032, Hall Carpenter Oral History Collection. Their mothers both joined KENRIC.

55. *Arena Three*, **2**(1), January 1965.

56. *Arena Three*, **2**(7), July 1965.

57. *Arena Three*, **2**(9), September 1965.
58. See 'Mailbag,' *Arena Three*, **2**(8), August 1965.
59. See *Arena Three*, **2**(9), September 1965, and subsequently *Arena Three*, **2**(10/11), October/November 1965.
60. Julie Switsur, C456/032, Hall Carpenter Oral History Collection.
61. Rene Sawyer, Hall Carpenter Oral History Collection, C456/068/01–03.
62. After 1966, *Arena Three* and the MRG did not have an office.
63. *Arena Three* **5**(5), May 1968.
64. *Arena Three* **2**(7), July 1965.
65. *Arena Three* **5**(1), January 1968.
66. *Arena Three* **8**(4), April 1971. A 'conservative estimate' of the readership is given as 1000, based on a print run of 1000 copies a month. The print run never exceeded this figure.
67. Rene Sawyer, Hall Carpenter Oral History Collection, C456/068/01–03.
68. Hunter Davies (ed.), *The New London Spy* (London: Anthony Blond, 1966), p.237.
69. *Arena Three* **4**(4), April 1967.
70. Eighty per cent of subscribers in 1971: *Arena Three* **8**(3). Total response was only 50 subscribers.
71. F. E. Kenyon, 'Studies in female homosexualities. v: Sexual development, attitudes and experiences', *British Journal of Psychiatry*, **114** (1968), 1337–50.
72. *Arena Three* **5**(7), July 1968.
73. *Arena Three* **4**(1 and 2), January and February 1967.
74. Montgomery Hyde, *The Other Love*, p.285.
75. Davies, *The New London Spy*, p.23.
76. *Arena Three*, **9**(2/3), February/March 1972.
77. Brighton Ourstory Project, *Daring Hearts: Lesbian and Gay Lives of 50s and 60s Brighton* (Brighton: QueenSpark Books, 1992), p.59, and Diana Chapman, Hall Carpenter Oral History Archive.
78. Brighton Ourstory Project, *Daring Hearts*, p.236.
79. Davies, *The New London Spy*, p.236.
80. Elizabeth Wilson, *Only Halfway to Paradise: Women in Postwar Britain 1945–1968* (London: Tavistock, 1980), p.158.
81. *Arena Three*, **4**(7), July 1967, pp.2–3, re panel discussion the same evening as the *Man Alive* programme, 14 June 1967.
82. For KENRIC's involvement see Julie Switsur, C456/032, Hall Carpenter Oral History Collection.
83. See, for instance, *Arena Three*, **4**(1), January 1967.
84. F. E. Kenyon, 'Studies in female homosexualities. iv: Social and psychological aspects', and 'v: Sexual development, attitudes and experience', *British Journal of Psychiatry*, **114** (1968), 1342.
85. June Hopkins, 'The lesbian personality', *British Journal of Psychiatry*, **115** (1969), 1433–6.

10 the politics of lesbianism

'I will sing with a clear voice to enchant you'
Sappho, Fragment 98

In 1968 the recommendations of the Wolfenden Report were finally taken up and sex, in private, between men over the age of twenty-one was decriminalized. The low-key tactics of the HLRS had apparently been effective. In the ten years between its establishment and 1968, the HLRS had been the major voice calling for changes in the law against homosexuality in Britain. Those involved with the HLRS were convinced that they knew what was best for Britain's homosexuals. This sometimes led to clashes with more radical individuals and organizations, as the clash between the HLRS and the Male and Female Homosexual Association of Britain in the late 1960s illustrates.

MANDFHAB, as it was rather clumsily acronymed, was set up by a young gay man and a lesbian, John Holland and Elizabeth Cooke, in Wolverhampton. Elizabeth Cooke had previously been a subscriber to *Arena Three*. Initially it was successful: by April 1968 it apparently had over 50 members.[1] Problems started, however, when the draft of a proposed constitution for MANDFHAB reached the HLRS. This set the minimum age for membership as sixteen, which outraged the HLRS, who subsequently produced a second draft of the constitution which it circulated to interested parties. This draft raised the minimum age for membership to twenty-one and debarred service personnel and married people.

As this indicates, MANDFHAB wanted more radical reform than the HLRS, and perhaps as a result their views received media coverage in Wolverhampton and eventually in the *News of the World*.[2] This prompted gay men allied to the HLRS to write letters to the press and to other possible sympathizers, attacking MANDFHAB, and stressing the HLRS belief in assimilation, a softly-softly approach, and acceptance of the limited gains which the Wolfenden Report offered. There was real anger expressed at the supposed naïvete of Holland and Cooke; this anger seems to have been rooted in the belief that no public discussion of homosexuality, let alone the formation of a new group, should occur without the express permission of HLRS.[3] MANDFHAB appears to have subsequently collapsed, and this can be, at least partially, attributed to the behaviour of the HLRS.

Although the HLRS may have been a powerful organization in the 1960s, it folded after the enactment of the Wolfenden Report, its work having been done. Its direct heir, CHE, the Committee for Homosexual Equality, established from the HLRS's North Western Committee in 1969, was to struggle for survival in the 1970s as it was increasingly seen as staid and timid. The difficulties which CHE and the old-style organizations faced in the 1970s were largely due to the eruption in London in the autumn of 1970 of the Gay Liberation Front.[4] The GLF had emerged as a semi-organized political force in New York following the Stonewall riots in 1969. It was a grass-roots movement which spontaneously organized itself to demonstrate, protest and organize parties.

The GLF offered a new way of life for lesbians and gay men. Like the second wave of feminism, which it paralleled, the GLF made the personal political; it protested against the silence forced on lesbians and gay men, and demanded respect for lesbians and gay men. The GLF encouraged lesbians and gay men to come out in all areas of their lives and literally stand up and be counted. The GLF organized the first lesbian and gay demonstrations in Britain, and the first public lesbian and gay dances. The direct action politics of the GLF were tremendously invigorating after years of politeness, quietness and good behaviour by lesbians and gay men.

While the GLF itself was to be short-lived (it had collapsed by the end of 1972), the idea of Gay Liberation that it articulated continues to live on, most obviously in the activities of OutRage!. The particular nature of the GLF was influenced by the radical politics which appeared throughout Europe and America in the late 1960s. The GLF was influenced by anti-imperialism, Marxism and anarchism and inevitably it drew its support largely from lesbians and gay men who were already politically radicalized.

The GLF was a largely *ad hoc* organization with no formal hierarchy or precise agenda. It quite quickly became factionalized on issues other than those of lesbian and gay liberation, most obviously hard-left politics. The GLF was concerned with showing the broad nature of homosexual oppression, self-oppression and oppression by society, and demonstrated publicly against this; it was less concerned with producing a detailed pragmatic agenda for change.

The GLF analysis that homosexuals were oppressed as a social group was not new; Radclyffe Hall had clearly seen it in 1928. Esmé Langley had actually suggested that in comparison with homosexuals, other oppressed groups, like Jews and blacks, had it relatively easy:

> no Jew or Negro is (a) reared from infancy, willy-nilly as if he was Gentile or White (b) obliged to conceal, even from his father or mother, the fundamental fact of his Jewishness or colour.[5]

It was not the GLF analysis that was liberating so much as the empowerment of mass action by lesbians and gay men that it provided. Never before had lesbians and gay men declared their sexuality with pride on the streets of Britain.

The emergence of the GLF was probably a more important intellectual force for gay men, given the pusillanimous approach of the gay male organizations, than it was for lesbians. There was already a relatively political lesbian voice in *Arena Three*, which had been published for six years by the time the GLF appeared. Discussions about coming out and lesbian pride had, as I have said, taken up increasing space in *Arena Three* from the late 1960s. Moreover, the early 1970s also marked the beginning of the 'second wave' of feminism, which offered lesbians, as women, an alternative set of ways of analysing their position in society and the meaning of lesbianism.

The 'second wave' of feminism is usually dated from the publication of Kate Millet's *Sexual Politics* in 1970, although it was foreshadowed by the publication of Betty Friedan's *The Feminine Mystique* in 1963. These books initiated an avalanche of books, articles and public meetings where it was shown that women had not gained equality with men through the granting of the suffrage; that women earned less, had lower status jobs, received less education than men, and still bore almost the entire burden of child-care and housework. Particular attention was also paid to the constriction of women's freedom by the demands of conventional femininity, and it was this that led to the protests at the Miss World competition and to the occasional public burning of bras.

The key to this new mass feminist movement was the realization that the public sphere of politics routinely and consistently ignored, belittled or personalized issues which affected significant numbers of women. For instance, in cases of rape, women were often criticized for inviting attack by wearing short skirts or by being drunk. Women, and even girls, were often presented as complicit in sexual assault against them. Generally, many deeply unpleasant things that women regularly experienced, like rape and domestic violence, were portrayed as unalterable facts of life and not as social or political problems which demanded attention.

The development of a new feminist consciousness in the 1970s was formed by women meeting together to discuss their experiences and analysing the invidious, as well as obvious, ways in which women were oppressed. Throughout Britain consciousness-raising groups were established where women worked to articulate female experience and develop an agenda for change. Like gay liberation, the women's liberation movement in the 1970s was grass-roots-led, anarchic, factional and largely unorganized.

The belief that the personal was political was prime. This meant that women's private and individual experience was significant and reflected broad political realities. It also meant that women's actions in the putatively private realms of the family, love, dress, and the home were politically important. Not wearing make-up, for instance, became a political act, a public manifestation of a view on the artificial nature of conventional femininity and on conventional notions of beauty. As the issues with which feminists were concerned were not up for debate within traditional political circles, the politicization of the 'private' sphere was the main forum for feminist politics.

Lesbians were attracted to the feminist movement in the 1970s just as they had been attracted to suffrage campaigning seventy years before. Again for lesbians, equal wages and equal access to education were of particular importance since lesbians could not rely on being supported by a male partner. The feminist attack on conventional notions of femininity also presumably attracted lesbians, who felt constricted by the beautiful, passive, domestic and heterosexual image of women which was still held up as the model of good womanhood.

For lesbians, then, the 1970s offered considerable opportunities. Lesbians could work with gay men in the GLF; they could work with straight feminists in the women's liberation movement; or they could create a lesbian political agenda via *Arena Three*, and later *Sappho*. Many lesbians, of course, did not engage in the new politics and continued with their lives. This was not necessarily because they were self-oppressed, but because they personally felt no need: they were busy and happy with the lives that they had built.

In 1970 *Arena Three* was in the process of a radical overhaul; membership and income had become moribund and urgent action was obviously required.[6] A Press Freedom Group was established to urge newspapers to take advertisements for *Arena Three*. This was to be immensely successful. The Press Freedom Group transformed *Arena Three* by introducing new and vigorous women into its hierarchy, most notably Jackie Forster, Elsa Beckett and Barbara Todd. *Arena Three* submitted a complaint to the Press Council: that they were discriminated against by newspapers which would feature them in scandalous articles but not take their advertisements.

The complaint was rejected in the spring of 1971 but it produced considerable publicity for *Arena Three* and showed that *Arena Three* was prepared to go public with its belief that lesbianism was not merely not criminal but actually legitimate. The only slightly bizarre note amid the radicalism was Jackie Forster's continued use of the title 'Mrs'.[7] By the spring of 1971 *Arena Three* had achieved a goal unimaginable two years earlier; it had limited distribution to the general public through high street newsagents. It cost 30 pence.

The 1970 winter issue of *Arena Three* had marked the start of a cultural revolution. Glossier, though still not glossy, it featured an Edna O'Brien lesbian-erotic story entitled 'Mouth of the Cave'. It also included a sketch of a woman with bare breasts, the first breasts to feature in *Arena Three*.[8] Snapshots of female nudes were to subsequently make regular appearances as 'illustrations'. Generally those women who produced *Arena Three*, if not the readership at large, were pro-GLF. The Stonewall riots and American Gay Lib received coverage in 1969, and there were subsequently articles on the GLF in Britain.[9]

However, Esmé Langley in particular was quick to articulate what was to become a familiar lesbian anxiety about the power dynamics in lesbian and gay organizations:

> GAY LIB – WOMEN'S LIB – YOUNG LIB – ANTI-APARTHEID . . . all the talk and most of the doing in Britain today is of liberation and freedom from age-old oppressions. And where do we stand on all this?
>
> Let's always remember that we are women first, homosexuals second. *ARENA THREE* has always stood up to be counted in the battle for equal status with men – and this whether the men are hetero, homo or bisexual. And if it comes to a straight choice between Women's Lib and Gay Lib, let's all take serious note of the Gay Lib scene in the USA. Not long ago, Del Martin, prominent in the US homophile movement for 15 years, felt obliged to resign from what has become merely a 'male-dominated' movement, in which men, outnumbering women by 10 to 1, have been treating lesbians as strictly second-class homosexuals since 1953. In 1966 at the second NACHO Conference, Shirley Willer (like Del Martin, a pillar of DOB) blasted off: 'If

you guys would stay out of the damned toilets and have your sex at home, the homophile movement might find time to discuss some of the more important problems facing us.'

Can this happen here in Britain, too? Signs are that the answer is an unmistakable YES. So, to all our Gay Lib sisters, we say again: 'We are women first, just as men are men first, even when they're got up in drag, even when we're got up in gents natty suiting. Fight for the rights of gay boys if you like – but don't forget to fight for ours, too.[10]

The politics of the GLF, and the experience of women within it, were complicated. Although the GLF was, no doubt, well-intentioned in relation to the experiences and desires of women and lesbians, in practice the GLF was home largely to white middle-class men with left-wing politics.[11] Left politics have notoriously been insensitive to women's experiences and prone to sexism. The make-up of the GLF meant that the concerns and experiences of lesbians were often ignored. The development of radical drag was a case in point. Walking down the street in hairy legs and a frock might be fun, and an effective way for a man to demonstrate political and social daring, but it did not seem to either acknowledge or advance the position of women in a sexist society.

Jeffrey Weeks, who was an active participant in the London GLF, admits that from the beginning women had a difficult time in the GLF:

Many women felt that the atmosphere of meetings was overwhelmingly male. Men who were accustomed to dominating meetings had little sympathy for the problems of women unused to public speaking, and many women felt that sexist attitudes were as prevalent among men in the gay movement as outside.[12]

It was not just lesbians within the GLF who found their position difficult; lesbians who were not involved in the new politics found some of the GLF actions bizarre. One of the GLF's revolutionary acts was a 'zap' at the Gateways in February 1971 by a group of both men and women. The leaflet they handed out stated:

The Gateways has made thousands of pounds out of women who come to the club (precisely how much money and publicity was gained from The Killing of Sister George?) . . . We are not sick and don't like people who condescendingly treat us as such – especially when they are making a living off us.[13]

This produced some surprise in the lesbian community; was the Gateways, a lesbian club run by lesbians, really the most pressing item on the liberation agenda?

In early 1972 the lesbians within the London GLF decided to leave the organization both because of the sexism they had experienced and because they believed that its political agenda was unduly narrow, and limited in aspiration. When the women in the GLF quit they found that the options that had appeared to be open to lesbians wanting to organize politically were more illusory than real. Initially feminist groups were not particularly supportive of lesbians or lesbianism. In the spring of 1971 the aims and objects of one group, the Women's Liberation Front, were published in *Arena Three*. This was an 'effort to set the record straight' by the WLF who were 'fed up with the man-hating, bra-slinging image that has nothing to do with Front'. No mention is made of lesbians or the liberation of female sexuality in the aims and objectives of the WLF.[14]

In Betty Friedan's memorable phrase lesbians were the 'lavender menace'; a dangerous fifth column who might destroy the political integrity of heterosexual feminists. As had happened before, feminist women wanted the support and energy of lesbians but only if they acted 'straight'. Many feminists were complicit in this, like Vera Brittain, a feminist of long-standing and a woman with a large number of lesbian friends. In 1968, she had published, rather surprisingly, a study of the 1928 trial of *The Well of Loneliness*, where she suggested that lesbianism was a result of glandular abnormality, or rape, or fear of pregnancy, and that illegitimate children were more likely to be homosexual.[15]

This time lesbians refused to toe the line and forced the women's movement, through some bloody battles, to publicly acknowledge and support the rights of lesbians. Lesbians from the GLF managed to get the issue of sexuality raised at the Women's Liberation Conference in Skegness in October 1971, and from then on it was, at least in theory, included in the demands of the women's liberation movement.[16] Some feminists, however, continued to be noticeably unsupportive of lesbians.

Although not a completely positive space the women's liberation movement was important for lesbians, and a significant number of lesbians came out via the women's movement:

> For both of us . . . [Sue Cartledge and Joanna Ryan], the women's liberation movement has been decisive in creating a shift to lesbian relationships after a substantial personal history of heterosexuality.[17]

The women's movement provided women-only events and parties which must have facilitated intimacy between women and it did provide some theoretical space in which lesbianism was viewed positively. Some branches of feminist thought in the 1970s did begin to link feminism explicitly with lesbianism, suggesting that lesbian sexual experience was politically sound. Even quite conservative feminism was committed to the idea that women were wonderful and this would seem to provide a positive culture for lesbian relationships to flourish.

Other lesbians remained sceptical about the linking of lesbianism to a broader feminist agenda. Lesbianism was for them a, sometimes difficult, way of life – a self-identity not a radical political strategy. *Arena Three*, which tried to hold the middle ground between the GLF and feminism, received a number of letters on the following lines: 'I am heartily against the GLF's slogan 'Gay Is Good'. It isn't, neither is it bad. It just IS.'[18]

In 1971 *Arena Three* folded: Esmé Langley appears to have felt that she was being squeezed out of her magazine and she went abroad, taking with her *Arena Three*'s financial assets. However, the new recruits to *Arena Three* quickly regrouped and, led by Jackie Forster, they established *Sappho* in 1972, a magazine with social activities. *Sappho* was explicitly feminist and political; point two of its five-point strategy was: 'To support all minority groups regardless of politics, colour or creed, who work to counteract oppression'.

Sappho was extremely active on behalf of lesbians. It helped to establish the London Lesbian and Gay Switchboard in 1974, donating £100, and helped to set up support groups for lesbian teachers, lesbian mothers and lesbian social workers among others. *Sappho* organized insemination by donor for lesbians, and their first baby was born in 1973. It also acted as a legal referral centre for servicewomen accused of lesbianism, and thus facing the loss of their jobs, providing them with names of sympathetic solicitors. Lesbians from *Sappho* were involved as well in lobbying for sexual orientation to be included in a Sex Discrimination Act.

Both the Albany Trust and CHE continued to operate, and did attract some lesbian support. In 1971 CHE changed its name from the Committee for Homosexual Equality to the Campaign for Homosexual Equality, and began to work more closely with members of the GLF.[19] The Albany Trust continued to operate during the 1970s although it seems to have been relatively unaffected by the new politics of gay liberation and feminism. It continued, for instance, to refuse to give the names of lesbian-friendly pubs to lesbian enquirers apparently because they were not 'suitable' places for lesbians to go to. Many of the records of CHE and the Albany

Trust for this period are closed in order to protect the privacy of the members, so it is impossible to tell precisely how many lesbians were involved with these organizations.

However, there are some letters in open files which are illuminating, such as a letter received in 1971 from a Miss Milburn of Northampton. This letter cancelled Miss Milburn's subscription to the Albany Trust, because at the age of eighty she felt she should try to wind down some of her commitments.[20] It seems likely that Albany Trust and CHE, like the GLF, were mainly made up of men. Jeffrey Weeks notes that at the CHE annual conference in 1976 only 50 of the 700 participants were women.

By 1972 homosexual organizations in Britain were numerous enough for a National Federation of Homophile Organisations to be established. KENRIC would not join the NFHO, purportedly because it was too political.[21] KENRIC in this period still required a married woman to produce an approval form signed by her husband if she wanted to join. Women were usually only accepted as members if they were over twenty-one; women aged between eighteen and twenty-one had to have the written approval of a doctor, parent or guardian.

In 1972 the commercial gay media was born with the establishment of *Gay News* by activists from CHE and the GLF. *Gay News* was published every fortnight until 1983. This had noticeable lesbian support, from lesbians such as Alison Hennegan. *Spare Rib*, the feminist magazine, was founded in the same year and it too covered lesbian issues. Feminist journalists, like Jill Tweedie, were also gaining space in mainstream newspapers and this increased the discussion, not always positively, of lesbianism.

Gay News shot into the mainstream when it was prosecuted for blasphemy for publishing the homoerotic poem featuring Jesus, 'Love That Dares to Speak Its Name'. The trial which took place in the summer of 1977 received considerable press coverage, partly because of the calibre of support that *Gay News* received; John Mortimer led the defence, and Margaret Drabble spoke for it.

By 1976 there were lesbian and gay groups within the Liberal party, the Tory party, the Labour party and the Communist party. When Maureen Colquhoun was outed in 1976 (she was having a relationship with Barbara Todd from *Sappho*), Britain had its first out MP. In the 1970s then, lesbians and gay men came roaring out of the closet, not just in terms of lesbian and gay organizations and the women's movement, but in mainstream public spaces. There were television programmes such as ATV's documentary *The Important Thing Is Love*, shown in 1971 and the BBC's *Play for Today* by Watson Gould, *The Other Woman*, shown in 1976.

The 1980s was a decade of lesbian and gay expansion based on these foundations. In London the lesbian and gay community received considerable financial help in creating a infrastructure of businesses and community resources from the Greater London Council (GLC) until its abolition in 1986. The growth of gay and lesbian cultural institutions and support systems in Britain has been phenomenal. From the desert of 1963 a wealth of infrastructure has emerged: lesbian and gay newspapers, book shops, publishers, cafés, travel agents, solicitors, carpenters, hotels, therapists, theatre companies – the list could go on.

Lesbians and gay men have also won apparently secure places within mainstream establishments, with events like London Lesbian and Gay Film Festival at the National Film Theatre. The gradual adoption of equal opportunities policies which include sexual orientation have also helped lesbians and gay men feel more secure in the workplace. This success in improving the quality of life for lesbians and gay men has undoubtedly encouraged them to come out. The number of lesbians and gay men marching at Lesbian and Gay Pride was in 1994 close to 100,000.

Alongside this physical expansion of lesbian and gay opportunities, there have been changes in how lesbians feel about their lesbianism and how they conceive it. An influential development for lesbians was the emergence of lesbian-feminist politics in the mid-1980s. Although lesbian-feminism is a school of thought rather than a political organ-ization, it has had some relatively well-known British advocates, like Sheila Jeffreys, the Lesbian History Group, Annabel Faraday and Celia Kitzinger. Lesbian-feminism has been an important catalyst in the development of lesbian politics.

Lesbian-feminism was formed from a feminist world view which placed lesbians as the army in the war against the oppression of women by men. It is a product of the historically specific period of its birth when both gay liberation and feminism were popular and accessible political movements. The first major public appearance of lesbian-feminism was in the book *Love Your Enemy?* produced by the Leeds Revolutionary Feminists in 1981. Lesbian-feminism argued that we live in a world where men hold power over women. This power is culturally, economically, sexually, politically and legally main-tained by violence against women. This violence can take the form of rape, domestic violence, the refusal to educate women, legal discrimination against women, and an infinite number of other forms. Lesbian-feminism saw men and women as fundamentally opposed groups of people.

The importance of lesbianism in this theory was that it was a bond between women which excluded men, and a bond which usurped heterosexuality. Lesbianism was a place of refuge from male violence, and a place where women could work to destroy male violence permanently. From this political perspective lesbians were women who did not support patriarchy and who were actively engaged in fighting to make the world a better place for women.

While the number of lesbian-feminists in Britain was never more than 10,000, and the number of lesbian separatists far fewer, their influence on what it meant to be a lesbian was profound. The media seized upon 'loony' lesbian stories as a way to attack not only all lesbians but all feminists. The stigmatization of lesbian-feminists as fat, ugly, women in dungarees was used to attack lesbians and feminists regardless of what they actually thought about lesbian-feminism. This meant that lesbianism quite generally came to be seen as a politicized identity, and many lesbians who had not seen their lesbianism as political had to accept that other people now did.

In one sense it is obviously true that lesbianism is feminist. If to be feminist is not to depend upon men, to believe women are important and not to be held back from developing all your potential by the weight of social beliefs about what is suitable for women, then most lesbians probably are feminists. However, lesbian-feminism involved much more than this; it involved believing that all men, including gay men, were actively engaged in the oppression of women, that masculinity and femininity as we know them both evolved in order to oppress women and, perhaps most problematically, that lesbianism is a feminist political strategy.

In lesbian-feminism, to be a lesbian was not necessarily to be a woman who desires women or who has sex with women. Desiring women or having sex with women does not, *per se*, undermine male hegemony. For lesbian-feminism, male power will be undercut and men will be forced to change when women withdraw all support, social, economic, sexual and political, from men. It is the total withdrawal from intercourse with men that lesbian-feminism described as lesbianism; lesbianism was 'resistance to male power'.[22] Lesbianism, then, originates not out of a foundational desire for women, but out of a power struggle with men.

Withdrawing from men is not a new feminist strategy. Many of the suffragettes publicly withdrew from relationships with men in order to make men change their behaviour. Many lesbians have also thought that the institution of heterosexuality and its potential for abuse of power unpleasant, as Kathlyn Oliver did. It was, however, new for lesbians to justify lesbianism in these terms. Lesbian-feminism, influenced by Adrienne Rich's essay *Compulsory Heterosexuality and the Lesbian Continuum*, did not require sexual desire for women to be an element in lesbian identity.

The importance of lesbian-feminism for lesbian identity, however, was based neither on its originality nor its verisimilitude, but on the debates it sparked off in Britain, and America, during the 1980s. Debates, discussion and indeed fights, about what lesbianism meant, what feminism meant to lesbians and who counted as lesbians, have subsequently been an influential public aspect of lesbianism. The lesbian and feminist media were enthralled as different groups of lesbians fought over such diverse issues as the politics of the London Lesbian Archive, the right of homosexual sado-masochists to use the London Lesbian and Gay Centre, and the morality of pornography.

These debates within the lesbian community have made lesbianism a profoundly political identity. Gay men have not sized each other up by running through a list of loaded questions: do you wear make-up, skirts or a dildo? How women perceive their lesbianism is an inalienable part of lesbian identity, and the 1980s lesbian sex wars were a more public version of debates that have recurred throughout this century. The different ways in which lesbians have created identities, and the debates they had about lesbian identity, are the very essence of the history of lesbianism.

A major battleground, as I have already examined, has been lesbian dress. From the turn of the century, if not earlier, lesbians have marked their identity by turning to masculine dress. We are not just talking here about Mary Allen, Radclyffe Hall and Valentine Ackland. A photo of Edy Craig, Chris St John and Tony Atwood taken in their old age, in 1943, shows Edy looking like a nice granny, and Chris and Tony looking like dapper old dykes.[23] A professional publicity shot of Lilian Barker shows her wearing little round glasses with an iron-grey Eton crop.[24] A photograph of Vera Holme, found among her private papers and taken in about 1960, shows her sitting in a chair wearing full male dinner dress.

Equally a significant but less obvious number of lesbians dressed unremarkably and even girlishly, just like any other women of their period, profession and class, as Clemence Dane did.[25] Some women, like Vita Sackville-West, did not wear lesbian clothes in public, but wore them regularly in private. It is impossible to know now precisely why these women did not feel that they wanted to look recognizably like lesbians. Perhaps Dane, as a feminist, did see women assuming the accoutrements of masculinity as problematic, or perhaps she did not want to advertise her lesbianism to the straight world or to other lesbians. Perhaps she had a femme identity and butch lovers.

Mannish lesbians, I have argued, wore men's clothes in order to show that they were laying claim to that which was kept for men: sexual desire and women. Mannishness also marked the erotic space that they occupied as lesbians. This has always been contentious within the lesbian community. Some lesbians have not wanted to stress the difference of lesbians from other people, as shown in *Arena Three*. Some lesbians have believed that we should seek to eliminate gender altogether, and hence presumably the 'butchness' of butch dykes; this seems to have been the agenda manifested in *Urania*. Others have believed that it is a small step from dressing in men's clothes to becoming more profoundly like a man, and, as lesbian-feminists have argued, thus reproducing the male oppression of women.

These responses to mannish lesbians actually reveal as much about the lesbian identities of the respondents as they do about why lesbians dressed mannishly. Mannish lesbians may have had a myriad different reasons for choosing to dress as they did. Perhaps one of the most important was that by dressing as a lesbian, whatever that consisted of in a particular period, one was identifiable to other lesbians. In recent years sex, exactly what lesbians do in bed, has been debated in similar kinds of ways as dress had previously been within the lesbian community.

The debate about pornography was representative of much of the rest of the lesbian sex wars of the 1980s. Lesbian-feminists had a strong position on pornography; they believed that pornography was inalienably tied to the maintenance of male power. Sheila Jeffreys, said for instance:

> Pornography gave the lie to any idea that women were gradually achieving equality. Pornography made it clear that what constituted sex under male supremacy was precisely the eroticised subordination of women. Inequality was sexy and the sexiness of this equality was the grease that oiled the machinery of male supremacy. The sexiness of inequality, it became clear, was the unacknowledged motor force of male supremacy. Through sexual fantasy men were able to reinforce the sense of their power and of women's inferiority daily and be rewarded for every thought and image of women subordinated with sexual pleasure; a pleasure acknowledged to be the most valuable form of pleasure in male-supremacist culture.[26]

Pornography, according to this analysis, is an instruction manual from which men learn to terrorize women and a cultural artefact that also teaches women to love their own degradation: 'Women raped and tortured in pornography claimed to love and seek their abuse. Incest was shown as harmless and good fun for all the family.'[27] For lesbian-feminism one answer to the problem of pornography was to ban it.

Other lesbians, some of whom identified as feminist and some not, have argued that pornography, the explicit depiction of sexual acts and sexualized bodies, need not necessarily oppress women. To concentrate just on the case of lesbian pornography made by consenting lesbians for lesbians, lesbians have argued that this is lesbian-positive and not oppressive. Historically the best known depictions of lesbian sexuality were created by men for titillatory purposes. Lesbian sex appeared to be for men, not for lesbians. With lesbian-positive pornography lesbians got their sex back.

In Britain the publication of Sheba's *Serious Pleasure* in 1989 was a landmark; it was the first generally available sexually explicit book written for lesbians by lesbians. The success of *Serious Pleasure* was probably due as much to the fact that it actually gave lesbians a context in which to place their own sexual experience, as to unsatisfied demand for lesbian-positive pornography. It is interesting to wonder what earlier lesbians would have made of lesbian-positive pornography. Mary Allen would probably have written to *The Times* condemning it; Radclyffe Hall on the other hand would probably have written the introduction.

For lesbian-feminists, lesbian-positive pornography like *Quim*, *Serious Pleasure* and Pat Califia's writings were just as pernicious and as damaging to women as snuff-movies. Jeffreys has argued that 'The selling of the idea of pornography to women in the 1980s is a more sophisticated and effective way of bolstering male power.'[28] In terms of the lesbian-feminist analysis, it was impossible to make pornography which did not damage women. On the issue of pornography, lesbian-feminists have found common cause with a number of organizations which were also supported by the political and religious right, such as the Campaign Against Pornography (CAP).

This kind of alliance angered many feminists and lesbians. When, in the late 1980s, CAP seemed to be on the brink of actually succeeding in banning all shops except sex-shops from selling pornography, a counter-group with significant lesbian involvement, Feminists Against Censorship (FAC), was formed. FAC, and the lesbians involved with it such as Elizabeth Wilson, offered two main arguments against the lesbian-feminist position on pornography. One was a pragmatic point that it could not be in the interests of lesbians to seek to ban explicit depictions of sex, for such a measure could very easily be turned against lesbians and gay men. It could be argued that all public representations of homosexuality were an 'explicit' depiction of sex; homosexuality could be perceived as nothing but the display of perverse sexual desire.

The more theoretical point was that for women, including lesbians, sex itself and the discussion of what it meant and felt like have been culturally disallowed. Women have often been alienated from their own sexual desire and from sex and for this to change there needed to be a safe space for women to talk about what they do want sexually. If one of the things that women find that they want is pornography and they feel happy with this desire how then can this pornography be said to oppress them? As Bea Campbell has said 'it would seem that an essential component of feminist sexual politics should be a feminist erotica'.[29]

The lesbian-feminist reaction to FAC was to argue that the 'prosex' lesbians have just bought into their own oppression. In short lesbian-feminism did not accept that women can have a desire for rough sex, penetration or 'butch' dykes which is genuinely their own. All such desires, lesbian-feminism believed, were misogynistic desires imported from male hegemony. It is a major theoretical flaw in lesbian-feminism that no evidence can serve to disprove it. Lesbians who disagree with lesbian-feminism are not credited with rationality but with having internalized the false consciousness perpetuated by the structures of male power.

Lesbians talking about what lesbians do in bed and what lesbians feel about sex has produced a whole new area of discussion about lesbian identity. Lesbian sex, from 'vanilla' to sexual rôle-playing, dildos, sex toys, and sado-masochism, has been brought out into the open. The major difficulty with debates about lesbian sexual practices, as with dress, is that it is so emotionally loaded for the lesbians involved that they are hardly rational debates at all. If you are a lesbian the kind of sex that you like with women, and the sex you do not like, is fundamental to your identity as a lesbian. If being a lesbian *like this* is a core part of your self-identity, it is unlikely that you are going to be sympathetic to another lesbian who suggests that you are being a bad lesbian, or that you are doing it wrong.

It seems that much of what has passed as debate in the lesbian community is more like the marking of different territories within it. The medium of politics has allowed lesbians to really show what they are, what they do and how they feel: 'I am a lesbian, I do this, and it's OK'. What has clearly been demonstrated is that lesbians are socially, culturally, geographically, politically, and erotically diverse. If the basis of lesbianism is an erotic desire for women, this need not be manifested in exactly the same way; we do not all need to do it in the same position or wearing the same clothes.

By the 1990s lesbian-feminists appeared to have largely lost their position as the best known representatives of lesbianism. The lesbian commercial scene and how lesbians present themselves has become much more overtly sexualized in the last few years. The public image of lesbianism has become more glamorized and sexy and less political. This is probably partly in reaction to the consuming lesbian politics of the last 20 years. Perhaps for the moment we have marked our different lesbian identities well enough. Lesbian politics have largely occurred within the lesbian and feminist communities; lesbians appear to have left the main stage to gay men.

The issues which lesbian and gay political organizations have campaigned on since 1968, including work within Stonewall and OutRage!, have been overwhelmingly gay male issues, principally the age of consent for gay men. Of course, in some circumstances, the interests of lesbians are clearly conterminous with those of gay men, or straight women. The community of lesbians and gay men unites most effectively when it is the community as a whole which is under attack, as during the campaign against Clause 28 of the Local Government Act. The legislation proposed, and passed here, did not differentiate between lesbians and gay men. On issues of rape and sexual assault, and other 'women's issues' lesbians have greater community with straight women.

In some areas gay men and their beliefs and identities have become increasingly instituted as the norm, and lesbians are fitted in to a gay male agenda. Lesbian and Gay Studies in universities is increasingly dominated by 'queer theory', which has little connection with lesbian experience and ignores the importance of the fact that lesbians are *women*. This is a point that Sheila Jeffreys has noted with some acuity in *Lesbian Heresy*. In Britain the reclaiming of the word 'queer' appears to have been linked to the post-feminist reclamation of male sexuality by gay men.

There are few lesbians and fewer feminists working with 'queer theory'. It is overwhelmingly the preserve of gay men, and some straight women. 'Queer theory' as direct action politics seems, like gay liberation, to focus on the desires of gay men and to have little analytical force behind it. No one seems to know what it means. Terry Castle believes that the move away from 'lesbian and gay' to 'queer' is generally disturbing:

> The term *queer* has lately become popular in activist and progressive academic circles in part, it seems to me, precisely because it makes it easy to enfold female homosexuality back 'into' male homosexuality and disembody the lesbian once again.[30]

Lesbian lives today have more potential for happiness and success, however measured, than ever before. This does not mean, however, that we can afford to lose our politics or ignore the fact that there are serious threats to lesbian communities. The issue of reproductive rights is one of the most pressing concerns affecting lesbians, and an issue on which lesbians can expect to find little help from gay men or straight women.

Class, race, religion, geography, politics and sexual practices segment the lesbian community, yet these differences do not negate the existence of a lesbian community itself. The lesbian community is united by a common erotic desire, however expressed, for women. Debates about the very nature of our politics and identities as lesbian unite us just as they may appear to divide us. I have tried to show in this book that diversity and difference among lesbians in how they think of their lives and what they do with their lives is not new.

Lesbians have fought in wars and fought against war, and they have tended the casualties of war as the lives of Toupie Lowther, Esther Roper, Louisa Martindale and their comrades show. Lesbians have fought the police and been arrested, from the suffragettes to Pat Arrowsmith. Yet with Mary Allen and Isobel Goldingham they were also among the first policewomen. Lesbians have worked for the state in the civil service, the education system and the armed forces, and their sisters have worked to destroy the British Establishment. Some women have moved through a spectrum of political and politicized positions over the course of their lives.

Mary Allen went from being an enemy of the state as a suffragette, to servant of the state as a policewoman, back to enemy of the state as a fascist sympathizer. Allen's lesbianism determined some of her politics, but not all of them; she had political beliefs which came from outside her feminism and lesbianism. For most women, even Radclyffe Hall, their lesbianism was not the sum of their lives, but a significant part of their identity, and a significant influence on their politics and interests. The politics of lesbians affect the politicization of lesbianism, and both are interwoven in lesbian history and lives.

Lesbians have thought themselves beyond gender, they have thought themselves men in women's bodies, and they have thought themselves made by God. Lesbians have struggled to find public and private identities which make sense of their sexual desire for women. Sex with women was an important part of their lesbianism but not the totality of their lesbianism: Hilda Matheson said, as did, no doubt, other lesbians: 'I don't think I agree that the physical side is the *only* magic part of love – I don't feel it is with us'.[31]

We are not the first generation to tell our mothers that we are lesbians. Vita Sackville-West may have given dissembling talks on the radio about the importance and joys of heterosexual marriage but she did tell her mother that she was a lesbian. Nor are we the first to believe in the reality of a lesbian community. Lesbians have always accepted responsibility for their own, as Radclyffe Hall said: 'I have also stood for fidelity in inverted unions'. Vita Sackville-West accepted without hesitation the duty of providing for Chris St John and Tony Atwood in their old age when their future looked precarious.[32] Lesbian communities existed as networks of women rather than geographical concentrations of lesbians, although there were geographical communities around Brighton, in London, and apparently in Lyme Regis.

Lesbians have always been involved in British feminism and were the backbone of the suffrage movement from the constitutionalism of Eleanor Rathbone to the radicalism of Esther Roper and the anarchism of Mary Allen. Lesbians have worked to improve the lives of women and other lesbians. The pioneering work Eleanor Rathbone did in order to gain the family allowance has not been irrelevant to lesbians; Rathbone made lesbian motherhood much easier by insisting that child benefit be paid to mothers not fathers.

The politicization of lesbianism has not stopped with feminism; lesbianism is closely identified today with pacifism, the ecology movement, animal rights activism, vegetarianism and spirituality. This can be irritating, as lesbian is not an exact synonym for vegetarian. Yet these issues have consistently been ones which have concerned lesbians in Britain over the last century. The new explicit politicization of lesbianism has great similarities with the politics that lesbians have always had.

Consider pacifism as just one of the many possible examples. The lesbians and feminists protesting against nuclear weapons at Greenham Common in the 1980s were inheritors of a tradition passed on from lesbians and feminists like Esther Roper, Eva Gore-Booth and Sybil Morrison. There is not just a symbolic link between these women, there is a real link of friendship and knowledge. Through Myrtle Soloman, lesbian peace protesters of the 1980s had a direct tie to lesbian peace protesters of the 1950s, like Sybil Morrison, and from Morrison to the ex-suffragist lesbian peace campaigners of the Great War, like Esther Roper.

The politics of lesbians have a real history which can be mapped via the networks of friendship and political involvement of lesbians in Britain during the last century. Lesbian politics are today the culmination of the politics of individual lesbians who were linked through networks of love, friendship and respect. The intricacies of lesbian politics that we face today only differ from the past in that we are able to *say*, as we act politically, *we are lesbians*.

We should remember that some responses to lesbianism have remained remarkably consistent. In 1915 Stella Browne, writing from the viewpoint of a 'professional' observer, wrote:

> I repudiate all wish to slight or depreciate the love-life of the real homosexual; but it cannot be advisable to force the growth of that habit in heterosexual people.[33]

In 'Studies in feminine inversion' Stella Browne reiterates this point:

> I think it is perhaps not wholly uncalled-for, to underline very strongly in my opinion that the homosexual impulse *is not in any way superior* to the normal; it has a fully equal right to existence and expression, it is no worse, no lower; *but no better.*[34]

This nervousness about lesbians, and fear of lesbian strength, has not disappeared. Lesbians and lesbianism are troubling to the straight world, regardless of how they conceptualize their lesbianism. We should remember that we are more vulnerable to attack if we forget that we have a community of interests and a shared identity. However, lesbian life and community have survived incomprehension and outright attack. British lesbians have a long tradition of diversity, action, success and pride. This is our history and we should take note of it. It can be our guide to how we build a future.

NOTES

1. *Arena Three*, **5**(4), April 1968.
2. *The News of the World*, 21 January 1968, by Ron Mount.
3. Hall Carpenter Archives: Albany Trust 14/75, Male and Female Homosexual Association of Britain.
4. Jeffrey Weeks, *Coming Out: Homosexual Politics in Britain from the Nineteenth Century to the Present* (London: Quartet, 1990, revised edition), p.185.
5. *Arena Three*, **1**(12), December 1964.
6. *Arena Three*, **7**(6), June 1970.
7. *Arena Three*, **8**(3, 4, 5 and 6), March, April, May and June 1971.
8. *Arena Three*, **7**(11/12), November/December 1970.
9. *Arena Three*, **6**(9/10), October/November 1969, **7**(3), March 1970 and **8**(2), February 1971.
10. *Arena Three*, **8**(2), February 1971. DOB is the American lesbian organization The Daughters of Bilitis, founded in 1955. NACHO was the North American Conference of Homophile Organizations, which existed between 1966 and 1970.
11. Weeks, *Coming Out*, p.191.
12. *Ibid.*, pp.199–200.
13. *Ibid.*, p.193.
14. *Arena Three*, **8**(3), March 1971.
15. Vera Brittain, *Radclyffe Hall: A Case of Obscenity?* (London: Femina Books, 1968).
16. Weeks, *Coming Out*, p.200.
17. Sue Cartledge and Jo Ryan, *Sex and Love: New Thoughts on Old Contradictions* (London: The Women's Press, 1983), p.4.
18. *Arena Three*, **8**(5), May 1971.
19. Weeks, *Coming Out*, pp.211–12.
20. Albany Trust 9/17 subscriptions, Hall Carpenter Archives.
21. *Arena Three*, **9**(3), March 1972.
22. Annabel Faraday, 'Social Definitions of Lesbians in Britain 1914–1939', unpublished PhD thesis, University of Essex, 1985, p.6.
23. Eleanor Adland (ed.), *Edy: Recollections of Edith Craig* (London: Frederick Muller, 1949), p.97.
24. Lilian Barker collection, National Portrait Gallery Archive.
25. Clemence Dane collection, National Portrait Gallery Archive.
26. Sheila Jeffreys, *The Lesbian Heresy* (London: The Women's Press, 1994), pp.251–2.
27. *Ibid.*, p.252.
28. *Ibid.*, p.260.
29. Beatrix Campbell, 'A feminist sexual politics: now you see it, now you don't', in *Feminist Review* (ed.), *Sexuality: A Reader* (London: Virago, 1987), p.34.
30. Terry Castle, *The Apparitional Lesbian: Female Homosexuality and Modern Culture* (New York: Columbia University Press, 1993), p.12.

31. Victoria Glendinning, *Vita: The Life of* V. *Sackville-West* (London: Penguin, 1984), p.212.
32. *Ibid.*, p.349.
33. Stella Browne, 'The sexual variety and variability among women', in Sheila Rowbotham, A *New World of Women: Stella Browne – Socialist Feminist* (London: Pluto Press, 1977), pp.102–3.
34. Stella Browne's emphasis in 'Studies in feminine inversion' (1923), in Sheila Jeffreys *et al.*, (eds), *The Sexuality Papers* (London: Hutchinson, 1984), p.61 ↑.

bibliography

Ackland, Valentine, *For Sylvia: An Honest Account*. London: Chatto & Windus, 1985.

Adlard, Eleanor (ed.), *Edy: Recollections of Edith Craig*. London: Frederick Muller, 1949.

Allen, Mary Sophia, *Lady in Blue*, London: Stanley Paul & Co., 1936.

Allen, Mary Sophia, *The Pioneer Policewoman*. London: Chatto and Windus, 1925.

Allen, Mary Sophia, *Woman at the Crossroads*. London: Unicorn Press, 1934.

Altman, Dennis, *et al.*, *Which Homosexuality?* London: Gay Men's Press, 1989.

A.J.R. (ed.), *The Suffrage Annual and Women's Who's Who*. London: Hutchinson, 1913.

Arena Three, London, January 1964–1968.

Auchmuty, Rosemary, 'By their friends we shall know them: the lives and networks of some women in North Lambeth, 1880–1940', in Lesbian History Group (1989).

Baker, Michael, *Our Three Selves: A Life of Radclyffe Hall*. London: Hamish Hamilton, 1985.

Banks, Olive, *The Biographical Dictionary of British Feminists 1800–1930*. Brighton: Wheatsheaf, 1985.

Banks, Olive, *The Biographical Dictionary of British Feminists 1900–1945*. London: Harvester Wheatsheaf, 1990.

Bellis, Hannah, *Heroines of Our Time*. London: W & R Chambers, 1939.

Brandon, Ruth, *The New Women and the Old Men: Love. Sex and the Woman Question*. London: Secker and Warburg, 1990.

Braybon, Gail and Summerfield, Penny, *Out of the Cage: Women's Experiences in Two World Wars*. London: Pandora, 1987.

Brighton Ourstory Project, *Daring Hearts: Lesbian and Gay Lives of 50s and 60s Brighton*. Brighton: QueenSpark Books, 1992.

Browne, Stella, 'Studies in feminine inversion', in Jeffreys *et al.* (1984) (first published 1923).

Browne, Stella, 'The sexual variety and variability among women', in Rowbotham (1977) (first published 1915).

Bullough, V. and Bullough, B., 'Lesbianism in the 1920 and 1930s: a newfound study', *Signs*, Summer **2**(4), 1977.

Caine, Barbara, 'Feminism, suffrage and the nineteenth century English women's movement', *Women's Studies International Forum*, **5**(6), 1982.

Campbell, Beatrix, 'A feminist sexual politics: now you see it, now you don't', in Feminist Review (1987).

Caplan, Pat (ed.), *The Cultural Construction of Sexuality*. London: Tavistock, 1987.

Cartledge, Sue, 'Duty and desire: creating a feminist morality', in Cartledge and Ryan (1983).

Cartledge, Sue and Ryan, Jo (eds), *Sex and Love: New Thoughts on Old Contradictions*. London: The Women's Press, 1983.

Castle, Terry, *The Apparitional Lesbian: Female Homosexuality and Modern Culture*. New York: Columbia University Press, 1993.

Claus, Ruth F., 'Confronting homosexuality: a letter from Frances Wilder', *Signs*, **2**(4), Summer 1977.

Clyde, Irene, *Beatrice the Sixteenth*. London: George Bell & Sons, 1909.

Clyde, Irene, *Eve's Sour Apples*. London: Eric Partridge, 1934.

Collis, Maurice, *Somerville and Ross*. London: Faber & Faber, 1968.

Colquhoun, Maureen, *A Woman in the House*. Shoreham-by-Sea: Scan, 1980.

Compton-Burnett, Ivy, *More Women than Men*. London: Alison & Busby, 1983 (first published 1933).

Costello, John, *Love, Sex and War: Changing Values 1939–45*. London: Collins, 1985.

Cowper, J.M. (ed.), *The Auxiliary Territorial Service*. 1949.

Crompton, Louis, 'The myth of lesbian impunity: capital laws from 1270–1791', in Licarta and Peterson (1985).

Cutbill, Jonathan, Introduction to A.T. Fitzroy, *Despised and Rejected*. London: Gay Men's Press, 1988.

Dane, Clemence, preface to *The Hepzibah Omnibus* by Olwen Bowen [Davies]. London: T. Nelson & Sons, 1936.

Dane, Clemence, *Regiment of Women*. London: Heinemann, 1966 (first published 1917).

Dane, Clemence, *The Woman's Side*. London: Herbert Jenkins, 1926.

Dangerfield, George, *The Strange Death of Liberal England*. London: Constable, 1936.

Davies, Hunter (ed.), *The New London Spy*. London: Antony Blond, 1966.

de Vries, Jacqueline, 'Gendering patriotism: Emmeline and Christabel Pankhurst and World War One', in Oldfield (1994).

DeJean, Joan, *Fictions of Sappho 1546–1937*. Chicago: University of Chicago Press, 1989.

Dickson, Lovat, *Radclyffe Hall at the Well of Loneliness: A Sapphic Chronicle*. London: Collins, 1975.

Donisthorpe, G. Sheila, *Loveliest of Friends*. London: Old Royalty Book Publishers, 1931.

Donoghue, Emma, *Passions between Women: British Lesbian Culture 1668–1801*. London: Scarlet Press, 1994.

Doughan, David, *Lobbying for Liberation: British Feminism 1918–1968*. London: LLRS Publications, 1980.

Douie, Vera, *Daughters of Britain*. Oxford (published by the author), 1949.

du Maurier, Angela, *It's Only the Sister*. London: Peter Davies, 1951.

du Maurier, Angela, *Old Maids Remember*. London: Peter Davies, 1966.

du Maurier, Angela, *The Little Less*. London: Michael Joseph, 1941.

Duberman, Martin, Vicinus, Martha and Chauncy, George, Jr. (eds), *Hidden from History: Reclaiming the Lesbian and Gay Past*. New York: Meridian, 1990.

Dyhouse, Carol, *Feminism and the Family in England 1880–1939*. Oxford: Blackwell, 1989.

Echols, Alice, 'The new feminism of yin and yang ', in Vance (1992).

Elliman, Michael, *The Pink Plaque Guide to London*. London: Gay Men's Press, 1986.

Epstein, Julia and Straub, Kristina, *Body Guards: The Cultural Politics of Gender Ambiguity*. London: Routledge, 1991.

Ettorre, Elizabeth, *Lesbians, Women and Society*. London: Routledge, 1980.

Ettorre, Elizabeth, 'Sappho revisited: a new look at lesbians', *Women's Studies International Forum*, **3**(4), 1980.

Faderman, Lillian, *Odd Girls and Twilight Lovers*. London: Penguin, 1992.

Faderman, Lillian, *Scotch Verdict*. London: Quartet, 1985.

Faderman, Lillian, *Surpassing the Love of Men: Romantic Friendship and Love between Women from the Renaissance to the Present*. London: The Women's Press, 1985.

Faraday, Annabel, 'Liberating lesbian research', in Plummer (1981).

Faraday, Annabel, Social Definitions of Lesbians in Britain 1914–1939: 'Subject to Query'. Unpublished PhD thesis, University of Essex, 1985.

Feminist Review (ed.), *Sexuality: A Reader*. London: Virago, 1987.

Fitzroy, A.T., *Despised and Rejected*. London: Gay Men's Press, 1988 (first published 1918).

Forster, Margaret, *Daphne du Maurier*. London: Chatto & Windus, 1993.

Foster, Janette, *Sex Variant Women in Literature*. London: Frederick Muller, 1958.

Freedman, E.B., *et al.* (eds), *The Lesbian Issue: Essays from Signs*. Chicago and London: University of Chicago Press, 1985.

Freewoman, The, London: 1911–12, Vol. 1. no 1 to Vol. 2. no 47.

Fuss, Diana (ed.), *Inside/Out: Lesbian Theories, Gay Theories*. New York: Routledge, 1991.

Garber, *Lesbian Sources: A Bibliography of Periodical Articles 1970–1990*. New York: Garland, 1993.

Glendinning, Victoria, *Elizabeth Bowen: Portrait of a Writer*. London: Phoenix, 1993 (first published 1977).

Glendinning, Victoria, *Vita: The Life of V. Sackville-West*. London: Penguin, 1984.

Gordon, Linda and DuBois, Ellen, 'Seeking ecstasy on the battlefield: danger and pleasure in nineteenth century feminist sexual thought', *Feminist Review*, **13**, Spring 1983.

Gore, Elizabeth, *The Better Fight: The Story of Dame Lilian Barker*. London: G. Bles, 1965.

Green, Sarah, The Politics of Gender, Sexuality and Identity: An Ethnography of Lesbian Feminists. Unpublished PhD thesis, Cambridge University, 1992.

Grier, Barbara, *The Lesbian in Literature*, 3rd edn. Florida: The Naiad Press, 1981.

Grundy, Isobel *et al.*(eds), *The Feminist Companion to Literature in English*. London: Batsford, 1990.

Hall Carpenter Lesbian Oral History Group (ed.), *Inventing Ourselves*. London: Routledge, 1989.

Hall, Radclyffe, *The Well of Loneliness*. London: Virago, 1982 (first published 1928).

Holledge, Julie, *Innocent Flowers: Women in the Edwardian Theatre*. London: Virago, 1981.

Hanscombe, Gillian, and Forster, Jackie, *Rocking the Cradle: Lesbian Mothers a Challenge in Family Living*. London: Peter Owen, 1981.

Harman, Claire, *Sylvia Townsend Warner: A Biography*. London: Minerva, 1991.

Harman, Claire, *The Diaries of Sylvia Townsend Warner*. London: Chatto & Windus, 1994.

Hemmings, S. and Cant, B., *Radical Records: Thirty Years of Lesbian and Gay History 1957–1987*. London: Routledge, 1988.

Hitchman, Janet, *Such a Strange Lady: A Biography of Dorothy L. Sayers*. Sevenoaks: New English Library, 1979.

Hobby, Elaine and White, Chris (eds), *What Lesbians Do in Books*, London: The Women's Press, 1991.

Hopkins, June, 'The lesbian personality', *British Journal of Psychiatry*, **115** (1969), 1433–6.

Hunt, Agnes, *This Is My Life*. London: Blackie, 1938.

Hunt, Agnes, *Reminiscences*. Shrewsbury: Wilding & Son, 1935.

Hunter, Fred, 'Hilda Matheson and the BBC, 1926–1940', in Oldfield (1994).

Hyde, H. Montgomery, *The Other Love: A Historical and Contemporary Survey of Homosexuality in Britain*. London: Heinemann, 1970.

Ingram, Angela and Patai, Daphne (eds), *Rediscovering Forgotten Radicals: British Women Writers 1889–1939*. Chapel Hill and London, University of North Carolina Press, 1993.

Ingram, Angela and Patai, Daphne, 'Fantasy and identity: the double life of a Victorian sexual radical', in Ingram and Patai (1993).

Iremonger, Lucille, *Ghosts of Versailles: Miss Moberly and Miss Jourdain and Their Adventure*. London: Faber, 1957.

Jacob, Naomi, *Me – Again*. London: Hutchison, 1937.

Jacob, Naomi, *Me – and the Stags*. London: William Kimber, 1964.

Jacob, Naomi, *Me – and the Swans*. London: William Kimber, 1963.

Jacob, Naomi, *Me in War-Time*. London: Hutchinson, 1940.

Jacob, Naomi, *Me: A Chronicle about Other People*. London: Hutchinson, 1933.

Jackson, Margaret, '"Facts of life" or the eroticisation of women's oppression? Sexology and the social construction of heterosexuality', in Caplan (1987).

Jeffreys, Sheila, *Anticlimax*. London: The Women's Press, 1990.

Jeffreys, Sheila, *The Spinster and Her Enemies: Feminism and Sexuality 1880–1930*. London: Pandora, 1985.

Jeffreys, Sheila, *The Lesbian Heresy*. London: The Women's Press, 1994.

Jeffreys, Sheila, *et al.* (eds) *The Sexuality Papers*. London: Hutchinson, 1984.

Kenyon, F.E., 'Studies in female homosexuals. iv: social and psychological aspects', and 'Studies in female homosexuals. v: Sexual development, attitudes and experience', *British Journal of Psychiatry*, **114** (1968), 1337–50.

King, Francis, *Yesterday Came Suddenly*. London: Constable, 1993.

Kitzinger, Celia, *The Social Construction of Lesbianism*. London: Sage, 1987.

Krippner, Celia, *Quality of Mercy: Women at War Serbia 1915–1918*. Newton Abbot: David & Charles, 1980.

Larkin, Philip (ed.), *The Oxford Book of Twentieth-century English Verse*. Oxford: Clarendon Press, 1973.

Leaska, Mitchell A. and Phillips, John (eds), *Violet to Vita; The Letters of Violet Trefusis to Vita Sackville-West*. London: Methuen, 1989.

Leonardi, Susan J., *Dangerous by Degrees: Women at Oxford and the Somerville College Novelists*. New York: Rutgers University Press, 1989.

Lesbian History Group (ed.), *Not a Passing Phase: Reclaiming Lesbians in History 1840–1985*. London: The Women's Press, 1989.

Levine, Philippa, *Feminist Lives in Victorian England*. Oxford: Blackwell, 1990.

Lewis, Gifford, *Eva Gore-Booth and Esther Roper*. London: Pandora, 1988.

Lewis, Gifford, *Somerville and Ross: The World of the Irish R.M.* London: Viking, 1985.

Licarta, J. and Peterson, R.P. (eds), *The Gay Past: A Collection of Historical Essays*. New York: Harrington Park Press, 1985.

Liddington, J. and Norris, J., *One Hand Tied behind Us: The Rise of the Women's Suffrage Movement*. London: Virago, 1978.

Lock, Joan, *The British Policewoman. Her Story*. London: Robert Hale, 1979.

Mannin, Ethel, *Young in the Twenties*. London: Hutchinson, 1971.

Manning, Rosemary, *A Time and a Time: An Autobiography*. London: Marion Boyars, 1986.

Manning, Rosemary, *A Corridor of Mirrors: An Autobiography*. London: The Women's Press, 1987.

Martindale, Hilda, *From One Generation to Another*. London: G. Allen & Unwin, 1944.

Martindale, Louisa, *A Woman Surgeon*. London: Gollancz, 1951.

The Forum Club. London: C. W. May, 1955.

Mayne, Xavier [Edward Stephenson], *The Intersexes*. Italy, published privately, 1908.

McIntosh, Mary, 'The homosexual role', in Plummer (1981).

Melville, Joy, *Ellen & Edy: A Biography of Ellen Terry and Her Daughter, Edith Craig. 1847–1947*. London: Pandora, 1987.

Mitchell, David, *Women on the War Path*. London: Cape, 1966.

Mohin, Lilian and Wilson, Anna, *Past Participants: A Lesbian History Diary for 1984*. London: Onlywomen Press, 1983.

Morley, Ann with Stanley, Liz, *The Life and Death of Emily Wilding Davison*. London: The Women's Press, 1988.

Morrison, Sybil, *I Renounce War: The Story of the Peace Pledge Union*. London: Sheppard Press, 1962.

Mulford, Wendy, *This Narrow Place: Sylvia Townsend Warner and Valentine Ackland*. London: Pandora, 1988.

Neild, Suzanne and Pearson, Rosalind, *Women Like Us*. London: The Women's Press, 1992.

Nestle, Joan, *A Restricted Country*. London: Sheba, 1987.

Newton, Esther, 'The mythic mannish lesbian: Radcliffe Hall and the new woman', in Duberman *et al.*(1990).

Nicolson, Nigel, *Portrait of a Marriage*. London: Weidenfeld & Nicolson, 1973.

O'Sullivan, Sue, 'Passionate beginnings: ideological politics 1969–72', in Feminist Review (ed.) (1987).

Oldfield, Sybil (ed.), *This Working-day World: Women's Lives and Culture(s) in Britain* 1914–45. London: Taylor & Francis, 1994.

Oldfield, Sybil, 'England's Cassandras in World War One' in Oldfield (1994).

Onlywoman (ed.), *Love Your Enemy? The Debate between Heterosexual Feminism and Political Lesbianism*. London: Onlywoman Press, 1981.

Oram, Alison, '"Embittered, sexless or homosexual": Attacks on spinster teachers 1918–1939', in Lesbian History Group (1989).

Pankhurst, Sylvia, *The Suffragette Movement*. London: Virago, 1977 (first published 1931).

Plummer, Douglas, *Queer People: The Truth about Homosexuals*. London: W.H. Allen, 1963.

Plummer, Ken, *The Making of the Modern Homosexual*. London: Hutchinson, 1981.

Pugh, Martin, *Women and the Women's Movement in Britain* 1914–1959. London: Macmillan, 1992.

Quorum, The. London: privately published, 1920.

Raitt, Suzanne, *Vita & Virginia: The Work and Friendship of Vita Sackville-West and Virginia Woolf*. Oxford, Oxford University Press, 1993.

Reassessments of 'First Wave' Feminism, Special Issue, Women's Studies International Forum, **5**(6), 1982.

Renault, Mary, Afterword to *The Friendly Young Ladies*. London: Virago, 1984.

Renault, Mary, *The Friendly Young Ladies*. London: Virago, 1984 (first published 1944).

Reynolds, Barbara, *Dorothy L. Sayers: Her Life and Soul*. London: Hodder & Stoughton, 1993.

Rich, Adrienne, 'The lesbian continuum and compulsory heterosexuality', in Sinitow *et al.* (1984).

Richards, Dell, *Lesbian Lists*. Boston: Allison, 1990.

Rolley, Katrina, 'Cutting a dash: the dress of Radclyffe Hall and Una Troubridge', *Feminist Review*, **35** (Summer 1990).

Rolley, Katrina, 'The lesbian sixth sense', *Feminist Art News*, **3**(5).

Roper, Esther (ed.), *The Prison Letters of Countess Markievicz*. London: Longman, 1934.

Rose, Jacqueline, 'Femininity and its discontents', in Feminist Review (ed.) (1987).

Rowbotham, Sheila, *A New World of Women: Stella Browne – Socialist Feminist*. London: Pluto Press, 1977.

Rowbotham, Sheila and Weeks, Jeffrey, *Socialism and the New Life: The Personal and Sexual Politics of Edward Carpenter and Havelock Ellis*. London: Pluto Press, 1977.

Ruehl, Sonja, 'Inverts and experts: Radclyffe Hall and the lesbian identity', in Brunt and Rowan (1982).

Ruehl, Sonja, 'Sexual theory and practice: another double standard', in Cartledge and Ryan (1983).

Rule, Jane, *Lesbian Images*. London: Pluto Press, 1989.

Rupp, Leila J., '"Imagine my surprise": women's relationships in mid-twentieth century America', in Duberman *et al.* (1990).

Russell, Dora, *The Tamarisk Tree: Vol. 3. Challenge to the Cold War*. London: Virago, 1985.

Sappho, *Poems and Fragments*, translated Josephine Balmer. Newcastle upon Tyne: Bloodaxe Books, 1992.

Showalter, Elaine, *Sexual Anarchy*. London: Virago, 1992.

Showalter, Elaine, *A Literature of Their Own: British Women Novelists from Brontë to Lessing*. London: Virago, 1984.

Sinitow, Anne *et al.* (eds), *Desire: The Politics of Sexuality*. London: Virago, 1984.

Smith, Harold (ed.), *British Feminism in the Twentieth Century*. Aldershot: Elgar, 1990.

Smith, Timothy d'Arch, *Love in Earnest: Some Notes on the Lives and Writings of English 'Uranian' Poets from 1889–1930*. London: Routledge & Kegan Paul, 1970.

Smith-Rosenberg, Carroll, *Disorderly Conduct: Visions of Gender in Victorian America*. New York and London: Oxford University Press, 1986.

Smyth, Cherry, *Lesbians Talk Queer Notions*. London: Scarlet Press, 1992.

Somerville College Record 1879–1971. Oxford: Somerville College.

Souhami, Diana, *Gertrude and Alice*. London: Pandora, 1991.

Souhami, Diana, *Gluck: Her Biography*. London: Pandora, 1988.

Spain, Nancy, *A Funny Thing Happened on the Way*. London: Hutchinson, 1964.

Spain, Nancy, *Why I'm Not a Millionaire*. London: Hutchinson, 1956.

Sprigge, Elizabeth, *The Life of Ivy Compton-Burnett*. London: Gollancz, 1973.

Spurling, Hilary, *Ivy When Young: The Early Life of I. Compton-Burnett 1884–1919*. London: Gollancz, 1974.

Spurling, Hilary, *Secrets of a Woman's Heart: The Later Life of I. Compton-Burnett 1920–1969*. London: Hodder & Stoughton, 1984.

St John, Christopher, *Christine Murrell, M.D.* London: Williams and Norgate, 1935.

St John, Christopher, *Hungerheart*. London: Methuen, 1915.

Stanley, Liz, 'Romantic friendship? Some issues in researching lesbian history and biography', *Women's History Review*, **1**(2), 1992.

Stearn, Jess, *The Grapevine: A Report on the Secret World of the Lesbian*. London: Frederick Muller, 1965.

Stein, Arlene (ed.), *Sisters, Sexperts, Queers*. New York: Plume, 1993.

Stewart-Pack, Angela, and Cassidy, Jules, *We're Here: Conversations with Lesbian Women*. London: Quartet, 1977.

Stocks, Mary, *Eleanor Rathbone*. London: Victor Gollancz, 1949.

Stott, Mary, *Organisation Woman: The Story of the National Union of Townswomen's Guilds*. London: Heinemann, 1978.

Sturtevan, Katherine, *Our Sisters' London: Nineteen Feminist Walks*. London: The Women's Press, 1991.

Sweetman, David, *Mary Renault*. London: Chatto & Windus, 1993.

Terry, Roy, *Women in Khaki: The Story of the British Woman Soldier*. London: Columbus, 1988.

Troubridge, Una, *The Life and Death of Radclyffe Hall*. London: Hammond & Hammond, 1961.

Vance, Carole (ed.), *Pleasure and Danger: Exploring Female Sexuality*. London: Pandora, 1992.

Vance, Carole, 'Social construction theory: Problems in the history of sexuality', in Altman *et al.* (1989).

Vicinus Martha, '"One life to stand besides Me": Emotional conflicts in first-generation college women in England', *Feminist Studies*, **8**(3) (Fall 1982).

Vicinus Martha, '"They wonder to which sex I belong". The historical routes of modern lesbian identity', in Altman *et al.* (1989).

Vicinus, Martha (ed.), *A Widening Sphere: Changing Roles of Victorian Women*. London: Methuen, 1980.

Vicinus, Martha (ed.), *Suffer and Be Still: Women in the Victorian Age*. London: Methuen, 1980.

Vicinus, Martha, *Independent Women: Work and Community for Single Women 1850–1920*. London: Virago, 1985.

Vicinus, Martha, 'Distance and desire: English boarding school friendships', in Duberman *et al.* (1990).

Weeks, Jeffrey, *Coming Out: Homosexual Politics in Britain from the Nineteenth Century to the Present*. London: Quartet, 1990 (revised edition).

Whitbread, Helena (ed.), *I Know My Own Heart: The Diaries of Anne Lister*. London: Virago, 1988.

Whitbread, Helena (ed.), *No Priest But Love: The Journals of Anne Lister from 1824–1826*. Yorkshire: Smith Settle, 1992.

Whitelaw, Lis, *The Life and Rebellious Times of Cicely Hamilton*. London: The Women's Press, 1990.

Wilson, Elizabeth, 'I'll climb the stairway to heaven: lesbianism in the seventies', in Cartledge and Ryan (1983).

Wilson, Elizabeth, *Only Halfway to Paradise: Women in Postwar Britain 1945–1968*. London: Tavistock, 1980.

Wilson, Elizabeth, 'Psychoanalysis: Psychic law and order?', in Feminist Review (1987).

Wiltsher, Anne, *Most Dangerous Women: Feminist Peace Campaigners of the Great War*. London: Pandora, 1985.

Woman's Leader, The, "Cripicus" letter to the editor, 11 January 1929, p.383.

ARCHIVAL SOURCES

Carpenter Collection, Sheffield City Archives
Carp.01/MSS 386/355 Chambers letter 19/8/1921
Carp. 01/MSS 386/262 Oliver letter 25/10/1915
Carp. 01/MSS 386/409 Rodgers letter 16/3/1925
Carp. 01/MSS 386/410 Rodgers letter 18/5/1925
Carp. 01/MSS 386/218 Tasker letter 21/7/1913

Fawcett Library Archives, Fawcett Library, London Guildhall University
Vera 'Jack' Holme collection, 7/VJH, 1A Box – papers uncatalogued
Fawcett collection, letters from Thomas Baty to Mrs Fawcett and material on Aëthenic Union and *Phoenix*, Box 295, Folder 4
Alice Williams collection 7/AHW including *The Forum Club Record*
Press cuttings collection

Hall Carpenter Oral History Collection, National Sound Archive, British Library
Diana Chapman, C456/015
M. H., C456/014
Cynnie Reid, C456/023
Julie Switsur, C4 5 6/033
Rene Sawyer, C456/068/01–03
Pat Arrowsmith, C456/067/01–02
Myrtle Soloman, C456/010/01–02

Hall Carpenter Collection, Library of the London School of Economics
Urania
Papers of the CHE
Papers of the Albany Trust:
    9/17 subscriptions
14/75 Male and Female Homosexual Association of Britain
14/80 'Minorities Research Trust', by Esmé Langley (1964)

Women at War Collection, The Imperial War Museum, London
The Hackett-Lowther Papers

Publishers' Archive, Reading University
Letters from Thomas Baty to George Bell, publishers

Public Records
Will of Winifred Ashton (Clemence Dane) of 20 Tavistock St, Covent Garden,
    London, 10 September 1956
Probate order of the estate of Winifred Ashton (Clemence Dane) of 1 Draycott
    Place, Chelsea, London, 23 September 1965

National Portrait Gallery Archive
Mabel Batten collection, catalogue description
Lilian Barker collection
Clemence Dane collection

index